WINTER AT MORRISTOWN 1779-1780 THE DARKEST HOUR

Samuel Stelle Smith

"There never was a darker hour in American prospects than this."

Maj. Gen. Nathanael Greene to
Maj. Gen. Alexander McDougall
February 1780.

PHILIP FRENEAU PRESS
Monmouth Beach N.J.
1979

In print titles in the Philip Freneau Press
Bicentennial Series on the American Revolution

THE BATTLE OF LONG ISLAND
Eric I. Manders
LC No. 78-72581/ISBN 0-912480-14-9

THE BATTLES OF SARATOGA
John R. Elting
LC No. 77-89325/ISBN 0-912480-13-0

THE BATTLE OF BRANDYWINE
Samuel S. Smith
LC No. 76-9405/ISBN 0-912480-12-2

THE BATTLE OF BUNKER'S HILL
John R. Elting
LC No. 75-3540/ISBN 0-912480-11-4

AT GENERAL HOWE'S SIDE 1776-1778
Friedrich von Muenchhausen/Ernst Kipping, trans.
LC No. 73-94002/ISBN 0-912480-09-2

BRITISH MAPS OF THE AMERICAN REVOLUTION
Peter J. Guthorn
LC No. 72-79889/ISBN 0-912480-07-6

THE HESSIAN VIEW OF AMERICA 1776-1783
Ernst Kipping
LC No. 72-161384/ISBN 0-912480-06-8

FIGHT FOR THE DELAWARE 1777
Samuel S. Smith
LC No. 74-130878/ISBN 0-912480-05-X

VALLEY FORGE CRUCIBLE OF VICTORY
John F. Reed
LC No. 70-76769/ISBN 0-912480-04-1

THE BATTLE OF PRINCETON
Samuel S. Smith
LC No. 67-31149/ISBN 0-912480-03-3

AMERICAN MAPS AND MAP MAKERS OF THE REVOLUTION
Peter J. Guthorn
LC No. 66-30330/ISBN 0-912480-02-5

THE BATTLE OF TRENTON
Samuel S. Smith
LC No. 65-28860/ISBN 0-912480-01-7

THE BATTLE OF MONMOUTH
Samuel S. Smith
LC No. 64-56379/ISBN 0-912480-00-9

This Bicentennial Series
on the American Revolution
has been designed throughout by Paul R. Smith

Photography by Daniel I. Hennessey.

Library of Congress No. 79-52313
International Standard Book No. 0-912480-15-7

Library of Congress Cataloging in Publication Data
Smith, Samuel Stelle.
Winter at Morristown, 1779-1780.
(Philip Freneau Press Bicentennial series
on the American Revolution)
Bibliography: p.
Includes index.
1. Washington, George, Pres. U.S., 1732-1799—
Headquarters, Morristown, N.J. 2. United States—
History—Revolution, 1775-1783—Campaigns and battles.
3. Morristown, N.J.—History—Revolution, 1775-1783.
I. Title. II. Series.
F144.M9S6 973.3'36 79-52313
ISBN 0-912480-15-7

TABLE OF CONTENTS

Chapter I

MORRISTOWN ENCAMPMENT

*''Those who have only been in Valley Forge or Middlebrook during the last two winters, but have not tasted the cruelties of this one, know not what it is to suffer.''**

Major General John Kalb
Morristown, February 12, 1780.

Winter Deployment

In September 1779, a French fleet under Vice Admiral Charles Henry Hector Count d' Estaing appeared off British held Savannah, Georgia, and joined with an American land force under Major General Benjamin Lincoln in a siege of Savannah. On September 29, American commander in chief, General George Washington, at his West Point, New York, headquarters, learned of Admiral D' Estaing's presence off Savannah, but weeks were to pass without receipt of further information.

Washington had hoped that D' Estaing eventually would sail north from Savannah to join with him in some action against the large British force stationed in and about New York City under the command of General Henry Clinton. But, having received no new information from the south for weeks, Washington noted on November 12, that ''From present appearances and the season of the year, there is little reason to believe that a co-operation with the French Admiral can possibly take place'' before winter set in. Three days later, on November 15, Washington learned that on October 9, a combined French-American attack had been made against Savannah, but that it had failed, whereupon D' Estaing and his fleet had departed for ''the West Indies.''

Upon receipt of this unfavorable news from the south, Washington quickly put into action his plan for winter quartering his army. He would leave some troops behind in the New York Highlands, mainly at West Point, send a small force to Connecticut, and take the bulk of his army to Morristown, New Jersey, where he had made his winter headquarters two years earlier.

Although Gen. Washington had made his headquarters in Morristown during the winter of 1776-77, the bulk of his small army of about ''3,500 rank and file'' had been in the front lines, opposite the enemy at Brunswick and Amboy, quite some distance from Morristown. (See Appendix VI.) During this winter of 1779-80 it would be different. From the day of their arrival, ''8,433 rank and file'' would be quartered in and on the outskirts of Morristown.

Morristown and the neighboring area could not provide essential food and forage for such a large number of men and their many horses. A contemporary record states that the village of Morristown, in 1780, consisted of only ''sixty or eighty [houses] round the meeting house.'' This would suggest a total village population of 200 to 300 people.

The village was the county seat of Morris County, and the courthouse and county jail stood on the town green around which was centered most of the town's activity. Within a mile of the green, there were located ''two churches, two schools, two taverns, two saw mills, three grist mills, one fulling mill, five iron works, and one powder mill.''

There was one comparatively large merchantile store in Morristown, which boasted of selling everything from ''alum and awls to watch chains and wool cards.'' The store appears to have made a specialty of taking farm products in trade for merchandise, or giving cash for same. It was noted in their advertisement of March 14, 1780, that we ''give the highest prices for bees-wax and hog bristles.''

Neighboring communities, within three or four miles of Morristown were Parsippany, Troy, Hanover, Whippany, Bottle Hill (now Madison), and Mendham. These were slightly more than crossroad communities. Farther removed, and within a distance of ten miles of Morristown, were the other small settlements of Boonton to the north, Chatham to the east, Veal Town (now Bernardsville) and Basking Ridge to the south, and Succasunna to the west.

Between these communities were small farms located along the principal roads every half mile or so. As a rule, the farmers grew enough vegetables and raised enough livestock for their own use. They also cultivated a field or two of grain that took care of their needs for grist and flour in addition to providing a small surplus of both grain and livestock for use to barter with local merchants or to sell for cash.

Probably not over one acre in a hundred within ten miles of Morristown was under cultivation; the balance was swamp and timber land. Thus, in 1779-80, Morristown and vicinity were in no way equipped to supply even minimum essential needs of the army, with the exception of timber and wood with which to build their huts and feed their fires.

Gen. Washington had selected Morristown to be the site of his encampment for, as he said, ''the double purposes of security and subsistence.'' As to security, Washington noted that Morristown lay back of a low range of mountains, which will ''preserve us from the insults of the collected force of the enemy.'' Regarding subsistence, he said ''I very well know that a supply of Forage will be difficult at this post, and so it will be wherever the Bulk of the Army shall sit down'' for the winter.

Further, there was a critical shortage of grain throughout the mid-Atlantic area during the winter of 1779-80, and Washington took this into consideration when he ordered the various divisions of his army to be sent from West Point to Morristown over different routes. To this end, on November 16, Quartermaster General Nathanael Greene issued marching orders as follows: ''The Virginia Division to move . . . from Haverstraw by the Road under the Mountain [High Tor] to Suffrans [Suffern], Pompton [Plains] and

** In this volume there are 988 direct quotes from primary sources. Rather than reference these quotes by the use of superior numbers, the author has chosen to key the first three words of each quote in the text to documentation placed in the back of the book under ''References,'' i.e., ''Those who have . . .'' Kalb 183. Kalb is the ''Short Title'' for the primary source,* The Life of John Kalb, *by Friedrich Kapp, New York, 1870.*

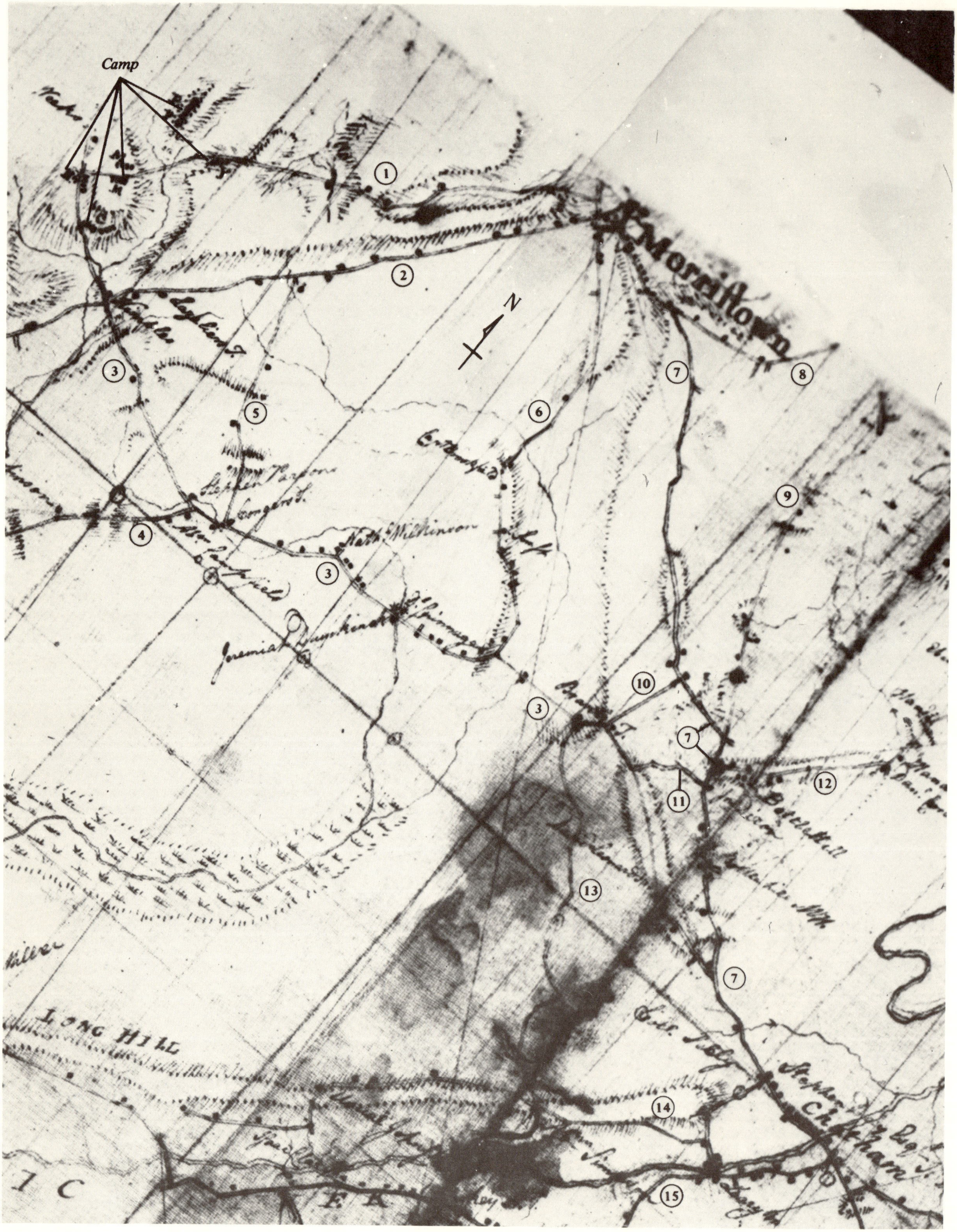
Camp
Morristown
N
LONG HILL
Chatham
1
2
3
4
5
6
7
8
9
10
11
12
13
14
15

Rockaway bridge [North Beverwick crossing of Rockaway River] to Morristown . . . the Maryland and Pennsylvania Divisions to be sent from West point to New Windsor . . . through the wood to Haverstraw-iron work, thence to Suffrans and to Pompton . . . and proceed to Morristown. The Connecticut Division to cross at Kings ferry [Crugers to Grassy Point], and proceed . . . by the Road under the Mountain to Suffrans, Pompton and Rockaway bridge to Morristown. The New York and . . . Hand's Brigades to March from Pompton [where they were presently stationed] . . . to Morristown."

ROAD COMPLEX IN MORRISTOWN–CHATHAM AREA 1779-1780–Reproduced here is a section of a map by Assistant Geographer to the United States Army Simeon De Witt made during the 1779-80 winter encampment at and near Morristown. The map, numbered 106A, is entitled Contraction in the Jerseys, *(AmM 14/106A)–reproduced here through the courtesy of* The New York Historical Society. *Road identifications, in terms of modern road names, were made by Mr. Henry Pilch of Madison, New Jersey, an attorney who has spent many years in land title and road survey work in Morris County. Mr. Pilch is presently a member of the Morris County Heritage Commission.*
(1) ROAD FROM MORRISTOWN TO MAIN CAMP—Roughly present Washington Street as far as and continuing southwesterly along Western Avenue or Jockey Hollow Road.
(2) ROAD FROM MORRISTOWN TO MAIN CAMP AND TOWARD VEALTOWN (Bernardsville)—Roughly present Mt. Kemble Avenue or U.S. 202.
(3) ROAD FROM MAIN CAMP TO CHATHAM—Roughly present Tempe Wick Road, Glen Alpine Road, Blue Mill Road, Loantaka Way, Woodland Road and Kings Road.
(4) ROAD FROM VEALTOWN TO CHATHAM—Roughly present Madisonville Road, Lees Hill Road, thence via (3).
(5) CUTOFF ROAD—Roughly present Sand Spring Road in Harding Township.
(6) BACK ROAD FROM MORRISTOWN TO CHATHAM—Roughly present South Street and Spring Valley Road, Feebletown Road in 1779, thence via (3).
(7) MAIN ROAD FROM MORRISTOWN TO CHATHAM—Roughly present Morris Avenue, Washington Avenue and Madison Avenue in Morristown and Morris Township; Elm Street, Park Avenue and Kings Road in Madison; Kings Road and Main Street in Chatham.
(8) ROAD FROM MORRISTOWN TOWARD WHIPPANY—Roughly present Morris Avenue and Whippany Road.
(9) ROAD FROM BOTTLE HILL (Madison) TOWARD WHIPPANY —Roughly present Park Avenue, earlier known as Division Road because it divided the original townships of Morris and Hanover.
(10) CUTOFF ROAD—Roughly present Loantaka Way between Madison Avenue and Woodland Road in Madison.
(11) CUTOFF ROAD—Roughly present Green Village Road between Kings Road and Woodland Road in Madison.
(12) ROAD FROM BOTTLE HILL TOWARD HANOVER AND WHIPPANY—Roughly present Ridgedale Avenue in Madison and Florham Park.
(13) ROAD FROM BOTTLE HILL TOWARD TURKEY (New Providence) AND SCOTCH PLAINS—Roughly present Loantaka Way, Southern Boulevard, mostly in Chatham Township, and Passaic Street in New Providence.
(14) ROAD FROM CHATHAM TOWARD BASKING RIDGE—Roughly Hillside Avenue, Fairmont Avenue and Long Hill Road in Chatham and Passaic Townships.
(15) ROAD FROM CHATHAM TOWARD TURKEY AND SCOTCH PLAINS—Roughly present Main Street in Chatham and River Road and Passaic Avenue in Summit. Circled numerals and CAMP, with extending lines, are additions to the map.

The North Carolina brigade was ordered to go from West Point "by water to King's ferry and thence to march by Kakiate [New Hempstead, New York] to Paramus." The post that the North Carolina brigade was to occupy was at Paramus Church, now Ridgewood, New Jersey, so as "to cover the communication between this [Washington's Morristown headquarters] and Kings Ferry," a most strategic crossing of the Hudson River.

Two days after the North Carolina brigade was given their orders, they were altered. The change was made on November 19 as a result of "Congress having directed the two Regts. of North Carolina with the Army to proceed to the State of South Carolina," and put themselves under the command of Major General Benjamin Lincoln, commander of the American southern army. It was, however, not until "November 23," that the North Carolina troops began their march. In order not to leave the important Paramus post unmanned, Washington ordered Lieutenant Colonel William De Hart of the 2nd New Jersey regiment, already in New Jersey, to "proceed with the detachment under your command to Paramus."

To Connecticut, went the New England brigade under Brigadier General Enoch Poor, consisting of "three regiments," all from New Hampshire. Gen. Poor's brigade would replace Brigadier General John Stark's Rhode Island brigade, which was ordered to proceed to Morristown from "Danbury," by way of "Kings Ferry, Suffrans and Pompton & c." Like Stark, Poor would make his headquarters "at Danbury," and would take "orders generally from the Officer commanding at the [New York] Highlands post," namely Major General William Heath. One of Poor's main duties would be to keep "an eye on the [Long Island] Sound."

Also to "Paramus," New Jersey, went a detachment of Moylan's dragoons, to keep communications open from Morristown to the Highlands. To Connecticut went the balance of the horse troops—"Moylans, Sheldons and Baylors Regiments of light Dragoons . . . to be quartered as near to this [Poor's] Brigade as the Country on acct. of Forage & ca. will admit." These were the continental dragoon regiments of Colonel Stephen Moylan, Colonel Elisha Sheldon and Colonel George Baylor.

Ordered to remain in the Highlands were the "Fifteen Massachusetts Regiments," making up the "1st, 2d, 3d, and 4th Massachusetts Brigades." One Massachusetts brigade was to be "Incamped near the Continental Village, [about three miles north of Peekskill] the other three quartered at West point." The three brigades at West Point were to "furnish garrisons for Kings ferry on both sides, [of the Hudson] and 4 or 500 light Troops in advance towards the enemy lines" in lower Westchester County.

Even before winter quartering plans were made for the main army to go to New Jersey, the Jersey shore opposite the enemy was guarded by continental troops under the command of Major General William Alexander, known as Lord Stirling. His force consisted of detachments under Brigadier General Anthony Wayne, Brigadier General William Maxwell and Major-Commandant Henry Lee. Wayne's light infantry was headquartered "in the neighbourhood of Acquacanack," now Passaic. His detachment was guarding the lower Hudson River and keeping watch over the enemy outpost at "Paulus Hook," now Jersey City. Maxwell's New Jersey brigade was encamped at "Scotch Plains," and was guarding "the country from Newark to Perth Amboy," opposite enemy held Staten Island. Lee's detachment of dragoons and infantry was headquartered at "Burlington." It was guarding the country south of the Raritan River, keeping communications open to Philadelphia, and trying to contain the enemy outpost on "Sandy Hook."

Supporting and coordinating with American continental forces throughout the colonies were numerous regiments of state militia, under the command of the various state governors. Duties of militia units were usually confined to their own states. In New Jersey, where the main American army was to quarter for the winter, William Livingston was the governor and commander in chief of militia. Serving under him, and heading the militia infantry regiments, plus miscellaneous artillery and cavalry units, was Major General Philemon Dickinson.

Settling-in

On November 28, after getting his army in march, General Washington left West Point enroute to Morristown. On his arrival at Peekskill on the 29th, he received "Reports worthy of credit, that the Enemy are making or preparing for a pretty considerable embarkation of Troops from New York." Washington was sure that these were preparations for a move southward, with the destination most likely Georgia or South Carolina. To offset such a move, Washington wrote to Congress from Peekskill that "I have determined, illy as they can be spared, to put the whole of the Virginia Troops in motion" to the southward.

After sending off his letter to Congress, Washington rode on toward Morristown via "Sufferan's [and] Pompton." Upon his arrival at Morristown on December 1, where he took up quarters in the home of Theodosia Ford, widow of Jacob Ford, Jr., Washington learned that the British fleet had not yet sailed out of New York Harbor, whereupon he delayed sending off the Virginia troops. On the 2nd, however, he did order a part of Baylor's dragoons who were at Paramus under "Lieutenant Colonel [William] Washington," to the southward with about "125 men."

On the 9th, although the British fleet was still in New York Harbor, Washington decided to act. He ordered "the whole of the Virginia Troops to be immediately put in motion." By this date, the Virginians had already arrived at the camp site near Morristown and had begun cutting logs for their huts. Consequently, Washington made it clear that "The logs and other materials prepared for the use of the Virginia troops are not to be applied to any other purpose without an order from Head Quarters."

On the 13th, despite the fact that the British fleet still lay at anchor, Gen. Washington decided that he could no longer delay the overdue replacement of Gen. Maxwell's detachment, which was watching the possible movement of the enemy fleet. To relieve Maxwell, Washington sent forward a mixed detachment under the command of Connecticut's Brigadier General Samuel Parsons. At the same time, Washington wrote Maxwell that when Parsons "arrives at the place of his destination he will give you notice, and, you will march your brigade immediately to camp."

Days continued to pass with no movement of the British fleet. Then, on December 23, Brig. Gen. Wayne sent off a hurried note to Gen. Washington that from lookout posts on the Bergen Peninsula, his men reported that "the fleet has sailed from New York." On the 26th, Wayne sent another message that "the second division of the Fleet put to sea yesterday." Although not known to the Americans, their destination was Charleston, South Carolina, where the British planned to open up a new front.

The departing fleet consisted of "88" ships. They carried a fighting force made up of "the [British and Hessian] grenadiers, [British] light infantry, five English [foot] regiments and several light corps." The light corps were mainly Provincial or Loyalists troops. General Henry Clinton was in command, and his force totaled "7,258 [regulars and] 1,450" Provincials.

Left behind in New York were "6,613 British and 6,427 German auxiliary" rank and file, under the command of Lieutenant General Wilhelm von Knyphausen. This remaining New York

JOCKEY HOLLOW ENCAMPMENT—This is a map of the 1779-80 winter encampment of the American Army, now called "Jockey Hollow." (AmM 40/1) The origin of the name Jockey Hollow is not precisely known. It was used as a road name on 8.26.77 in a deed of property, "Situate at Morristown afsd in the Jockey Hollow Road." (M. C. Records, Deed Bk A p. 44) It was used as a place name in 1779 by Col. Robert Erskine, geographer to the army in a map, #104B, titled Road from Morristown thro' Jockey Hollow. *(AmM 17/104B) During the 1779-80 encampment, the actual camp site was called by various names i.e., "Kembles"—"Back of Kembles"—"Camp near Morristown"—"Camp Mendham"—"Camp at Basking Ridge" —but most often just "Camp" or "Hutts." This camp site map was made by Capt. Etinne de Rochefontaine, a French volunteer on the staff of Col. Louis Duportail, commandant of engineers, pursuant to Gen. Washington's order of "December 15, 1779." (WW 17:271) The map, untitled, is signed by Rochefontaine and the text reads: "a. Pennsylvania Division b.c. 1t and 2d Maryland Brigades d.e. 1t and 2d Connecticut Brigades f. Genl Hand's Brigade g. New York Brigade h. Rhodisland [Stark's] Brigade i. Mjr Genl St Clair's Quarters. k. Brd Genl Smallwood's Quarters. 1. Brd Genl Stark's Quarters. m. Mill." Smallwood occupied his quarters only until the latter part of December when he went on a "journey" (WW 17:288,297) to Maryland. The mill indicated on the map was a saw mill as shown on the William Gray map reproduced in Appendix I.*

The Rochefontaine map accompanied a letter written to Gen. Washington from Col. Duportail, endorsed by Qm. Gen. Greene. The letter discusses methods of defending the camp against possible enemy attack, as follows: "Morristown 16th Jany 1780, Sir: To locate the army to any particular spots, may facilitate the Enemies getting possession of advantageous grounds, either upon one or the other of our flanks. It appears to us more proper therefore, that we move the troops upon the high and advantageous grounds, according as the motions of the enemy may indicate an intention to make an impression at particular places. Having examined the grounds, in and about camp, agreeable to your Excellency's order of the 15th of December, we are of the opinion, that the range of hills marked P.O.N. is that upon which the troops may be most advantageously posted, to receive the enemy, should they present themselves in front of the mountains from Morristown to Kemble's. Should the enemy approach us by Baskingridge and that quarter, we must occupy the grounds from the hill P. to the hill R., but if they approach us by Pluckemin, Blackriver and Mendham, we must draw up in the form of two sides of a square from hill R. to hill S. and from hill S. to hill T., the last of which lies a little in front of the Pennsylvania Line. Should the enemy attempt to penetrate our rear, by the way of the [New] York Brigade, we must take post from the hill U. to the hill N. Some of the positions are weaker than others, and some parts of each, weaker than the rest: such are the intervals between the mountain Q. to the mountain R. and between the mountain R. and the mountain S. Therefore to be safe in those positions (should we be greatly inferior to the Enemy) it will be necessary to strengthen these places by art [artillery]; and for this purpose it would be well to preserve as much of the wood as possible standing on the ground [for breastworks]. The several positions we have marked, being composed of a chain of hills have this advantage, that we never can be brought to a general action; the hills being divided by deep valleys, which form each, in a manner, a distinct post. We may govern our retreat according to the enemies approach. If they approach us by the way of Morris[Town], we can retreat by the way of Mendham, but if they approach us by the way of Baskingridge, or Mendham we may retreat by the way of Morris[Town]. However the position of the army is at such a remove [distance removed?] from the enemy and so difficult of access, that there is little probability of their attempting any thing against us without a great diminution of our force than we have reason to expect. We are with great respect your Excellency's most obedient humble servant Duportail Commdr of the Corps of the engineers [endorsed] Nath Greene QMG [To] Excellency Washington." (WP Dup/GW 1.16.80) Map courtesy Geography and Map Division, Library of Congress.

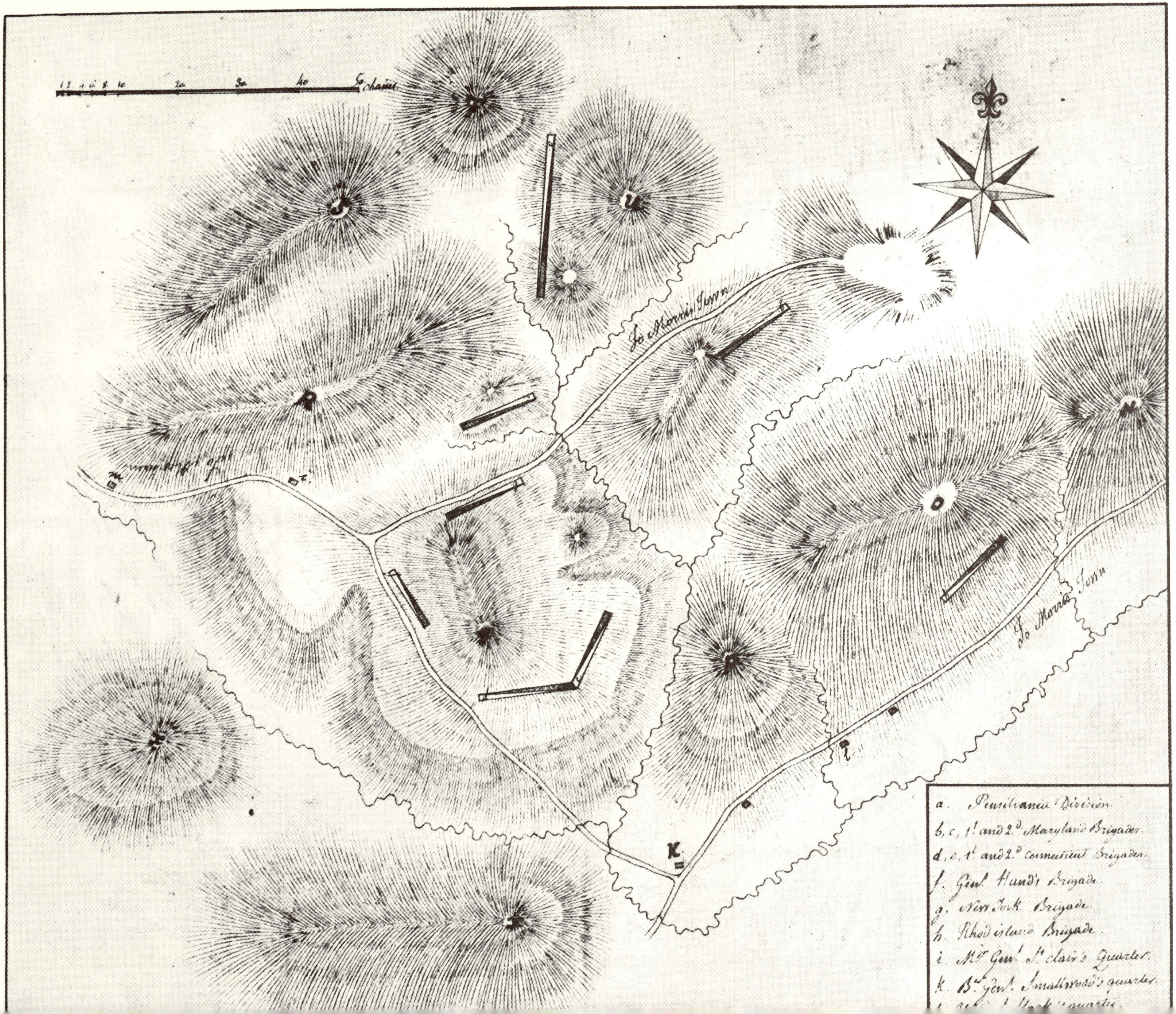
12 4 6 8 10 20 30 40 50 chains
To Morris Town
To Morris Town
a. Pensilvania Division.
b, c, 1st and 2d Maryland Brigades.
d, e, 1st and 2d Connecticut Brigades.
f. Genl. Hand's Brigade.
g. New York Brigade.
h. Rhod island Brigade.
i. Mr Genl. St clair's Quarter.
k. Br. Genl. Smallwood's quarter.

force of 13,040 regulars was still considerably larger than Washington's "8,433 rank and file" at Morristown.

Despite this continuing threat present in New York, Gen. Washington, upon the departure of the Clinton force, sent orders to Gen. Wayne to disband his light infantry detachment and prepare them to go into winter quarters. Specifically, he ordered Wayne to "detach the Massachusetts Troops to the Highlands and march the rest to this Camp," where they would report to their regular units. Upon receipt of these orders to disband his light infantry, Wayne asked "for leave of absence," which was granted.

While Washington had been so much concerned with the movement of the British fleet, his army, division by division, had arrived at Morristown. Although the various units had begun their march over different routes so that food and forage might be obtained locally as the troops moved forward, they found supplies inadequate. For example, Brigadier General William Irvine of the Pennsylvania division, said, "We had a tedious and severe march from West Point . . . being . . . four days without Bread." The shortage of flour to make bread was "owing to the uncommon drought which [for lack of waterpower] has stopped most of the Mills."

It was difficult enough to march without bread, but it was made much worse when men were called upon to march in cold November weather without sufficient clothing, and, in many cases, without shoes. As Gen. Washington observed, "the deficiency of Shoes is so extensive, that a great portion of the Army is totally incapable of duty."

The New York brigade and Hand's brigade had been the first to reach the Morristown area. They had the shortest distance to march, having come only from Pompton, New Jersey. As James Abeel of the quartermaster department wrote to Qm. Gen. Greene from Morristown on November 23, Lieutenant Colonel Marinus "Willetts & [Colonel Peter] Gansevoorts Regt. are come in and Quartered Two Miles from Town in a very good situation." As noted by Lieutenant Robert Parker of artillery, who marched with this contingent, this temporary camp was "near Hanover."

The Maryland division seems to have been the first of the West Point contingent to complete its march. On November 30, Lt. Parker said, "The First Maryland arrived today." It is presumed that the 2nd Maryland was not far behind.

Next to arrive may have been the Connecticut troops. The two brigades of the Connecticut division were issued orders at Parsippany on December 1, as follows: "The Division will march tomorrow morning to the ground assigned for Winter Quarters." In the Morristown area, however, there was "a severe storm" on December 1, which could have delayed them until the 3rd. This storm also may have delayed the Pennsylvania division until the 3rd, when Lt. Parker noted that a "Great part of the Army arrived today."

Next to the last unit to reach Morristown was Stark's brigade. It had not received marching orders until November 25, and as late as the 29th, Washington noted that Stark had not yet reached Peekskill from his starting point, Danbury, but was expected there "in a day or two." By December 8, Stark's brigade had reached "Pumpton." Surgeon James Thacher, of Stark's brigade said that "on the 14th [we] reached this wilderness [the American camp] about three miles from Morristown."

The last unit to arrive at camp was the New Jersey brigade, which had been at the front opposite Staten Island and had been relieved by a detachment under Brig. Gen. Parsons on the 14th and 15th. According to Sergeant Major George Grant, the 3rd New Jersey regiment marched on December "17 To Eyre's [Ayer's] Forge and encamped and began building huts." "Ayer's Forge" was on the Passaic River, about two miles southwest of the main camp.

The main camp, now designated Jockey Hollow, lay "about three miles" southwest of Morristown. Qm. Gen. Greene had suggested the site to New Jersey Deputy Quartermaster General James Abeel, who was in Morristown examining possible sites. On November 23, the day that the New York brigade had arrived near Morristown, and had encamped temporarily near Hanover, Abeel wrote Greene that he had viewed "the ground you mention . . . back of Mr. Kembles & find a pretty large Spott . . . well covered with Timber & pretty well watered the Ground is dry & if the Tract is large enough I believe will be the best I have as yet seen." Abeel spent some time "laying out the ground" for the various units of the army, then he wrote Greene assuring him that "the Troops as they arrive will be properly quartered."

Qm. Gen. Greene later described the camp site as follows: "The ground is mountainous and uneven; and, therefore, will not be so agreeable as I could wish. There is wood I am in hopes sufficient for the purpose of hutting and firing, if it is used properly. There is water in plenty, tho in some places it will be some distance to fetch. The ground I think will be pretty dry."

As Greene had noted, there was sufficient wood on the camp site and nearby to supply the needs of the army. Thus, as each unit had arrived in camp, they set about cutting logs for their huts. On December 3, two days after Washington's arrival at Morristown, he issued orders regarding the assignment of huts. His instructions were in part as follows: "All regimental officers to hut with their respective regiments. The regimental and brigade staff are also to be with their respective Corps; and the brigadiers if they do not hut with their brigades are to be as convenient to them as possible."

Commanding officers of divisions and brigades of the army in camp as they began building huts were "Generals St Clair, De Kalb, Woodford, Clinton, and Colonel Weyllis." More specifically these men were Major General Arthur St. Clair, commander of the Pennsylvania division; Major General John Kalb, commander of the Maryland division; Brigadier General George Clinton, commander of the New York brigade; Brigadier General William Woodford, senior officer present with the Virginia division, (which division was about to leave for the south) and Colonel Samuel Wyllys senior officer present in camp with the Connecticut division.

Additional units to be hutted were Brigadier John Stark's Rhode Island brigade, and a newly formed division made up of Brigadier General William Maxwell's New Jersey brigade and Brigadier General Edward Hand's Pennsylvania brigade. As of December 15, "Maxwell's and Hand's brigades" were formed into a division under Major General Lord Stirling.

The above commanders in charge of building huts soon found that weather conditions slowed their work. Although most of the troops began cutting logs early in December, it would not be until the end of the month that the bulk of the enlisted men would be hutted. Almost the whole of December the men slept "on the frozen ground," in tents. Some of the men, at first, did not even have tents to shelter them. Such was the fate of Stark's brigade whose "baggage [including tents] is left in the rear for want of wagons."

The enlisted men of Stark's brigade did not move into their huts until Christmas day. Lieutenant Colonel Ebenezer Huntington of Colonel Samuel Webb's Additional regiment of that brigade noted in a letter dated December 24, "expect, if good weather, to have the men's Hutts so far compleated that they may go into them on Sunday or Monday . . . The severity of the weather hath been such that the men suffer'd much without shoes and stockings, and working half leg deep in snow."

Even as the troops had begun their march to Morristown the weather had taken a turn for the worse. Following are entries in Lt. Parker's journal: "November 25 . . . The roads very bad & the weather cold . . . November 26 . . . about 11 o'clock it began to snow & continued all day, at night it cleared up very cold . . . December 1 . . . arrived at Morristown today; very severe storm . . . December 5 Snow all day and the weather very cold . . . December 6 . . . the snow knee deep & the weather very cold."

The weather continued generally bad throughout December

and into January. On January 3, Surgeon Thacher noted in his diary, "experienced one of the most tremendeous snow-storms ever remembered; no man could endure its violence many minutes without danger of his life." But this storm would not cease. As Lieutenant John Barr noted in his diary on January 7, "the storm continues from the N. W. Saturday 8th excessive Cold and wind from the N.W." Again on January 10, Gen. Washington noted that "the snow set in pretty briskly."

During this long and severe storm, Surgeon Thacher, who was doing what he could to attend the men of his regiment, said, "the sufferings of the poor soldiers can scarcely be described, while on duty they are unavoidably exposed to all the inclemency of storms and severe cold; at night they now have a bed of straw on the ground, and a single blanket to each man; they are badly clad, and some are destitute of shoes . . . the soldiers are so enfeebled from hunger and cold, as to be almost unable to perform their military duty."

There was not one day during the whole of January that the thermometer in the general area registered above freezing, averaging "22.1 degrees" for the month. Snow piled upon snow throughout December and January, making it almost impossible for the men to get about.

Although Thacher spoke for the common soldier, most of the officers were suffering many of the same hardships. Washington had ordered that officers's huts were not to be started until the enlisted men's huts were completed. As a result, colonels and those of lesser rank, lived in tents well into January—some of them into February. One soldier wrote from camp on February 11, "A number of officers are still in tents."

Generals, however, were expected to lodge in neighboring houses, but quarters were hard to find. Because Brig. Gen. Smallwood and his 1st Maryland brigade had been the first to arrive at the camp site, apparently he had the first choice, and he selected Peter "Kembles" substantial house on the southern outskirts of the camp. Maj. Gen. St. Clair, who may have had the second choice, decided on Henry "Wick's" house on the western outskirts of the camp. Brig. Gen. Stark, who was one of the last of the generals to reach camp, was compelled to settle for quarters in "Lazaliers" (Jacob Larzelaer's) Tavern. Although these were not ideal quarters, they were near the huts of his brigade in the southeast sector of the camp.

Brig. Gen. Knox did not live near the main camp because his artillery brigade was quartered "about a mile west" of Morristown, on Mendham Road. To be near his troops, Knox took up residence in the Samuel "Roberts" house or the nearby house of Roberts' son-in-law "Jonathan Ogden." Both of these houses stood north of the present Mendham Road and west of Kahdena Road.

Qm. Gen. Greene had been the first general officer to arrive in the Morristown area while in search of a campsite for the army. He had taken up quarters in the home of "Jacob Arnold," located in Washington Valley, north of the present Sussex Avenue and just west of Ketch Road.

Surgeon General John Cochran took residence in the home of Dr. Jabez Campfield, now called the Schuyler-Hamilton House, presently located at 5 Olyphant Place, having been moved there from a position along present Morris Avenue, nearer the Jacob Ford house where Washington was headquartered.

As late as December 22, Gen. Washington, advised Qm. Gen. Greene that he was "extremely concerned to find that you meet with such difficulties in quartering the Officers whose rank and situation require they should be lodged in the Houses in the vicinity of the Army."

Perhaps it was, in part, this inability to find accommodations for Washington's general officers that persuaded so many of them to take furloughs. As of January 24, Washington complained that "We have at this time but two Brigadiers of the line [out of eleven] in Camp and one of them, General Irvine has pressing calls to see his family."

Furlough-fever seems to have been infectious, for it spread to regimental officers. As of January 22, Washington said that "There are in some of the Regiments too many officers absent on furlough, so that they are left without a sufficient number to preserve order, and perform the common routine of service."

General Washington was also having trouble maintaining an adequate number of major generals in camp. Before leaving West Point his most senior officer, Major General Horatio Gates "expressed his wishes to go to Virginia for a few months on account of the situation of his private Affairs." Major General Alexander Mc Dougall also asked to be excused from going to Morristown because of "some alarming Symptoms of the stone he imagines" in his kidney. Major General John Sullivan, at about the same time, asked "to retire from the service." Major General Gilbert du Motier de Lafayette was still in France, Major General Benjamin Lincoln was commanding the southern army, and Major General Friedrich Steuben was on detached duty in Philadelphia.

Of the major generals who did go to Morristown, Nathanael Greene was temporarily serving as quartermaster general and Robert Howe was serving as president of the court-martial of Major General Benedict Arnold. And, as soon as Arnold's trial was over, Howe would take over command in the New York Highlands from Major General William Heath who had asked for retirement for "health" reasons.

Only three major generals were available for line duty at Morristown. They were Lord Stirling, Arthur St. Clair and John Kalb. As to Stirling, who lived southeast of Basking Ridge about nine miles from Morristown headquarters, he spent considerable time at home. As late as March 19, he wrote Gen. Washington from Basking Ridge that "I have not for these two months been able to be on horseback with so firm a Seat as was necessary in extreme Bad roads." As to St. Clair, he spent most of his time in camp or on front line duty, but eventually took a short furlough in "Philada." So did John Kalb finally succumb to furlough-fever. He said that "Being entirely in rags, I shall go to Philadelphia as soon as I can, to purchase new clothes, especially linen." But Kalb lamented that he would not be able to buy much, as prices were so dear; "A hat costs four hundred dollars, a pair of boots the same."

Chapter II

ENDLESS BURDENS

Soaring Inflation

The fact that Major General Kalb was forced to pay an exorbitant $400. for a new hat was brought about by the loss in acceptable value of United States paper money when it was offered in payment for goods in place of gold or silver. The situation as it existed in 1780, when Kalb purchased his hat, had not come about over night, but had developed over the past five years of the war.

In the colonies there long had been a shortage of gold or silver, called specie, coin or hard money, for there were no known gold or silver mines in the colonies during the 18th century. Barter had developed as a general practice because of this shortage. For example, it was customary for a storekeeper to give a farmer long-term credit, with payment to be made in crops at the threshing season, or in livestock when of marketable size and quality.

When the war started in 1775, what little gold and silver there was in circulation in the colonies soon began to disappear from the market place, mainly as a result of hoarding.

Although there had been some paper money printed in the colonies before the war, when war came, Congress began printing large quantities of money, called Continental Currency, in order to finance the war. As Congress was forced to print more and more money to buy supplies for the army, it became less acceptable in trade or exchange. By the fall of 1778, if someone wanted to buy a

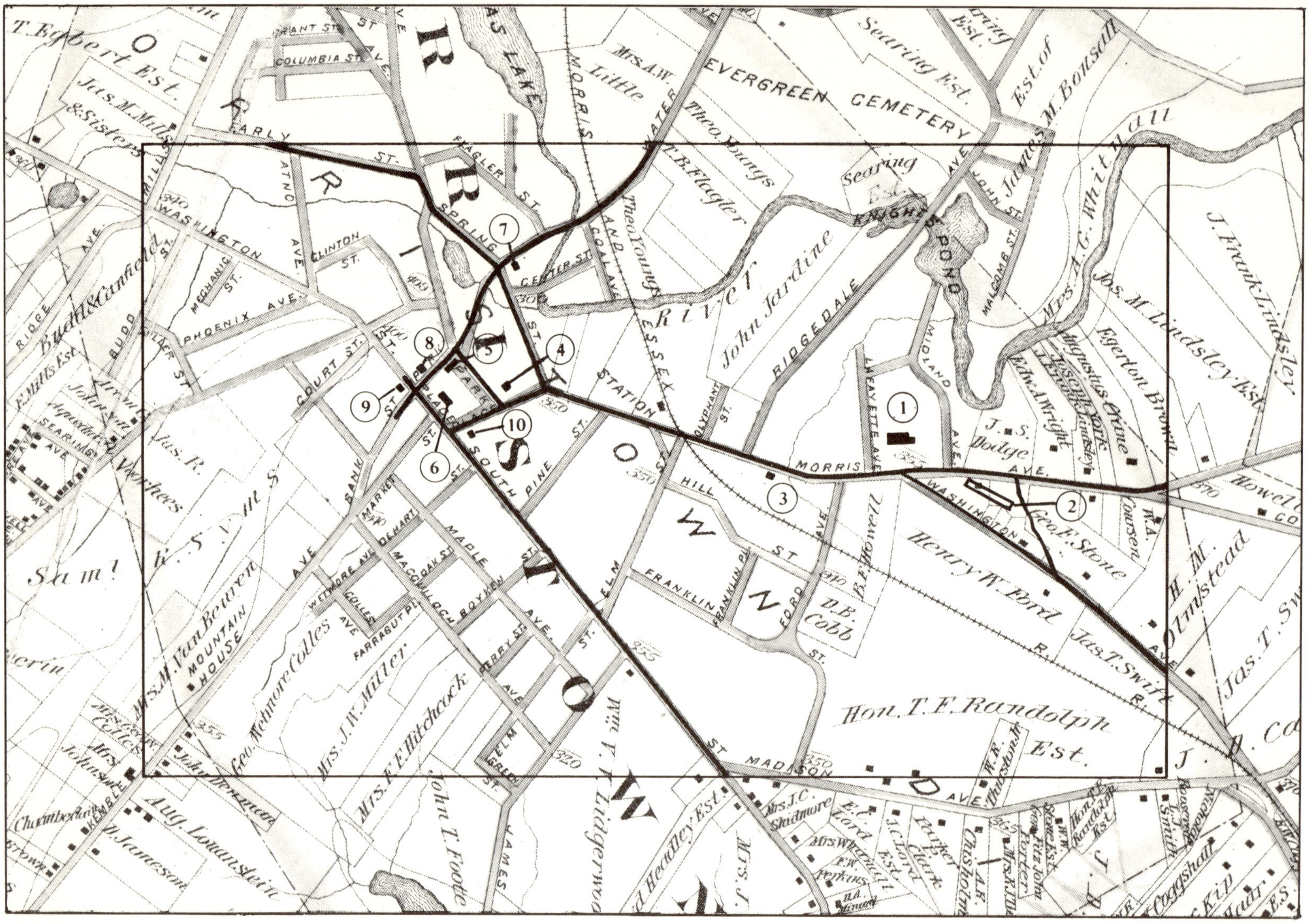

MORRISTOWN VILLAGE 1779-1780—On December 9, 1779, eight days after Gen. Washington's arrival at Morristown to winter quarter his army there, he instructed his aide, Lt. Col. Tench Tilghman, to write to Col. Robert Erskine, geographer and surveyor to the army, as follows: "His Excellency is extremely anxious to have the Roads in front and rear of the Camp accurately surveyed as speedily as possible." (WW 17:240) This resulted in a series of six maps. (See AmM 17/104, A,B,C,D,E and 17/105.) Map #105 is titled Survey of Morristown by the chain only, *and is dated December 12, 1779. It is reproduced on the opposite page, courtesy* The New York Historical Society. *To interpret this map, we have roughly outlined it upon a section of* Robinson's Atlas of Morris County, *printed in 1887, plate #6. We have also indicated the location of buildings that are mentioned in the text and that lie within the area of the map. (1) Jacob Ford house, occupied by Gen. Washington, (2) Barracks of Washington's Guard, (3) Jabez Campfield house (original site), occupied by Surg. Gen. John Cochran, (4) Presbyterian Church, (5) Courthouse and jail, (6) Continental storehouse, (7) Norris's Tavern, (8) Arnold's Tavern, (9) Samuel Tuthill's house, (10) Alexander Carmichael's house.*

dollar item, he could get it for that price if he had gold or silver, but if he had to pay in paper money, he would have to give "four for one."

As a consequence of this lack of confidence in paper money, farmers throughout the states began withholding their crops or livestock from the market for ever higher prices that were sure to come. Under these conditions, army commissary agents found it almost impossible to convince the farmer to sell his crops.

When the farmer eventually did decide that he must take paper money for some of his crops in order to buy something he needed, there usually was a speculator near at hand who would give him just a trifle more paper money than the going rate that the army commissary agents were authorized to pay. Sometimes a load of grain would change ownership four or five times before it came to the fair market in which the army commissary agents were dealing. The agents, finally, were forced to pay the inflated price in order to feed the army. This practice was called "forestalling." It was illegal, but it was a fact of life.

Forestalling was practiced so close to the Morristown camp that even the common soldier could observe it. The Morris County Court Minute Books of the period document case upon case of forestalling, but the practice went on, and prices rose higher and higher. Sometimes agents would have to range far from camp into southern New Jersey or into the back country of Pennsylvania in order to purchase needed supplies at acceptable prices. Even there, they often failed.

By mid-year 1779, paper money had become so depreciated that the difference in value between it and hard money was "upwards of 30" to one. Just to purchase enough forage for the horses of the army, now took an enormous amount of paper money. As one member of Congress scornfully put it, "Our public Horses [those of the army] have been starved for Want of Forage tho' there has been given to that [the Commissary] Department almost Paper [money] enough to litter [or bed-down] the whole number."

With the situation thus completely out of hand, Congress in

September 1779, resolved to stop printing paper money. The total had reached $200,000,000. plus, a huge sum for the times. On the face of this paper money it read "The Bearer is entitled to receive . . . Spanish milled dollars or an equivalent sum in Gold or Silver, according to a Resolution of Congress," but Congress had no gold or silver in the treasury to redeem this paper.

When Congress stopped printing money, that body found that its action had stimulated another industry, namely counterfeiting. As the number of counterfeiters grew, and as their product became mingled almost undetected with the government's paper money, the money market became even more depressed.

Gen. Washington deplored this additional assault on the integrity of Continental Currency. He wrote from Morristown to the President of Congress on December 7, 1779, that the ever-growing counterfeiting practice does nothing but "to increase the depression of our currency." Even the words describing the situation as it existed in 1779-80, still remain a part of our language—"not worth a continental."

On December 9, 1779, Gen. Washington wrote at length to the president of Congress stating that he had received reliable information from New York regarding "the indefatigable indeavours of the enemy to increase the depreciation of our currency, by increasing its quantity in Counterfeits. It [his informant] asserts, as a matter of certainty, that several Reams of the paper, made from the last emission [of Continental Currency] struck by Congress, have been procured [by the enemy] from Philadelphia . . . He observes, that the Enemy have great hopes of terminating the War in their favor in another Campaign, as they expect, confidently, the entire ruin of our Money and a failure of provisions for the supply of the Army."

What Gen. Washington claimed was the enemy's objective of destroying the American army by destroying the value of its currency, seemed to be taking effect. Since the government had stopped printing money, its only source of revenue was taxes, and these were slow in coming in. As Comm. Gen. Ephraim Blaine explained it on January 29, "I have done all in my Power to obtain Mony from the Treasury for my Department but have been disappointed the Treasury being of monies emitted [all the money collected had been paid out] and the Taxes coming in so very slow . . . I have not been able to obtain one shilling."

Royal Flint, assistant commissary of purchases, informed Gen. Washington when he complained about the lack of food for the army, "The purchasers here [at Morristown] say that they could buy cattle if they had money; of which I can neither give nor promise them any . . . and our credit is totally exhausted."

Even if Royal Flint had been given money, paper money that is, it would not have purchased much. In January 1780, prices were as follows: "Wheat pr bushel $50. Rye pr bushel $35. Corn pr bushel $30. Buckwheat & Oats pr bushel $20." And prices were going up every day.

As early as the first week in January 1780, a few states had enacted legislation "for the regulation of prices," but these curbs had little effect. By the middle of March, New Jersey "suspended the operation of the act" that they had passed because New York, Pennsylvania and Delaware had not passed similar acts as recommended in resolutions of Congress.

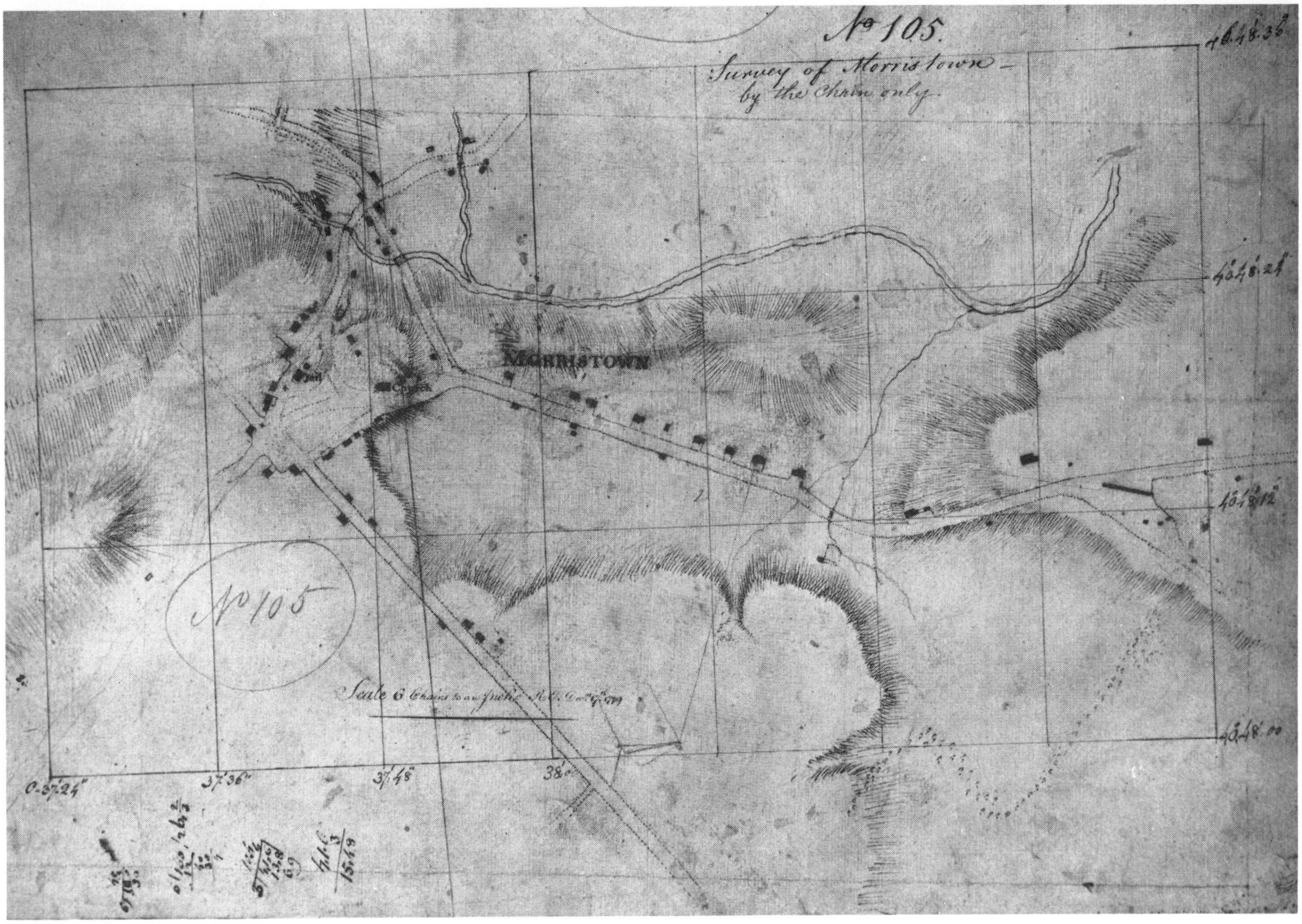

By spring, Gen. Kalb sadly noted that "Provisions and other articles . . . are growing dearer and dearer, being now double what they were a year ago, even if paid in gold one dollar of which is now equal to sixty in paper." These Kalb comments were made about the time he was purchasing his new hat for $400. with the paper money that he had received from the army in pay.

London Trade

What were the alternatives for the farmer regarding the sale of his produce during this period of extreme inflation? If the ratio of acceptability in the marketplace of hard money to paper money had risen from $1. to $1.50 in 1775, to $1. to $60. in 1780, what was there in the future to stop it from going higher and higher as long as the war continued? This reasoning turned out to be correct, for by 1781, it would be $1. to $150. And what if the cause of liberty would eventually be lost? Paper money would be worthless.

If the farmer could find a way of selling at least some of his crops or his livestock for hard money instead of paper money, he reasoned that he should do so. Thus, the farmer sought out what he considered any fair way to sell his goods for gold or silver instead of paper.

Where then could the farmer find these buyers with hard money? This was not difficult. There were numerous anonymous agents plying the countryside with hard money in hand. The British had hard money and they saw to it that sympathetic traders were well supplied. When a sale was made to one of these traders, there was no mention as to where the product eventually might be consumed. This was no business of the farmer, and even though the farmer might favor the Patriot side, he usually did not ask the question.

In all too many cases, however, the agent would quietly move the product down toward Staten Island or another convenient crossing place. Then, on some dark night, it would be moved across the front lines, sometimes under enemy escort, to be sold at a very considerable profit. This was called "London Trade."

Gen. St. Clair described one fully escorted large scale dash through enemy lines. This particular instance occurred in early February when Newark Bay and the Staten Island Sound, now Arthur Kill, were frozen over. St. Clair said, "They came by ice from Bergen Point [now Bayonne] passed up towards De Harts Point [now Elizabeth], about half way, and then moved off and landed near Deckers Ferry [now Port Richmond] on Staten Island. The sleighs were in number about one hundred and the escort consisted of about sixty infantry and twenty horse."

Of course, knowingly to sell to the enemy was against the law, but was it unlawful for the farmer to sell to one man for hard money and not to the army for paper money. Had not Congressman John Lovell stood up in Congress and spoken out that "It lays with the Farmer to say whether he will at any Rate furnish the Army."

From the very beginning of the Morristown encampment, Gen. Washington had deplored this trade with the enemy. When he had sent Gen. Parsons to the front opposite Staten Island in December, he instructed Parsons to "give protection to the well affected inhabitants and restrain the others by preventing all kind of intercourse with the enemy."

Washington's instructions to Maj. Lee, who covered the area below the Raritan River, were to keep watching the area of Monmouth County and British occupied "Sandy Hook" to the end of "cutting off the intercourse between the Country and the enemy." For example, it was reported from Monmouth County "that there are always considerable quantities of cattle brought from West Jersey, and lodged near the shore to be handy to send off to New York as a good opportunity serves." To Lt. Col. De Hart, who was sent to Paramus in December, Washington pointed out that "The detestable and pernicious traffic carried on with the Enemy will demand your greatest vigilance and attention." Likewise, in Connecticut, Governor Jonathan Trumbull was instructed to use his militia to "take the most vigorous measures for stopping the intercourse between the Inhabitants of that State and the Enemy in New York and upon Long Island."

Despite efforts to control this illicit traffic, it continued in all areas bordering on British held territory. Gen. Kalb noted in a letter to Washington that to stop the traffic, or at least to cut it down, he had taken new and stronger measures. He reported that "Besides the Guards and Patrolles, I have established . . . two . . . boats . . . one on the Rahway River the other on Bound Creek near Newark to be out all night plying to and fro. I intend to have another at Amboy . . . This method . . . to prevent more effectually the Traffick, called London Trade, which is mostly carried on at night."

It was difficult to regulate the movement of civilians. A soldier was not allowed just to confront a private citizen and demand to know where he got his goods or where he was taking them. It was now a free country, and he had to be caught in some illegal act before he could be apprehended. William Burnet, probably Dr. William Burnet of Newark, commented on this subject in a report to Brig. Gen. Huntington who was at the time commanding American forces at the front. He said, "There are a number of boats in the Passaic River which . . . may safely be made use of to . . . carry on London Trade . . . [however] Private property ought not to be touched unless Public Safety requires it."

London traders knew that they had the law on their side until the law was broken by their final dash across enemy lines. Consequently, this illegal movement of goods was extremely difficult to control, and London Trade flourished throughout the period of the Morristown encampment.

Starving Soldiers

General Washington was much aware that London Trade was drawing off a considerable amount of food that ordinarily would have gone to the army. Further, it was being drawn from an already diminished food supply as compared to former years, because of the drought during the fall of 1779. Inflation and the shortage of money further complicated the supply system of the army.

As early as December 19, Washington had appealed to the governors of the middle states for needed supplies, in the absence of adequate help from Congress. He pointed out to the states that his army had been for "five or six weeks past on half allowance and we have not more than three days bread at a third allowance on hand, nor anywhere within reach. When this is exhausted, we must depend on the precarious gleanings of the neighbouring country. Our magazines are absolutely empty everywhere, and our commissaries entirely destitute of money or credit to replenish them. We have never experienced a like extremity at any period of the war."

Strong as Washington's appeal had been, no immediate relief came. Then, on January 1, New Year's Day, it happened. The army was completely out of food, and would remain so for several days. On January 2, Nathan Beers of Stark's brigade wrote in his diary "no provisions for two days past." On the fourth day Qm. Gen. Greene wrote dejectedly from Morristown to one of his subordinates in the field, "Poor Fellows! they exhibit a picture truly distressing—More than half naked and above two thirds starved."

Private Joseph Plumb Martin of the Connecticut line, recalled that "We are absolutely, literally starved. I do solemly declare that I did not put a single morsel of victuals into my mouth for four days and as many nights, except a little black birch bark which I gnawed off a stick of wood, if that can be called victuals. I saw several of the men roast their old shoes and eat them, and I was afterwards informed by one of the officers' waiters, that some of the officers killed and ate a favourite little dog that belonged to one of them."

On the fifth day a small trickle of food came into camp. On the sixth day another trickle came in, but not enough to relieve even a regiment or two. By the seventh day of starvation week, there was chaos in camp as the common soldier took matters into his own hands. Officers were helpless as they observed "Gangs of Soldiers Going out of Camp and Committing every Species of Robery" in order to keep from starving.

Washington appears to have looked the other way at this action, stating that the men "have been at last brought to such a dreadful extremity, that no authority or influence of the officers no virtue or patience of the men themselves could any longer restrain them from obeying the dictates of their sufferings." The general said further "and I have not in my power to punish or to repress the practice."

The first week in January was a horrible one for the American army at Morristown. Even the weather turned against them. During that week, Morris County experienced the most extreme weather. As one soldier noted in his diary, "January 2 violent snow storme . . . January 3 the snow drifts mightily . . . January 4 very cold weather . . . January 6 continues very cold."

By January 8, Washington realized that his appeal to the governors of the middle states back in middle December was not bringing results, whereupon he was forced to levy on each county in New Jersey for food and forage, working through magistrates. To each New Jersey county he sent a quota, and he instructed the county officials to "impress till you make up the quantity required."

Impressed farmers would be given "certificates specifying the quantity of each article and the terms of payment" at some future date. These were drastic measures that Washington never expected he would have to take.

Although levying upon counties did cease when quotas were reached, food and forage that had been taken under this process soon was consumed, and men were again on the verge of starvation. By January 28, the inhabitants near camp once more became "a prey to the plundering & licentious spirit of the Soldiers." By March 3, Richard Peters, a member of Congress who had come to Morristown to observe conditions at first hand, noted "Unless the speediest Relief is afforded it is by no Means improbable that the Army will be obliged to disband."

The army did not disband but it was badly battered. As Gen. William Irvine wrote to Governor Joseph Reed of Pennsylvania as late as April 18, "We are still shockingly supplied with provisions."

Lagging Enlistments

As the year 1780 had begun, General Washington was confronted with still another serious problem. He feared that his army would fall apart due to expiring enlistments. In addition to the "Cambridge Army," there had been two so-called Continental "Establishments," or enlistment periods up to this point in the war. The "First Establishment" had ended December 31, 1776. This was followed by the "Second Establishment" beginning January 1, 1777. For this establishment, enlistments and reenlistments had been solicited for three years or the duration of the war. Thus, these Second Establishment terms began to expire on December 31, 1779, and they would continue to expire for the next four or five months, which had been the period of time it had taken to recruit enough troops.

As the reenlistment program of the army began for the "Third Establishment," Washington soon learned that an overwhelming number of men decided not to reenlist. They were poorly fed, poorly clothed, and most of them had not been paid since the "1st of Sepr." Washington knew precisely the magnitude of his problem. Scheduled enlistment expirations for the first five months of 1780 were, "January 969, February 621, March 1345, April 1725, May 1098."

Not only was Washington having difficulty in convincing the men of his present army to reenlist but he was having trouble with Congress in getting them to act on a program for obtaining new recruits. There had been prolonged debate in Congress about the Third Establishment, but as of January 1, 1780, when it was to begin, Congress's mind had not yet been made up as to how it should operate and what state quotas should be.

It was not until early February that Congress passed the needed legislation. And it was not until February 10, that Congress sent quotas to each state, along with a circular, which read in part, "It is recommended to each State respectively in the strongest Terms punctually to comply with this Requisition by furnishing their respective Quotas of Men Compleat without loss of Time."

Although Congress finally had acted, it would be weeks before state recruiting machinery could be put in motion. When at length this was accomplished, the recruiters found great resistance among possible enlistees. The states had planned to offer a "two hundred" dollar enlistment bonus, or bounty, authorized by Congress. The recruiters soon found, however, that because of inflation this figure was considered unrealistically low. It was argued by possible enlistees that if they were to be paid a bonus in paper money, it should reflect the current value ratio of hard to paper money. As a result of this pressure, some states were forced to raise bonus offers to as high as $2,000. in order to get recruits—the states making up the difference. Those states that resisted the pressure continued to fail in their recruiting efforts.

When these raw recruits began coming into camp at Morristown and telling of their $2,000. bonuses, the army's reenlistment program, which offered only $200., came to a sudden halt. Rather than reenlist, men decided to go home for a short while, then, possibly, come back into the army as new recruits so as to get the $2000. bonuses.

While all of these delays were occuring, Gen. Washington saw the strength of his army go down and down. On March 27, he reported to Congress that the "force at this post [Morristown] amounts to about 7000 rank and file, thirteen hundred of whom will have completed their terms of service the last of May." In the New York Highlands the situation was even worse. On March 27, out of 2,600 men at that post, there were "twelve hundred whose services will expire at the same period," namely the last of May.

Revengeful Refugees

Added to the burdens of soaring inflation, London Trade, starving soldiers and lagging enlistments, there was a fifth heavy burden that General Washington had to carry during his 1779-80 winter at Morristown. This was the control of refugees.

During the first five years of the war there had developed a growing intramural struggle between British and American protected colonies of civilian refugees, mainly in New York, New Jersey and Connecticut. The struggle between these civilian groups began shortly after July 3, 1776, which was the day before the Declaration of Independence was approved at Philadelphia. On this day, the British landed a large military force on Staten Island, and within two months, this force had extended its occupation to Long Island and Manhattan Island as well as lower Westchester County.

Soon after the British took these territories, there began a steady flow of British, or Loyalist, sympathizers from New York, New Jersey and Connecticut into British held areas. At the same time, there began a steady flow of Patriot sympathizers out of British held areas into Upper Westchester County, Connecticut and New Jersey, which were areas under the control of the forces of General Washington.

Most of the declared Loyalists or Patriots made their moves shortly after the British took New York. There were, however, a large number of undeclared Loyalists and Patriots, who feigned neutrality so as to remain where they had established homes, farms or businesses, in the hope that their side, eventually would prevail. Some even pretended to favor the other side so they could use this

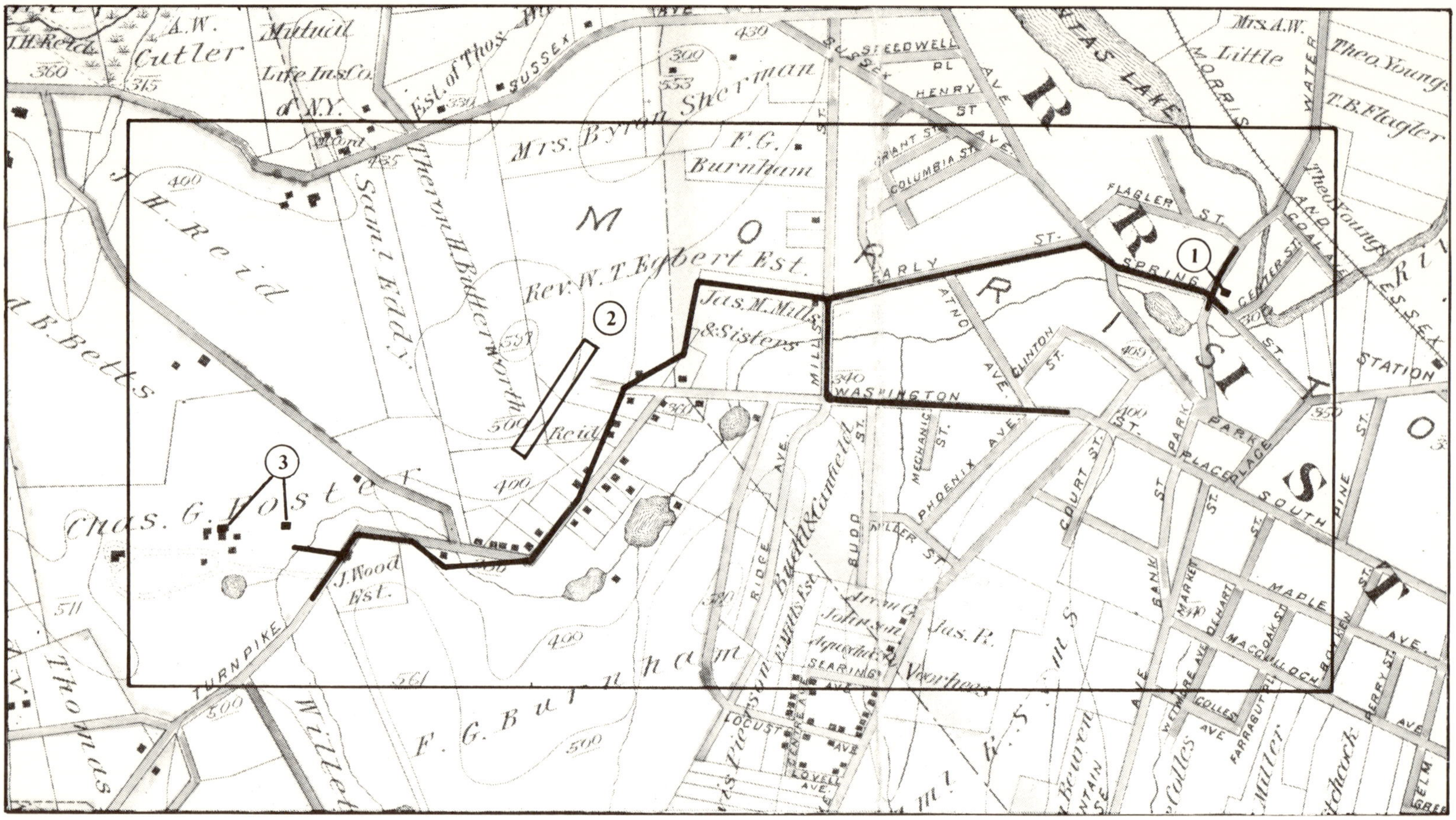

LOCATION OF ARTILLERY PARK—Roughly outlined on this section of plate #6, in the 1887 Robinson's Atlas of Morris County, *is Col. Robert Erskine's December 1779 map #104D (AmM 17/ 104D) reproduced on the opposite page, courtesy* The New York Historical Society. *The map is titled* Road from Norris's Tavern in Morristown past the Park of Artillery to Genl Knox's Quarters. *(1) Norris's Tavern was named for Robert Norris, the leasee in 1779. The owner of the tavern was Peter Dickerson who had been a captain in the 3rd New Jersey regiment of continentals prior to his resignation on 10.26.77. Maj. Gen. Benedict Arnold's trial was held in Norris's Tavern. In 1901 the tavern was described as "still standing, at the corner of Water and Morris streets, Morristown." (2 NJA 1:123) (2) The Artillery Park appears to have been located on a 500 foot hill, cresting at 597 feet, lying between present Egbert Avenue and Kahdena Road. (3) Knox's Quarters is somewhat in question as to exact location. A map of Washington Valley showing the old roads, the property lines and the location of houses in the 18th century, suggests that Brig. Gen. Knox lived in either the house of Samuel Roberts or that of Jonathan Ogden. (Hoskins map 114—115) The Hoskins map also shows the location of Jacob Arnold's house, which was occupied by Qm. Gen. Greene during the winter of 1779-1780.*

stance to help their side whenever it was possible to do so without being caught.

From the very beginning of their occupation, the British vigorously sought to uncover civilian enemies within their lines, but Gen. Washington tried to live with the same situation within his lines until it proved to be too dangerous. It was not until January 25, 1777, that Washington issued a proclamation declaring that all suspected Loyalists must either take the oath of allegiance to the United States of America or "granting full Liberty to all such as prefer the interest and protection of Great-Britain to the freedom and happiness of their country, forthwith to withdraw themselves and families within the enemy's lines."

Thus, there began another large movement of Loyalists out of Patriot held areas. Those who earlier had left voluntarily had been allowed to depart with all the personal property that they could carry with them, including livestock. With the issuance of the current proclamation, this practice would cease. It was ordered that "Such as go over to the Enemy, are not to take with them anything but their Cloathing and furniture, their Horses, Cattle and Forage must be left behind."

This was a severe blow to Loyalist refugees, but an even more severe blow would be struck. Their lands would be confiscated by the state and sold to the highest Patriot bidder. In New Jersey, this confiscation and sale was conducted pursuant to an act passed on December 11, 1778, described as "An Act for forfeiting to, and vesting in the State of New-Jersey, the real estates of certain fugitives and offenders." This act infuriated the deprived Loyalist landholders, and they vowed retaliation.

Some refugees, when they left their homes to be in exile, had friends or relatives who would take them in for the duration, or they had business connections that would occupy their interest. The bulk of the refugees, however, had no place to go and had nothing to do but mark time until they could return home. Thus, large numbers of refugees lived from day-to-day, close to the enemy lines, waiting to return home, or for an opportunity to help bring that day about.

Some refugees were not content just to wait. They joined the military forces of their chosen side. Those who had taken British sanctuary, except under extraordinary circumstances, were not permitted to join the regular British army. They could join only volunteer companies, regiments or brigades, called "Provincial" units. Although there were many of these units, the principal ones in the British held New York area were the New York brigade of Volunteers and the New Jersey brigade of Volunteers.

As their names suggested, the New York Volunteers was made up mainly of New York refugees and sympathetic citizens already residing in New York, while the New Jersey Volunteers was made up mainly of refugees from New Jersey. The New York brigade was stationed in and about New York City and the New Jersey brigade was stationed on Staten Island.

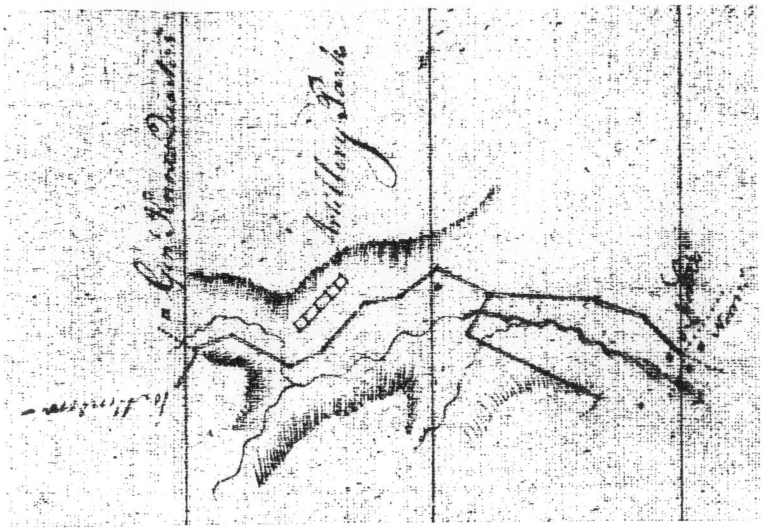

American policy regarding refugees was different. Refugees could join either the continental forces or the state militia. Most of them, however, preferred to join local militia units so they could stay close to home, and be ready for any favorable turn of events.

With so many refugees, both civilian and military, concentrated so near the front on both sides of the line, and under such volatile conditions, there were almost hourly disruptions at the front. Everyone spoke the same language; everyone wore the same type of clothes. One could easily slip over the lines at night and move great distances into the country, either to take revenge, to recover some property left behind, or for any one of a thousand reasons.

James Moody was one of the most daring of these refugees. And he was one of the few who wrote an account of some of his exploits. Moody had been a farmer in "Sussex County," New Jersey, before going into exile behind British lines. Moody tells how he frequently came back to New Jersey, undetected, and made raids deep into the country. Sometimes he came alone and sometimes with a small group of companions, carrying concealed arms of course, but looking and acting like any ordinary Patriot civilian, until the place to strike had been reached.

Moody was particularly active during the winter of 1779-80 while the American army was in camp near Morristown. On one occasion that winter, Moody actually penetrated the Morristown encampment proper and "obtained from their own books, an account of the rations which were drawn from them," which report was turned over to the British by Moody upon his return to Staten Island.

On one occasion he set out to kidnap Governor William Livingston of New Jersey who lived on the northern outskirts of Elizabethtown. On this venture, he "took with him four trusty men, and went into the Rebel Country with the intention of surprising Governor Livingston, a man whose whole conduct had been, in the most abandoned degree, cruel and oppressive to the loyal inhabitants [Loyalists] of New Jersey. When, with all necessary secrecy, Mr. Moody got into his immediate neighbourhood, information was received, that Mr. Livingston was gone to Trenton."

In addition to the countless raids by unauthorized personnel, like Moody, frequent raids or attacks were made into New Jersey and elsewhere, by Provincial military units. On these occasions, it was almost certain that matters would get out of hand, resulting in looting and burning. Although some depredations could be laid to Provincial units, it was usually the work of civilian refugees who always seemed to learn of an impending attack and trailed along behind the military, in large numbers.

The general staff of both British and American armies deplored burning and looting. British Major General James Robertson noted the indescriminate looting and burning "gave too good foundation to the rebels to represent us as inimical to the Country." General Washington said "Every thing of this kind should be prohibited as far as possible." Yet, as the war progressed, burning and looting became more widespread and more vicious. By 1780, the situation seemed to be completely out of control, particularly across the Staten Island-New Jersey front lines.

Chapter III

MORRISTOWN CAMP LIFE

In the Huts

Notwithstanding the hardships that General Washington and his army were experiencing at Morristown, somehow an organized army life was maintained. As much as possible, the men in camp were kept occupied from reveille to taps. Mess, exercise, roll call, drill, inspection, guard and fatigue duty were daily routines.

At times, during the winter of 1779-80, mess was pretty much on the basis of "eat when food arrives at the company kitchen." Some days there was no mess at all. On other days, mess call came at the oddest hour.

Exercise, first thing in the morning, was by companies in front of company huts. Exercise was a must, even in severe weather. It was spelled out in General Orders that "each Company be exercised by the Captain or officer commanding it. The Field Officer to superintend the whole and see that it is carried on agreeably to regulations." Roll call, by companies, was held at noon, "at which time the Officers commanding Companies shall cause their men to parade without arms, and their Rolls to be called."

Regimental reviews and inspections were numerous and scheduled by the commanding officers of regiments. They were in preparation for general inspections and reviews, which were held by brigades on the main camp parade ground. These were two-day affairs. First there was a general inspection of clothing, arms, accouterments, camp equipage, etc. followed by a review under the watchful eye of Inspector General Steuben, or his assistant. Notice to the brigades chosen for these two day affairs was given only three or four days in advance. For example, in the Headquarters Orderly Book under date of January 29 it stated, "Genl Clinton's brigade to be reviewed the 2nd & 3rd of Feby next—Genl Stark's the 4th & 5th."

When spring arrived, additional parades and reviews were held in town. These were by selected, well drilled, and well uniformed troops. They were small reviews consisting of two regiments or battalions with some artillery, and were more-or-less public relations gestures. As noted in General Orders of May 12, "Every Monday, Wednesday and Saturday beginning on Monday next the Inspector General or in his absence one of the Inspectors will exercise on the Green near Morristown two Battalions detached from the Line with four Field pieces."

Guard duty of several sorts was a principal occupation in camp. The main camp guard called for the greatest manpower. Ordinarily about 500 men were assigned to this duty on a 24 hour basis. The men were selected each day from the various divisions and brigades of the army, on a rotating basis, so as not to burden any one unit too severely.

At late afternoon retreat, traditionally at the setting of the sun, the new or incoming main camp guard would assemble and pass in review before it went out to relieve the old guard at the designated picket posts of the army. In March, with only 7,000 rank and file stationed at Morristown, 1,000 of whom were on front line duty, this meant that main camp guard duty for each man came up about once every two weeks.

At the changing of the main camp guard, there was a newly appointed commander of the guard or "officer of the day" calling

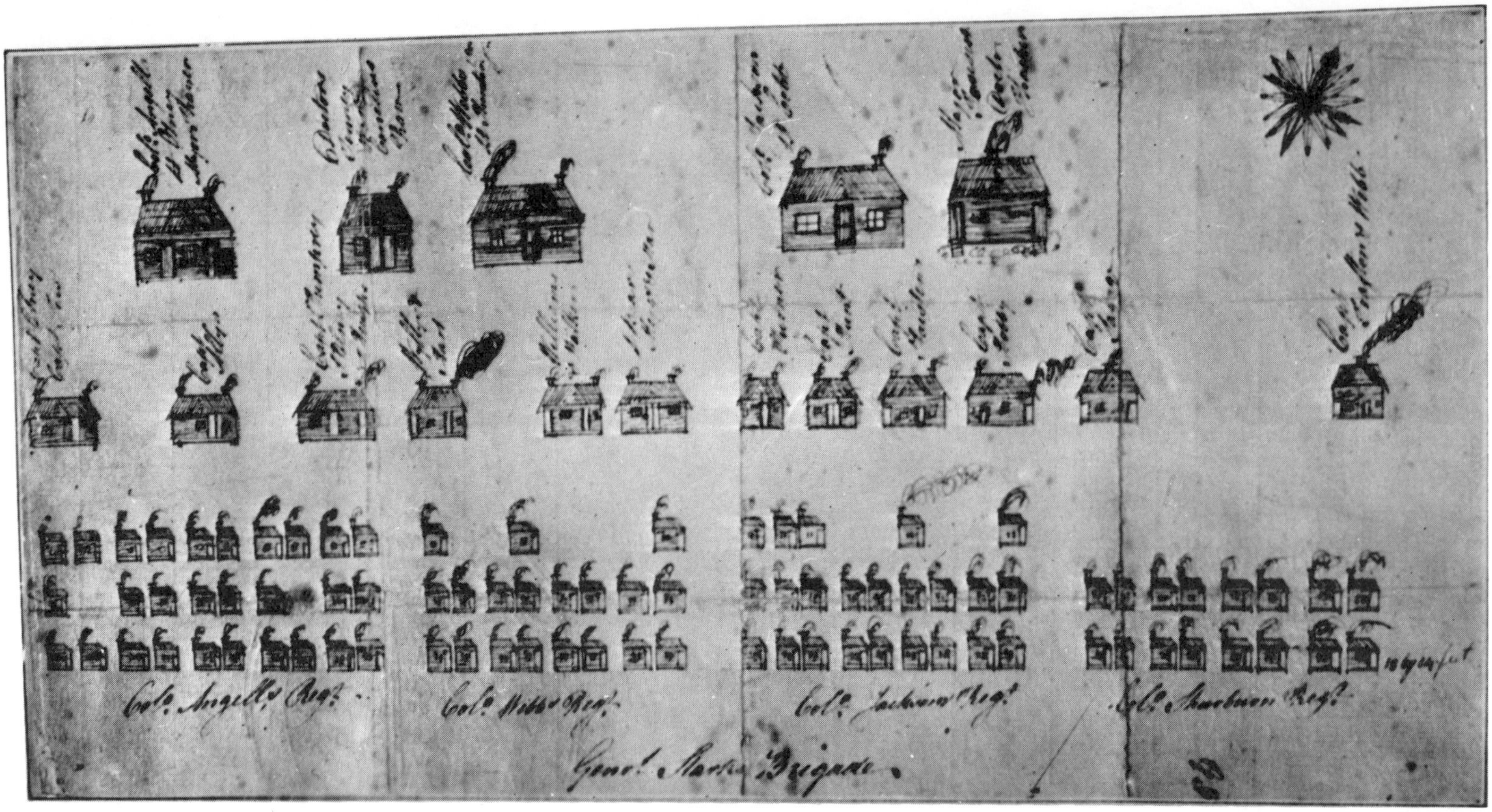

HUTTING ARRANGEMENT OF STARK'S BRIGADE—This drawing undoubtedly was made by someone who not only saw the Stark huts but knew the hutting assignments of Stark's brigade. The drawing most probably was made before 5.1.80 on which date Sherburne's regiment was disbanded and Sherburne's men were assigned to other regiments of the brigade. (WW 18:319) The regiments, from left to right, are labeled "Colo. Angell's, Colo. Webb's, Colo. Jackson's, Colo. Sherburne's." From bottom to top the first and second rows of huts were presumably for enlisted men and the third for ensigns and lieutenants. The fourth line was for captains and the fifth or top line was for majors, lieutenant colonels, colonels and doctors as labeled. The drawing was once owned by Erskine Hewitt of Ringwood, New Jersey, a Col. Robert Erskine namesake and a collector of his memorabilia. The drawing served as a guide for two very productive archeological digs, resulting in the Campbell report in 1967 and the Rutsch-Peters report in 1976.

for the rank of major or brigadier general. However, with the shortage of general officers in camp, some adjustment had to be made. Thus, on January 31, General Orders read, "In the present scarcity of General officers with the Army, the Colonels commanding brigades will roll in the duties of the day instead of brigadiers."

After the assignment from headquarters of the incoming officer of the day, it was required that "The old and new officer of the day will attend Head Quarters daily at one o'clock; the former to make report of the transactions of the preceding day and the latter to receive any new orders the Commander in Chief may have to give."

There were numerous other away-from-camp guard duties. One was the "Main Guard at Morristown." This duty was rotated "every two days." When the army first arrived at Morristown, the guard was small, but soon it was enlarged to consist of a "Capt, Sub. 3 Sergts 4 Corpls & 50" privates. Its principal task was to provide security for the guardhouse located in the county courthouse, on the town green. By the end of the winter there had been so much damage done to the facility that the magistrates applied to the government for funds to repair it. But it was not until the end of March 1782, when General Washington was again in Morristown for two days on his way to Newburgh, that he was reminded of the damage to "the Court House, which had been made use of as a Guard House and considerably injured by the public service."

It is possible that the "Main Guard at Morristown" also furnished a small detail to protect the commissary stores in town. The main commissary storehouse in Morristown was called the continental store or "continental building." It was located "on the parsonage lot between Mr. Carmichael's and Doct. Tuthill's," which would place it on the Morristown Green near the head of the present Market Street, which street, at that time, had not yet been laid out.

There also was a Quartermaster general store at nearby Succasunna, which called for a guard detail of "A Serjeant Corporal and 10 men." The guard "at Suckesuma [was] to be releiv'd weekly." Other around-the-clock guard details were required at the forage yard near Headquarters, just across the "Whippany River" and south of the present Evergreen Avenue. In addition, there was a forage depot at "Veal Town," now Bernardsville.

At Headquarters, "Fatigue at Orderly Room" was still another important duty assignment. This detail consisted of a "Sub., 2 Sergts & 40 R&F." As early as January 21, the orderly room at headquarters was being referred to as the "new orderly room" suggesting that a new one had been recently built. The duty here had nothing to do with guarding Headquarters, which was an assignment of Washington's Guard, but probably consisted of policing the grounds around Headquarters, and other similar tasks.

At the artillery park near what is now Burnham Park, Gen. Knox posted his own guard to watch the artillery stores. But, early in December, Gen. Washington requested Knox "to keep no more military Stores [related to artillery] in Camp, or very near it, than are absolutely necessary to answer immediate consumption or sudden calls." Thus, surplus stores should be moved to the artillery park at "Easton," Pennsylvania.

Guard and fatigue details also had to be furnished for the various army hospitals in the area. The "General Hospital [was at] Baskingridge," with a smaller facility "at Morristown." Guard details at hospitals in "Princeton, Trenton [and] Philadelphia" were probably on detached duty. Of course, each regiment in camp had its own hospital hut that called for several duty assignments.

Added to these regular duties that rotated, there were numerous special, one-time duty assignments called for by the supply departments to perform such tasks as clearing snow from roads, rebuilding bridges, transporting supplies etc. For example on December 7, it was ordered that "A Trusty Sergt with Sufficient Number of men are to be sent from Difft Brigades to drive the Wagon Horses."

Further, each regiment in camp had its own internal system of guard and fatigue duty. One hut was set aside in each regimental compound as a "guard house." A captain usually headed the guard house detail and he was called the "Police Captain." To the common soldier, there seemed to be a guard for almost everything in the world. There even was one, with a commissioned officer in charge, to examine, "Men's hutts at different hours of the Night and report all absentees."

The reason for this close surveillance of enlisted men was that they were not allowed to leave camp after retreat. If "aney Soldiers are found straggling out of the Chain of Centinals after Retreat beating thear to be brought by the Patrols to the officer of the Guard . . . to give them one Hundred Lashes on their Bare Back on the Spot."

Other offenses by enlisted men carried their appropriate treatment. Gaming with cards or dice for money was not allowed in camp, and when participants were caught they did not escape "exemplary punishment." Although it was not against orders to have liquor in camp, there was a regulation that "Strictly forbids aney Liquer to be Sold in the Hutts."

Punishment for gaming for money or selling drink in camp was to make the culprit or culprits run the gauntlet or receive a certain number of lashes. Running the gauntlet was accomplished by having "a company of soldiers standing in two lines, each one furnished with a switch, and the criminal is made to run between them and receive the scourge from their hands on his naked back." In getting the lash, "The culprit being securely tied to a tree, or post, receives on his naked back the number of lashes assigned to him, by a whip formed of several small knotted cords . . . It is always the duty of the drummers and fifers to inflict the chastisement."

Although sergeants and corporals were enlisted men, they, as noncommissioned officers, ordinarily did not receive the gauntlet or the lash. They were usually given a reduction in rank as punishment for minor offenses. Lower ranking commissoned officers who were charged with minor offenses usually were merely reprimanded by their superior officers.

Desertion, a serious offense, carried a severe penalty. A soldier "Deserting with his Arms and Accoutrements and loading his Arms," was a breech of the articles of war and punishable with death, usually hanging. Such hangings were well attended by large groups of men in camp. If a soldier just left camp for a few days to go home to see his wife and family, then returned to camp, he was not considered a deserter.

The lack of women in camp presented a very serious problem. During the day some women were allowed in camp to do washing, cooking, mending or hospital work. But none were allowed to stay over night, with the exception of some nurses. As one regimental order phrased it, "No provision is to be allowed to any Woman or Women whatever, but such as may be ordered by the Commanding officer of the Regiment."

Because all regimental commissioned officers, including colonels, were required "to hut with their respective regiments," officers were forced to abide by the rules laid down for enlisted men, particularily in regard to women in camp. This is one reason why so many officers took furloughs during the winter. Officer furloughs were relatively easy to obtain, as they were left to division, brigade or regiment command as long as "One Field officer [major or above was] to remain with every regiment." With enlisted men, it was a different matter. There were no furloughs for them, only an occasional short-duration pass issued to go home to visit a sick parent or wife or to attend to some emergency.

Unlike enlisted men who could not leave camp after retreat, commissioned officers were usually permitted to go wherever they pleased at any time of the day or night, as long as it was cleared with their commanding officer.

Going into Morristown of an evening, however, was no great opportunity of companionship for the average junior officer. Probably there were not over a couple of dozen eligible girls in town to date, and the three or four taverns within several miles were already doing a brisk business in local patronage, with little room for more than a few new customers from camp. As a result, most officers preferred getting together in camp for bachelor dinners in their huts. Dr. Thacher tells of one such get-together. "Dined with Colonel [Henry] Jackson, who entertained a party of gentlemen. Our table was not ornamented with numerous covers, our fare was frugal, but decent. Colonel Jackson posesses a liberal and generous spirit, and entertains his friends in the kindest manner. We sat at table till evening, enjoying the conversation of the Learned Doctor [William] Shippen, director-general of the hospital department."

General Washington did everything within his power to keep his men reasonably content in that barren camp of huts outside of Morristown—officers as well as enlisted men. For the officers, Washington planned a series of "dancing assemblies" for which young ladies from as far away as "Elizabethtown" were brought to Morristown for the occasion. Three of these dancing parties were held during the winter, on February 23, March 3 and April 24.

To finance this series of dances, Washington enlisted 34 officers, including himself, each one of whom subscribed $400. to defray expenses, with an agreement that if expenses exceeded the subscription, each would assume "an equal quota of any further Expence which may be incurred."

All three of these dancing parties were well attended, although the one held on March 3 had fewer girls in attendance than was expected, due to bad weather. The assembly on April 24 was a huge success, for it was held at a time the French Minister was visiting General Washington. Regarding this occasion, one diarist wrote, "General Washington and the French minister attended a ball, provided by the principal officers, at which were present a numerous collection of ladies and gentlemen of distinguished character. Fire-works were also exhibited by the officers of the artillery." The fireworks were an added attraction on this one special day and the enlisted men in camp were able to view the display. Otherwise, the dancing assemblies were strictly officer affairs.

Recreation or entertainment for the enlisted men was of equal concern to Washington—although more difficult to manage because of the large number of men involved. March 17, St. Patrick's Day, was one of those days that provided a good opportunity to involve the whole camp. A day of celebration was ordered from Headquarters to pay tribute to Ireland, which had recently recognized the independence of the new United States of America.

Orders on March 16, read in part, "All fatigue and working parties cease for tomorrow the 17th." According to a newspaper report of activities, the day was "ushered in with Music and the hoisting of Coulors, exhibiting the 13 Stripes, the favorite Harp, and an Inscription, declaring in capitals, THE INDEPENDENCE OF IRELAND." According to participating diarists, there was considerable drinking in camp during the festivities, and a number of soldiers had to be confined in the guard house.

FORD HOUSE THEN AND NOW—Shown here are two views of the Ford house or mansion as it is now called. The line drawing by Phyllis Mitchell shows the building with separate kitchen as it probably appeared during the winter of 1779-80 when Gen. Washington made his headquarters there. Below are "Some Thoughts on the Ford Mansion" by Mr. William L. Brown III, Staff Curator, Division of Reference Services, National Park Service, U. S. Department of Interior.

"On December 1, 1779, General Washington and his "military family" took up residence at the Ford Mansion; they left on June 23, 1780. It was this period of seven months that is of interest to the National Park Service. While working on the implementation of the Furnishing Plan, I had the pleasure of examining the house in detail, looking for clues to the interior appearance. Certain pieces of evidence presented themselves which lead me to believe that the exterior of the house appears now as it did in the 1830-40. These pieces of evidence are as follows:

"An examination of the attic and basement show that the kitchen was not originally attached to the main house. The main support beams do not continue through both buildings. This can also be seen in the hallway connecting the kitchen and the main house. A close look at the door moldings in Mrs. Ford's and the children's room reveals that they were original exterior doors. It is possible to see where the large hinges and locks were. The architectural reports show that before restoration, there was a doorway in the kitchen hallway where a window now is and a doorway also existed at one point in the kitchen (where it now is). While puzzling at first, what happened was that when the kitchen was built the doorway was placed where it now is, but when the kitchen hallway was constructed; after our period, a doorway was put in it and the doorway in the kitchen was sealed up, thus cutting down drafts in the kitchen. It was probably at this time that the kitchen was raised to a full two stories.

"Another interesting piece of information turned up to support the evidence that the kitchen hallway did not exist during Washington's occupation. When the siding was taken off the back of the house, the area of the hallway had wall paper on the external wall. This would indicate sections of an existing building were moved and utilized to connect the kitchen to the main house. Therefore, during the period December-June 1780, the kitchen was not connected to the house and it was probably only one and one-half stories high.

"Another area of interest is Washington's office. Again, the architectural reports show that at one point the window directly opposite the door was made into a doorway. This was either done originally in 1773 or later.

"On January 21, 1780, reference is made to the "new Orderly Room" and sending details to Headquarters to work on it. We have information that at one time a large room wrapped around the northwest corner of the house. This I believe was the "new Orderly Room" that is mentioned in the Day books. The room could be entered from General Washington's private office or through a common door in the new building. This would have freed the interior hallway of the mansion from the everyday coming and going of an army. Thus, the interior of the mansion, as it now stands, reflects the month of January, 1780."

At Headquarters

Life at Headquarters was quite different than it was in the huts. General Washington lived in and made his headquarters in a comparatively new eight room house, which had been completed by Colonel Jacob Ford Jr. about 1774. The house, then described as being on the outskirts of Morristown, is now almost in the heart of town, and is the headquarters of the Morristown National Historical Park.

General Washington and Colonel Jacob Ford had been closely associated in the war effort. In January 1776, 37 year old powder mill operator Jacob Ford became colonel of the Eastern Morris County New Jersey militia regiment. Then, in November 1776, he became colonel of a regiment of New Jersey "State Troops." (See Appendix VI).

By December 1776, Washington and his army were in great trouble, having been driven out of New York, through New Jersey, then across the Delaware River into Pennsylvania. With the enemy occupying most of New Jersey, Morristown became a focal point of resistance against the enemy.

It was under these conditions that Brigadier General Matthias Williamson, commander of New Jersey "State Troops," wrote to General Washington from Morristown as follows: "Colonel Ford's regiment makes up the principal part of the troops here and it is chiefly owing to his zeal in the American cause, as well as his influence with the people, that the appearance of defences at this post has been kept up."

Three weeks later, when General Washington made his attack on Trenton, followed the next week by his attack on Princeton, Colonel Ford marched his regiment south in a diversionary thrust against the enemy. In this operation, on January 4, 1777, the day after the Battle of Princeton, Col. Ford "was seized with sudden illness, lifted from his horse and brought home," to Morristown.

Two days later, on January 6, Gen. Washington and his army arrived at Morristown where he took up residence in "Arnold's Tavern," which faced the Morristown Green, a few blocks from the Ford house. Four days later, Colonel Jacob Ford Jr. died of pneumonia. On January 13, with Gen. Washington in attendance, they "Buried Col. Ford of the Jersey Militiar . . . with Honours of War."

With the army at Morristown was Benjamin Randolph, the famous Philadelphia cabinetmaker who was serving with the Philadelphia Light Horse Troop. Not only was Randolph a part of the army but he was a personal friend of both the General and Mrs. Washington. In 1777, "on her way up" to Morristown to visit the General, Mrs. Washington stayed at "Mr. Randolph's in Chestnut Street," and as noted by Randolph in his diary, the General and Mrs. Washington had stayed at "my house" on numerous occasions.

Although the Washington-Randolph connection was very close, there was a still closer Randolph-Ford connection. Benjamin Randolph and Mrs. Ford, the former Theodosia Johnes, were related, and close family friends. Theodosia and Benjamin were niece and nephew to "Stephen Johnes and Grace Fitz Randolph." In later years, Mrs. Ford's son, Gabriel would marry "Frances Gualdo," the ward of Benjamin Randolph, and Randolph's daughter, "Anna" would come to Morristown to live with the Fords, and she would die and be buried there.

Benjamin Randolph's Philadelphia Light Horse Troop was discharged at "Morris Town" late in January 1777 and Randolph returned to Philadelphia and to civilian life. Randolph, however, would return to Morristown as a civilian during the winter of 1777 and would be referred to by Gen. Washington as "Mr. Randolph."

Because of these strong Washington-Randolph-Ford connections, Gen. Washington, originally, may have intended to stay with the Fords during the winter of 1776-77, but changed his mind and moved into Arnold's Tavern on learning, upon his arrival in town, that Col. Ford had been taken seriously ill. On deciding to again make his headquarters at Morristown for the winter of 1779-80, surely Washington must have taken some part in making the decision to stay at the Ford house.

When, on December 1, 1779, Washington and his personal staff moved into the Ford house, Mrs. Ford and her four children limited their living quarters to two downstairs rooms. She occupied one room together with her daughter, Elizabeth, age 12. The other room was shared by the three Ford sons, Timothy 16, Gabriel 14 and Jacob 7.

Washington and his personal staff occupied the other six rooms of the house as sleeping quarters and offices, while sharing with the Fords a detached kitchen. The six members of Washington's personal staff who appear to have shared three upstairs sleeping rooms included George Augustine Washington, the General's nephew. He was a civilian aide, who on April 27 would receive a commission as "ensign." After this date he probably moved out of the Ford house and into the barracks of Washington's Guard to which unit he had become assigned. Other presumed members of the live-in personal staff were Lieutenant Colonel Robert Hanson Harrison, the General's personal secretary, and aides Lieutenant Colonels Tench Tilghman, Alexander Hamilton and Richard Meade, plus Captain James Mc Henry.

General Washington occupied one upstairs bedroom and shared it with Mrs. Washington when she came to visit. The other two rooms, both of them downstairs, were used as offices, one of which was capable of being converted into a dining room.

There were several additional members of Washington's personal staff who did not sleep at Headquarters but came there early each morning and spent the whole day in and about the house. One of these was Adjutant General Alexander Scammell, followed by Adjutant General Otho Williams who took over Scammell's duties about the first of the year and remained until the middle of April, when it was noted Scammell "resumes the duties of his office."

Other members of the non-live-in personal staff were Assistant Commissary General Royal Flint, Assistant Geographer Simeon DeWitt and Major Caleb Gibbs, commander of the General's Guard.

Members of Washington's general staff were frequent Headquarters visitors. These men were Quartermaster General Nathanael Greene, Commissary General Ephraim Blaine and his successor Jeremiah Wadsworth, Clothier General James Wilkinson, Foragemaster General Clement Biddle, Inspector General Friedrich Steuben, Surgeon General John Cochran, Judge Advocate General John Laurance, commander of artillery, Brigadier General Henry Knox, commandant of engineers and sappers, Brigadier General Louis Lebique Duportail and geographer and surveyor for the army, Colonel Robert Erskine.

It is not likely that general staff officers ate any meals at Headquarters, except under extraordinary circumstances. They had their own quarters and larders. Further, accommodations at Headquarters were very limited. The Ford kitchen, which was then not attached to the house as it presently is, measured only about 21 by 18 feet. In this small kitchen, most of the food was cooked for General Washington, for his personal staff and for the five Fords.

Sometime in December, Washington came to the conclusion that such shared facilities were inadequate, whereupon he asked Qm. Gen. Greene to build him a separate facility. Washington probably told Greene not to let Washington's personal need for this building interfere with the more important task of hutting the men in camp. Thus, there appears to have been some delay in getting the work under way.

After several weeks, Washington could see that his personal Guard already had finished building their nearby "eleven enlisted men's and three officers' huts," yet his building had not been started. The General then asked Maj. Gibbs of the Guards if his men would help. Soon, the logs were cut and the building roofed-off, but they could go no farther as they had no flooring. Thus, for some additional time, the building remained unfinished.

Finally, on January 22, Washington decided to put some pressure on Qm. Gen. Greene. He wrote him a very sharp letter in part as follows: "I have been in my prest. quarters since the 1st day of Decr. and have not a Kitchen to Cook a Dinner in, altho' the Logs have been put together some considerable time by my own Guard . . . Eighteen belonging to my family and all Mrs. Fords are crouded together in her Kitchen and scarce one of them able to speak for colds they have caught . . ." Washington's reference to as many as "Eighteen belonging to my family" eating in the kitchen would suggest that the number included personal servants and at least some personal staff.

Upon receipt of Washington's letter, Greene immediately got in touch with Moore Furman, New Jersey Deputy Quartermaster General, who in turn got in touch with his subordinate, Joseph Lewis. Lewis replied to Furman by letter on January 27, that the delay had been caused by his inability to find suitable boards for flooring. His letter stated, "I have been Ransacking this part of the world for a few (about 2,000 feet) of White pine boards to finish the Room for His Excellency." Apparently, shortly after the letter was written, Lewis did find the flooring and the building was completed.

Because 2,000 board feet of pine flooring would floor a building 40 by 50 feet, which is four times the size of the Ford kitchen, it is possible that it provided some dining facilities.

Despite the completion of the new kitchen and the return of the Ford kitchen to their exclusive use, there continued a close contact between the headquarters people and the Ford family, particularly with the children. Simeon De Witt, assistant surveyor, and a member of Washington's personal staff noted that 16 year old "Tim Ford . . . and I have got accidentally acquainted with each other and amuse ourselves by speaking composing playing on the flute—smoking together walking &c." It is further known that Tim Ford became good friends with Maj. Gibbs, commander of the General's Guard. On one occasion Tim was allowed to go along with the major on a very important mission against the enemy, during which Tim was wounded. Upon his return home, Tim had "a couple of Clever Marks to show for his Patriotism."

Mrs. Washington's arrival in Morristown on December "31st" 1779, for her second visit there, marked the beginning of what might be called the social season of the encampment, and the Washingtons appear to have done a modest amount of entertaining at Headquarters. Other general officers and high public officials, such as Governor William Livingston of New Jersey and his wife Susannah French Livingston entertained occasionally. During this period, in addition to a home in Elizabethtown, "Wm Livingston" had a residence in neighboring Parsippany.

Lord and Mrs. Stirling who lived at nearby Basking Ridge were frequent hosts to the Washingtons and others. Mrs. Stirling was the former Sarah Livingston, sister of the Governor. Major General Nathanael Greene and his wife Catherine Littlefield Greene did some entertaining and they attended most social functions as did Brigadier General Henry Knox and his wife Lucy Flucker Knox.

Colonel and Mrs. Clement Biddle were frequent hosts at small dinner and dancing parties. On one occasion at the Biddles, the gayety seems to have gotten a little out of hand when one "Deborah Olney" became involved in some altercation with General Washington and words flew. The matter was promptly hushed-up, but years later the incident came to light by an injudicious exchange of correspondence.

There is no record that Mrs. Ford attended any of these dancing parties, although she may have done so. Surely she was invited to state affairs held at Headquarters.

Dr. John Cochran, surgeon general, and his wife participated in most of the social events, both as guests and as hosts. Mrs. Cochran was the former Gertrude Schuyler, sister of Major General Philip Schuyler. When Gen. Schuyler and his wife, the former

Catherine Van Rensselaer, came to Morristown in April, they too joined the set.

It was, however, the Schuyler's daughter, Elizabeth, who would become the most exciting subject of conversation during the winter social season. Elizabeth or "Betsy" Schuyler had come to Morristown in January to visit her aunt Gertrude and Dr. Cochran. Shortly after Betsy's arrival in town, she met Susannah or "Sukey" Livingston, daughter of the Governor, and Catherine or "Kitty" Stirling, daughter of Lord and Mrs. Stirling. All three girls were in their early twenties.

Both Sukey Livingston and Kitty Stirling had known young 23 year old Lieutenant Colonel Alexander Hamilton, now Gen. Washington's aide, when he had attended school in Elizabethtown in 1773, and they promptly introduced him to Betsy Schuyler. Apparently it was love at first sight, for the two were together whenever possible for the remainder of the winter and they were married the following December.

The principal social and diplomatic event of the winter was the visit to Headquarters of the French Ambassador or Minister to the United States, Chevalier de la Luzerne. Minister Luzerne had been in Philadelphia meeting with members of Congress when he received an invitation from General Washington to visit him at Morristown.

Maj. Gen. Steuben, who was in Philadelphia on Congressional detached duty was asked to accompany the Minister and his party. As the entourage approached Morristown, Gen. Washington and several officers rode out about five miles to greet them. The Minister was "in a closed carriage drawn by four Horses & guarded by forty Light dragoons in beautiful uniforms."

The Minister arrived at Morristown on April 19 and he would leave on the 25th, giving him almost a week in camp. The whole time would be filled with consultations, tours, inspections, and in the evening, social gatherings. The stay would be capped on the 24th with a review of troops by the Minister and with his attendance, in the evening, at one of the scheduled officer assemblies or dances.

Gen. Steuben was put in charge of the review. It would be a small contingent of only four battalions but they would be the best drilled and best dressed men in the army. The troops to be selected were to come from several brigades. In the orders to have them prepare for the review, it was particularly specified that Maxwell's men should be wearing their "blue and buff" and Clinton's men their "blue and yellow." Colonels selected to command these four review battalions were "Colo. Johnston, Cortland, Ogden, Jackson." These were Cols. Francis Johnston, presumably Philip van Cortland, a militia colonel, Matthias Ogden and Henry Jackson.

For several days preceding the review, a large platform was being erected on the main parade grounds in camp. Then, on the 24th, in the afternoon, the distinguished guests started to arrive and finally the platform "was crowded by officers, ladies, and gentlemen of distinction from the country, among whom were Governor Livingston of New Jersey, and his lady." The review was a huge success and the Minister noted that it "met with his entire approbation."

There was, however, one marring note. The Spanish agent, Don Juan de Miralles, a member of the Minister's party, had been "seized the day of his arrival with a violent biliary complaint," whereupon he was put to bed "at head-quarters." Miralles did not recover from his illness but died at Headquarters on April 28, three days after the Minister had been compelled to return to his duties in Philadelphia. Two days later, on April 30, The Honorable Don Juan de Miralles was buried with full military honors.

Related to the French Minister's visit to discuss French assistance for the American cause, was a series of events at Headquarters that led to Maj. Gen. Benedict Arnold's betrayal of his country. Arnold's court-martial, which had begun in January, had been a long one, lasting over three months. The charges against him grew out of alleged personal business dealings contrary to military regulations while Arnold had been in command of Philadelphia after the British evacuation of that city back in June 1778.

Arnold's trial was finally concluded, with a verdict rendered on April 6, calling merely for the sentence of "a Reprimand from His Excellency the Commr. in Chief." But Benedict Arnold was already preparing to betray his country.

"On May 10," a little over a month after the French Minister's visit at Headquarters, Maj. Gen. Lafayette, arrived at Headquarters from an extended visit in France where he had been assured of increased French assistance for the American cause. Lafayette even brought Washington secret information as to the strength in manpower of this new French help and specific details as to where that force would land.

On May 12, two days after Lafayette gave Washington this secret information, Benedict Arnold came to Morristown and to Headquarters where he dined with the General. During dinner conversation, Washington told Arnold of the French plans. After dinner, Arnold secretly sent off information to the British high command in New York, detailing the French assistance, even to the planned French landing place at "Rhode Island."

Chapter IV

WINTER OPERATIONS

Staten Island

When the army came to its winter quarters near Morristown in early December 1779, Brig. Gen. William Maxwell and his brigade were guarding the New Jersey front opposite Staten Island. On December 14 and 15, Maxwell was relieved by a detachment under Brig. Gen. Samuel Parsons. After nearly two weeks at the front, on December 26, Parsons was relieved by a detachment of "750 men" under Brig. Gen. William Irvine.

Under Irvine's review of the situation, he decided that because of the increasing number of disturbances close to the front, he would move the front line headquarters to "Crane's Mills," now Cranford, where John Crane had a saw mill and a grist mill on the Rahway River. He chose this site because it was "convenient both to Elisabethtown & Rahway, about five miles from each of these places and ten from Woodbridge."

Irvine also altered the disposition of the troops along the front. He placed "about 200 men at Elisabethtown, 150 at Woodbridge and 50 at Newark with sundry other small guards on the [Staten Island] Sound," the present Arthur Kill. The remainder of his force would be kept at headquarters where they could be dispatched quickly to cover any disturbance of major consequence.

Gen. Knyphausen, the enemy commander at New York, soon learned the details of Irvine's realignment of troops. Knyphausen's informants also told him that on January 3 and 4, the Staten Island Sound had frozen over solidly. Thus, Staten Island was virtually joined to New Jersey. Men, horses and cannon could now cross to New Jersey on the ice.

With this new information, Knyphausen planned a large scale invasion of New Jersey to commence January 6. He would make "different movements into Jersey to take place at the same time." Objectives would be the American posts at "Perhamus . . . Hackensac . . . Newark Mountain Meeting [Orange] . . . Crane's Mills, Elizabethtown . . . Rahway and Woodbridge." Knyphausen had his entire force poised for action to move out from positions on Staten Island and Paulus Hook, when on "the night of the general incursion in Jersey . . . a sudden fall of Snow and Rain put a stop to the movement."

Brig. Gen. Irvine apparently did not learn of the intended invasion until after it was called off, but he too was told of the frozen sound, whereupon he transmitted information to Gen. Washington on the 8th that "the Sound appears to have a solid Bridge [of ice] over it—from Amboy to De harts Point." Amboy was the present Perth Amboy and De Harts Point was near the foot of what is now Trumbull Street, Elizabeth, where the sound begins to widen into Newark Bay.

Realizing that the frozen sound presented an opportunity to him as well as to Gen. Knyphausen, Gen. Washington decided to make a large scale raid on Staten Island "provided the state of the Ice affords a ready and safe passage and return." Maj. Gen. Lord Stirling, who knew the Staten Island terrain well, would be in command.

Lord Stirling's force would consist of about 2,500 men including "the detachment of 750 men already in the lines under the command of Brig. Genl. Irvine; the detachment of 1,000 Men, which marched this day under the command of Colo. [Moses] Hazen as relief to Genl. Irvine; a detachment of between three and four hundred, under the command of [ ] . . . and a fourth detachment of 500 Men under the command of Colo. Walter Stewart." The detachment commander not mentioned above was "Col. [Josias] Hall." (See Appendix II for troop breakdown).

There had been a "tremendeous snow-storm" and most of the roads were clogged with snow. But the raiding force would not be traveling over the roads, but over the fields, the snow having completely covered fences and hedgerows, except in spots where the wind had blown them bare or nearly so. To transport the force, Washington recruited "about five hundred sleighs." These were procured in the neighborhood of camp on the "pretence of going into the country after provisions." The men selected for the mission were issued special "caps and mittings" to protect them from the extreme cold.

The attack was to be made beginning "at five o clock" on the morning of January 15, from below Elizabethtown. The right column, under the command of Brig. Gen. Irvine, to consist of his own detachment plus Stewart's and Hall's, would cross "at Halsteds point" in what is now the Bayway area of Elizabeth. The left column, under the command of Col. Hazen, which was limited to his own detachment, would cross "at the Old point," being a local name for De Harts Point.

The New Jersey militia in and about Elizabethtown, which was well laced with refugees from Staten Island, learned of the impending action a day or so before it was scheduled to take place, whereupon they appealed to Gen. Washington to be allowed to participate. On the 14th, the day before the action was to begin, Washington agreed that the militia could participate and that they would be permitted to "share with the Continental Troops of whatever shall be brought off by authority."

By this Washington meant that only military stores must be taken in plunder and that no property could be taken from civilians on the island. There was, however, a fine line of distinction made between what was military and what was civilian property. Even Gen. Washington agreed that any civilian inhabitants of the island, "found in Arms must be expected to be treated as Enemies, and their Effects given up as plunder." Because almost every citizen carried arms, or had them in his home, this seemed to permit considerable latitude of action.

It was further explained to the men that anything taken on the island by anyone must be turned over to the authorities so that all would share. To this end, it was specifically spelled out that "if any Officer or Soldier [militia or continental] attempts to appropriate any thing to his own Particular use, he Shall be compell'd to Deliver it up, Shall forfeit all pretentions to a Common Share, and shall be punished at the Discreation of a Court Martial, for Disobediance of Orders."

Now that the militia had been allowed to participate in the raid, the word soon spread to civilian refugees from Staten Island in the Elizabethtown area, many of whom decided to follow the troops. Thus, when the attack got under way at 5 a. m. on the 15th, there was a "vast multitude who greedily rushed to plunder."

The two-day affair on Staten Island was militarily unsuccessful for the raiders. Major General Lord Stirling, American commander on the raid, and Brigadier General Thomas Stirling, British commander on Staten Island, both made detailed reports on the action.

Brig. Gen. Stirling's force on Staten Island consisted of "1800 men." Some of them occupied positions close to the New Jersey front but most of them were intrenched on the northeast corner of the island on high ground back of the present St. George and Tompkinsville.

Lord Stirling said that "The enemy having previous intelligence of our movements, a surprise was out of the question." With this advance notice, most of Brig. Gen. Stirling's forward posts were able to withdraw in front of the advancing enemy until they reached their main positions on the far side of the island. It was not until noon that Brig. Gen. Stirling, "observed them [the Americans] advancing in two Columns . . . the two Columns coming nearly at the same Time on each side of the Pond [the present Fresh Water Pond in Silver Lake Park] and took Possession of the Woody Heights in Front of the Center and left Hand Redoubts."

Brig. Gen. Stirling saw that soon after the American force arrived in front of his redoubts, "the Rebels began to light Fires and continued in that Position the whole Evening, and Night without any Alteration or attempt upon any of our advanced Parties. A little after Day break . . . the Enemy were discovered going off by Deckers Ferry," now Port Richmond.

The British pursued the retreating force with a party of "200 men . . . and 20 light dragoons." In the attack on Lord Stirling's rear, they "took a Serjeant & Sixteen Men Prisoners."

There had been one spin-off attack made by the raiders. It was made by Lieutenant Colonel Marinus Willett, on Decker's Ferry where Lieutenant Colonel Abraham Buskirk and his 4th New Jersey Volunteers were garrisoned. Buskirk and his men were able to escape but "The house [Decker's], as a garrison place, and 8 or 9 small vessels were burned. A considerable quantity of Blankets and other stores were found," and taken off.

The blankets and other stores taken at Decker's were certainly legitimate military plunder authorized by the American high command. But elsewhere little was taken legitimately. With the British force withdrawn to the far corner of the island, the civilian islanders had no protection, and as noted by Colonel Sylvanus Seely of the New Jersey militia, "the inhabitents of the Island are sorely Plundered." The plundering appears not to have been done by civilian refugees and militia alone, but also by continental soldiers. Ensign John Barr of the 4th New York continental regiment, who had not gone along on the Staten Island raid, noted in his diary at Morristown, "our Troops returned off the Island with 500 sleigh loads of Divers Articles."

According to a British account, the plunderers even stooped to "striping women of their body cloathes."

WINTER THEATER OF OPERATIONS—This is a section of a map by Maj. Michel Capitaine du Chesnoy, aide to Maj. Gen. Lafayette. The original is in the Ministry of Wars—Engineer, Paris 15-1-7 Pf. #2. In America, photo copies are in several Karpinski Collections, #141. Capitaine's principal function in America, according to Peter J. Guthorn, author of American Maps and Map Makers of the Revolution, *"was to record in maps the engagements in which Lafayette took part." (AmM 11/19) By 18th century standards, this is an extremely accurate map of northeastern New Jersey. The principal road structure is well delineated, and most of the place names mentioned in this chapter are located.*

CARTE
d'une partie de la Province
de Newyork
et des Jerseys
Hoppers
Peramus
Hanington
Closter
Scralenburg
Old Bridge
New Bridge
Liberty Pole
Hudsons River
Saddle River
Totawa
Great Falls
The Forks
Horseneck Bridge
Little Falls
the Notch
Wesel
Aquachminck
Hackensack
Pollifly
Fort Lee
English Neighbourhood
Fort Washington
North or Hudsons River
Troy
Moristown
Passaick River
Hanover
Mountains
Cranetown
Witsfeling
Second River
Schylers
Snake hill
Mountain Meeting house
Newark Mountains
Chatam
Newark
Bergen
Hobuck
Pawlus hook
Newyork Island
Harlem
Bulls Fy
Blomingdale
Hell Gate
Newyork
Springfield
Newark Bay
Barren Neck
Oyster Bay
NEWYOR
Brookland, or Brookli
Connecticut Farms
Govr Livingston
Elizabethtown
Bergen Point
Oyster Island
Cover'd at high water
Bedford
Point
Church
Yellow Hook
the heights of Guana
Rahway
Spanktown
Staten
Narrows
New Utrecht
Richmond
Gravesend
Island
Coney Isl
Atlant
Amboy
Billops Point
Oc

Elizabethtown—Newark

On January 16, the day his force returned from Staten Island, Lord Stirling's report to Gen. Washington was in part as follows: "While the troops were upon the Island, a number of persons from this side took advantage of the occasion to pass upon the Island, and plundered the people there in the most shameful and merciless manner."

Lord Stirling had learned of some of the depredations while he was still on the island but it was so wide spread and by so many people, both military and civilian, that he had no way of controlling it or estimating how extensive it was. His only recourse seemed to be to try to recover the property. To this end as reported to Washington, "Many of them were stopped on their return, and their booty taken from them. In addition to which, I have sent an order for publication, requiring those who had eluded the search to restore the articles in their possession, and exhorting the good people at large, to assist in detecting them."

Lord Stirling even specified how the loot was to be recovered. He ordered that "all persons possessed of any articles of plunder, taken on the island, do immediately deliver the same to Doctor Caldwell, at Springfield, to the end that they may be returned to the proper owners." Dr. Caldwell was the Reverend Mr. James Caldwell, minister of the Presbyterian Church of Elizabethtown, presently serving part time as assistant quartermaster general of the American army at Springfield and using the Presbyterian Church at Springfield as an army supply warehouse.

Caldwell's selection as the one to receive the plundered property may have been an unfortunate choice. The Loyalist refugees and others whose goods he was to recover and return, regarded him with contempt and distrust. They referred to him in his dual capacity of minister and quartermaster as a "Retailer of Sedition on Sundays; and Ammunition Shoes and Boots the Week Days; as Store-Keeper for the annoyance of the bodies of the Loyalists, military and civil."

After putting in motion the property recovery process, Lord Stirling sent a large portion of his force back to Morristown, then he departed for Basking Ridge, New Jersey, his home. Col. Hazen and his 1,000 men would remain at the front "as relief to Genl. Irvine" whose detachment had been guarding the front lines since December 26.

Col. Hazen did not use the Crane's Mills headquarters as his predecessor had done. He decided to spread his troops out by "drawing a line of cantonments from Connecticut Farms [Union] to Rahway about 7 miles in length . . . Secondly he established a Picquet of one Field officer and 100 men at Elizabeth Town, a Subt. and 20 men at Newark, a Capt. and fifty men at Woodbridge and sending other small guards on the Sound." These guards on the sound were "at De Harts and Halsted Points . . .[and] Blazing Star," now Carteret. He also had "11 men" of Captain Henry Bedkin's Independent Dragoons available for patrol duty.

One of Col. Hazen's numerous duties, was to keep an eye on how much loot was being brought into Rev. Caldwell for return to Staten Island. Hazen became very dissatisfied with results. By January 25, ten days after the raid, only one wagon load had been assembled, and "Morris Hatfield was sent with it" to Staten Island. The next day, Hatfield reported back to Col. Hazen that the loot had been delivered and that, while on the island, "he saw his brother."

Under ordinary circumstances, seeing one's brother would not have been of interest to Hazen, except that Morris Hatfield's two brothers were leading Loyalist refugees on the island. They were Job and Smith (the latter born John Smith Hatfield), sometimes spelled Hetfield. Job, Smith and Morris Hatfield were sons of "John Hetfield and Deborah Smith" of Elizabethtown.

Another Hatfield who was very active in Staten Island Loyalist circles, was Cornelius Hatfield Jr., son of "Cornelius Hatfield." Cornelius Jr. was a second cousin once removed to Job, Smith and Morris Hatfield. Cornelius Jr. had "managed the farm of his father in Elizabethtown" on Halsted's Point, before he escaped to Staten Island where he joined the New Jersey Volunteers as a captain in Col. Buskirk's regiment.

It was on the 25th, the night that Morris Hatfield returned the wagon load of loot to Staten Island, that Morris's cousin and two brothers, "Cornelius Hetfield, Job Hetfield and Smith Hetfield" acted as guides for a retaliatory raid against Elizabethtown. It was a relatively small operation involving only "120 men . . . with 12 dragoons" plus the usual complement of civilian hangers-on.

The place chosen to cross the sound on the ice was at "Trembley's Point," on the north bank of the Rahway River in present Linden. From there, they would move quickly up to the Lower Rahway Road, and they would enter the town from the west over what is now roughly Washington Avenue.

On the 25th, Gen. Washington had written Col. Hazen that "relief marches today." These troops, numbering "990 [would] parade at 9 o'clock" that morning at camp near Morristown and would reach the front sometime late in the day. Although Col. Hazen would remain as commander of the new detachment, there would be some confusion as the new troops took up their posts in relief of the old. Col. Buskirk may have learned of this change, and planned his raid to take place that night. (See Appendix II for breakdown of this detachment.)

In Col. Buskirk's report on the action, he said "guides led me without discovery to the rear of the Town, which I entered without any alarm . . . The surprise was compleat . . . I cannot pass unnoticed the good conduct of Capt. [Cornelius] Hatfield & those under his command, who led me thro Deep Snow, but with Judgment, to a Beaten Road that brought me into the Town & to effect the surprise."

Col. Buskirk continued in his report that "it was impossible to prevent the Refugees from Burning the Presbyterian Meeting House & the Court House, against both which (especially the former) the Refugees had particular Resentment." As to resentment of the courthouse, Cornelius Hatfield Jr., before escaping to Staten Island, had been lodged in jail located in the courthouse. And it was from the courthouse in "July 1779" that his farm had been sold to the highest Patriot bidder.

Regarding the burning of the Elizabethtown Presbyterian Church, of which Rev. Caldwell was the minister, when Caldwell heard of the burning, he made loud cries of injustice, but he was soon informed that the burning had been in reprisal for a church burning on Staten Island, during the recent raid under Lord Stirling.

Being told of this Staten Island burning, Caldwell wrote Gen. Washington as follows: "Burning a church seems indeed quite out of the line of military operatons. I did think of mentioning in my next [letter] to him [Lord Stirling] that unmilitary piece of savageness. But if your excellency could think it consistent, I had much desire you would call upon him to declare the avowal or disavowal of that conduct."

When Washington received Caldwell's letter, he promptly replied that "if Mr. Stirling, burns churches, the severest recrimination will be contained in the action." Of course Stirling did not authorize the burning of a church on Staten Island, and he may not even have known of it until told so by Caldwell, through Washington.

While burning was going on in Elizabethtown, there also was burning in Newark. Major Charles Lumm had made a simultaneous strike on Newark from Paulus Hook with a total of about 300 men consisting of "the Flank Companies of the 44th—100 of the 42d and 100 Hessians." As usual, a number of civilian refugees followed behind. The striking force arrived at their destination by traveling most of the way on frozen estuaries, "passing the Hackinsack, Head of New Ark Bay and Pissick Rivers on the Ice."

Maj. Lumm said in his after-report that "The Detachment after setting fire to the Accademy in which the Enemy were lodged, returned with their Prisoners to the Hook at half past three in the Morning." Of the prisoners taken at Newark and those taken at Elizabethtown, some were military personnel and some were civilians who had acted against the interests of the refugees.

At Elizabethtown, Col. Buskirk said he took "all the officers on Duty & 47 Men . . . without the loss of a man." In addition, he and his men took "a few Very Obnoxious Men," namely civilians. These men were "Mr. B. [elcher] Smith son of [the ardent Patriot] Mr. Peartree Smith . . . [and the] brother" of Major Matthias Williamson who was assistant quartermaster general and much involved with the disposal of "Staten Island plunder."

At Newark "About 12 of the Rebels were killed and wounded & 36 made Prisoners . . . [with the] loss of five Men." Among the prisoners were some civilians, including "Robert Neil [and] Joseph Hedden a justice commissioned to sell tory Estates." Robert Neil was "an acting commissary." According to a New York newspaper, Neil and Hedden were not captured by Maj. Lumm and his men, but by one of the civilian refugees. He was "one Walker a volunteer with them, who with many others had been inhumanly and barbarously treated by Justice Hedden."

Unstable Front

After the raids on Elizabethtown and Newark, Gen. Washington sent Maj. Gen. St. Clair to the front to investigate "the cause of the late misfortune." Upon a full inquiry, St. Clair found that it had been no fault of Col. Hazen.

Even as St. Clair's inquiry was in progress, a raid was launched from Staten Island. As St. Clair wrote to Washington on January 31, "A small Party of Refugees slipt in last night about nine o'clock behindst our guards, and carried off several of the Inhabitants . . . they were conducted by one of the Hatfields and the Villians have so perfect a knowledge of this part of the country."

The next day, February 1, there was a larger attack, this one by Lieutenant Colonel John Graves Simcoe and his Loyalist unit, known as the Queens Rangers. Simcoe's plan was to "march by very secret ways, made more so by the inclement season, and to arrive near Gen. Washington's Quarters by day-break, to tie up his horses in a swamp, and to storm the quarters," and hopefully take Washington a prisoner.

The attack started from Staten Island and got no farther than Woodbridge when Simcoe found "The snow prevented all possibility of marching, but on the beaten roads." With the mission called off the Queens Rangers and the inevitable band of followers began foraging and looting.

Because of the strenuous duty of responding to almost daily raids upon Hazen's advance posts, it was decided that Hazen's detachment should be relieved. To this end, on February 4, Maj. Gen. St. Clair, who was still at the front, reported to Gen. Washington that "Col. Star with the Connecticut Troops arrived last night." This was Colonel Josiah Starr, senior Connecticut officer in camp. So as to have a high ranking officer of experience with the forward troops, Washington asked St. Clair to stay on at the front until one of the Connecticut brigadiers returned from furlough.

St. Clair had his own idea for the proper disposition of the troops at the front so as to control the situation while the sound remained frozen solid. On February 7, he wrote to Gen. Washington that "The Body of Troops [are] now lying in a line from Spring Field to the southern part of West Field, with one hundred and twenty men advanced to Connecticut Farms [Union], and the same number in this neighborhood [Crane's Mills]; fifty men detached to New Ark, and fifty to Woodbridge. The different parties of militia horse are instructed to patrole the roads along the sound from New Ark to Amboy; fifteen of them stationed at New Ark, fifteen at Rahway and fifteen at Woodbridge." These last mentioned "militia horse" were the cavalry companies of "Capt. [Israel] Carle, Capt. [Peter] Stryker, Capt. [Samuel] Meeker," raised in Hunterdon, Somerset and Essex Counties, respectively.

On February 7, there was a deep penetration into New Jersey. St. Clair reported to Washington that "The enemy made an incursion into the State this morning about an hour before Day, in three different places from Staten Island and one from Paulus Hook . . . Their number are said to have been two thousand . . . They proceeded some distance into the Country and from the rout they pursued and . . . their Inquiries about the Situation of your Quarters," St. Clair believed that their destination was Morristown. The invasion force did not reach Morristown, but was compelled to stop their advance after moving inland only a few miles.

"Finding the snow very deep and the Roads not broken" the enemy abandoned their primary objective and began foraging and looting. Because the enemy on this occasion had come in such strength, "the guards at Elizabeth Town and Woodbridge . . . retreated" leaving the populace unprotected.

After the enemy had finished their looting and had withdrawn back across the sound, the guards returned to their stations. The returning Elizabethtown guards found "A number of houses in the Town have been stript of every thing and ten or twelve of the Inhabitants carried off . . . At Woodbridge [the enemy] carried off about thirty head of cattle . . . At Rahway [they] plundered the houses and carried off two men."

On February 19, there was yet another attack. As St. Clair reported to Washington, "The Enemy made another attempt last night about eleven o'clock to surprise the Party at New Ark and plundered the town." Upon taking leave with their booty, they were pursued by the American guard at Newark and had to leave behind "about twenty head of cattle they had collected and some horses."

St. Clair knew that as long as the sound remained frozen the raids would continue, and there was little he could do to protect such an extended front with so few troops. During January and February there had been "uninterrupted and unvarying cold," which kept the sound firmly frozen. At one time during the two month period, the entire New York Harbor was frozen over. "The passage of the North River, even in its widest part . . . was about the 19th [of February] practicable for the heaviest cannon, an event unknown in the memory of man." The ice was measured at "eleven feet thick."

Gen. St. Clair soon learned of the very thick ice and he reported to Gen. Washington that the enemy "horse passed on the ice to and from New York [to Paulus Hook] on the twentieth." On the basis of this information, St. Clair suggested that an attack be made on Paulus Hook, over the ice, from the relatively unprotected river side. Washington approved the plan, but on the 22nd it began to rain, which meant that the temperature had risen above freezing.

By the 23rd, St. Clair was forced to report to Washington that I am "extremely apprehensive that the Rains of yesterday, together with the high Winds from the eastward last Night have rendered the Enterprise on Paulus Hook impracticle."

By the 24th, the ice in the Hudson had broken up and so had the ice in the harbor and in Staten Island Sound, bringing to an end two months of terror along the Staten Island-New Jersey front.

Paramus—Hoppertown

With the breakup of the ice in the sound and harbor, Washington decided that he could now relieve Maj. Gen. St. Clair at the front, whereupon on "February 29," Maj. Gen. Kalb was sent forward to take over the command of the Connecticut detachment. Neither of the Connecticut brigadiers had yet returned from furlough.

Gen. Kalb would find the front along the sound less active than it had been during the freeze, which had permitted easy access by the British to New Jersey towns and farms along the sound for depredation as well as food and forage. Now, the British must return to old methods of securing supplies. One of these methods, and a very productive one, was London Trade. This trade had continued throughout the freeze, particularly in Bergen County, New Jersey, where Washington had noted there are "many disaffected people" eager and willing to do business with the enemy.

After the ice-breakup, a sizable increase in Bergen County London Trade was soon observed, whereupon Gen. Washington was determined to put a stop to it. Gen. Knyphausen, commander at New York, was equally determined to encourage the trade, even to increase it.

Since the beginning of the Morristown encampment, Gen. Washington had maintained a force of continentals in Bergen County with headquarters at Paramus, so as to keep the disaffected in the area under control. Present commander at Paramus was "Major Christopher Stuart" of the 5th Pennsylvania regiment.

The Paramus post was located in Paramus Church on what is now New Jersey Highway 17 and Glen Avenue, Ridgewood, where the church's 1800 successor presently stands. There was a breastwork around the church, manned at all times. Those men, not on actual duty there, resided in houses in nearby Hoppertown, now Hohokus, with headquarters in the home of "John A. Hopper, and his wife Mary."

Within a month after the thawing of the sound, Gen. Knyphausen became aware that Gen. Washington was putting too much pressure on the London Traders in Bergen County, and was harassing those who were trading with them. Knyphausen therefore decided that an attack on Paramus, and the capture of that garrison, would solve the problem. At least it would give encouragement to those willing to carry on the trade.

Knyphausen planned his attack for March 23. It would be a two-pronged movement. One force would cross from New York, land at Weehauken, hit Hackensack, then move on to Paramus. The other force would cross from New York to Closter Landing and proceed to Paramus. The two forces would reach the Paramus Church installation at the same time and would attack from the north and south.

The northern force consisted of "300 men" under the command of Lieutenant Colonel John Howard of the British Guards. The southern force also consisted of "300 men" under the command of Lieutenant Colonel Duncan Mc Pherson of the 42nd regiment. Both contingents were accompanied by a sizable complement of civilian refugees.

Both forces made their landings on schedule and in good order, but they could not make it to Paramus so as to arrive at the same time. Thus, the Paramus garrison was able to escape the pincers movement. Having failed in their primary objective, both enemy contingents began plundering the country. According to Maj. Stuart, commander of the Paramus garrison, "as soon as the Enemy found their Intentoons were frustrated, they seem'd more dispos'd to plunder than to pursue us, and immediately commenced their Retreat from the Church down the Hackinsack Road, plundering indescriminately."

In various places along their retreat, Mc Pherson's contingent took "Sixty four Prisoners," and there was the usual resort to burning. At Hackensack they "burnt the Court-house, and also Messers Boyd's and Chappele's dwelling-houses."

Having failed in the first attempt to wipe out the Paramus garrison, a second attempt was made on April 15. By this date, there was a new commander of the Paramus garrison. He was "Majr. [Thomas Langhorne] Byles," commanding his 3rd Pennsylvania regiment of "150 men." Maj. Byles had relieved "Majr. Anderson" and his detachment on the 4th.

This second attack was made by "300 Hessians" from New York and "105 men" from Staten Island, the latter mostly cavalry. In over-all command was Hessian Lieutenant Colonel Johann Du Buy. This time their objective was not the Paramus Church installation but the headquarters at Hoppertown where there was a considerable supply of "provisions, ammunition and stores."

The New York and Staten Island contingents of Du Buy's force landed separately in New Jersey, joined into one force shortly after landing, and proceeded toward Hoppertown. They arrived at Hoppertown "an hour after daylight" before word could reach Maj. Byles at headquarters—creating a complete surprise.

When Du Buy and his men reached headquarters and were discovered by Maj. Byles, he immediately barricaded the doors and began putting up a defense. The Hopper house headquarters was made of stone and quite defensible, but Du Buy soon set fire to the wood roof of the house. "Seeing it impossible to escape he [Byles] (on promise of good usage of his men) surrendered."

With the assurance of good treatment of his men, Byles came out of the front door of the Hopper house, and as he opened the door, "he was wounded in the breast." The one who did the shooting of Byles said that he did it because Byles did not come out of the house, as he should have, with his hands up. Three days later Major Byles died of his wound.

Men captured at and near headquarters were as follows: "Two Captains, three Subalterns and twenty one men were taken in this house [headquarters]—Nine in the next one and one hundred and fifty eight more and seven other officers in the town." Because Byle's regiment numbered only 150 men, 40 of the prisoners must have been civilians or militia.

As it had been on other raids, there was considerable burning in Hoppertown. Mrs. Hopper stated in a deposition relating to reimbursement for damages done by the raiders "The enemy . . . surprised the troops stationed at Hoppertown killed the major in command and wantonly burned two stone dwelling houses, one stone house and one grist mill with two run of stone . . . in consequence of this wanton destruction, your Petitioner's late husband was left homeless and peniless and destitute, not saving more than the clothes he stood in."

Chapter V

RIPE FOR INVASION

Melancholy Spring

In general, cold and raw weather stayed on in New Jersey well into May. Jerseyman John Hunt noted in his diary that it was "a Cold backward Spring . . . Some hundreds of Cattle & other Creatures have perished this Spring for want of food & the winter grain very much Destroyed with the hardness of ye winter, the wheat in particular many fields look as if there would not bee more than Sead gathered."

Over the winter, none of Gen. Washington's burdens had diminished. Soaring inflation, London Trade, starving soldiers, lagging enlistments and revengeful refugees were still with him. Qm. Gen. Greene summed up the situation in a letter on April 15, as follows: "Our treasury is empty—the business of finances in a doubtful snag—Public credit lost, and National confidence expiring—our army small and still upon the decline and little or no prospect of having it recruited this spring . . . I am happy for us that the Enemy are not able to push us here [at Morristown] as it is impossible to put the army in motion. We have neither the means of transportation nor provisions to subsist upon only from hand to mouth."

Despite all of his problems, particularly the one of declining forces at Morristown, Washington, on April 17, was forced to send the "Maryland division . . . with the first Regiment of Artillery" to the southward. The Maryland division, under the command of Maj. Gen. Kalb, was going south to offset an enemy force sent south in "ten Ships and Seven Brigs" that had sailed from New York on April 6, the suspected designation being Delaware or Chesapeake Bays. In order to depart with his division, Kalb was relieved of his temporary front line command of Connecticut troops, by Brig. Gen. Jedediah Huntington who was just returning from furlough. On May 28, Washington also would be compelled to send the New York brigade to Albany because of the "late incursion of the enemy upon the frontiers of New York."

Even before Washington had to give up so much of his force at Morristown, there had been concern as to whether the strength of the Morristown army, and the physical condition of the men, could resist an enemy attack of reasonable strength. Philip Schuyler who knew the situation well from an army point of view as a major general, and who was now in Congress, had warned that body on March 22, that "There never . . . since the Commencement of the Contest was an hour In which as It appears to me our Affairs were more Critical."

As a result of Schuyler's dire comments, and other information in hand, Congress voted to send an investigating committee to Morristown, designated the "Committee to Headquarters." Members of the committee were Philip Schuyler, John Mathews and Nathaniel Peabody.

There was some delay in getting to Morristown, and the committee did not reach there "until the 28th" of April. On arrival, the committee went right to work on their investigation. And for several weeks they made preliminary reports back to Congress, but little action was taken by Congress that could be observed as improvements in camp.

In its final report to Congress, on May 25, the committee found in part as follows: "That the commissaries cannot give any assurance of doing more than barely subsisting the Troops from day to day . . . That the Army is greatly deficient in Camp Equipage. That it is destitute of forage for the few horses which indespensable necessity has required, should be maintained in Camp. That it will require several Thousand horses to move the Army so as to promise any effectual operation from it . . . That as every department of the Army is without money, and not even the shadow of Credit left, consequently no article however necessary can be procured . . . That very few of the recruits required for the act of Congress of the 9th of February last have arrived.

"That from the information received there is no prospect that any considerable number will timely engage in the service as Voluntary inlistm'ts . . . That the patience of the soldiery who have endured every degree of conceivable hardship, and borne it with fortitude and perseverence, beyond the expectation of the most sanguine, is on the point of being exhausted. That the spirit of discontent is encouraged by the arts of the enemy, whose emissaries hold up in printed papers distributed among the soldiery the most flattering prospects and promises to induce them to desert their coulors."

Gen. Knyphausen, in New York, soon learned of this congressional report. In fact, he was aware of much of its content even before the committee made its final report. Knyphausen had very carefully questioned the "one hundred and sixty deserters" who had come over to the enemy, just during the first two months of the year. Further, Knyphausen had innumerable spies in New Jersey, many of whom were in the American army itself.

One of these spies was John Cunningham, age 26, who had come from Scotland to New Jersey in 1775, just before the war broke out. When war came and the Jersey militia was called out, Cunningham entered the service, but he became disheartened and began spying for the British. On February 26, while apparently still in New Jersey militia service, Cunningham reported to Gen. Knyphausen that "The Army is very discontented and dwindles very fast. Many desert homewards and elsewhere. None whose times are out, can be prevailed on to reinlist at any rate . . . Washington is at Ford's . . . the chief [or main portion] of his Army are desirous to leave him . . . They are sick of the war . . . The people of the Country are loud in their Complaints . . . They openly say the country has been cheated by the Cry of Liberty."

Although these were the words of an enemy spy, they were in part echoed by men of high rank in the American army. Brig. Gen. Irvine, on April 18, wrote, "Tis too melancholy a truth that our regts. are reduced to mere skeletons . . . Some have gone to the Enemy—many have gone on furlough, who I fear will never return."

The Last Straw

Although poorly equipped with winter clothing, the Connecticut troops had been ordered early in February to take over the front line duty of the American army. They arrived opposite Staten Island on February 4, and immediately were assigned to posts along the sound from Newark to Amboy.

From February 4 until the 24th, which was the date the Staten Island Sound opened up from its deep freeze, there were almost daily enemy forays across the sound that called for action. Following the breakup, there were fewer disturbances, but there were enough of them to be extremely fatiguing to those on front line duty.

After about a month and a half of difficult duty, Brig. Gen. Jedediah Huntington became impatient for relief of his troops. Thus, on April 17, he wrote Gen. Washington as follows: "The Connecticut Line becomes weaker every Day by the three year men leaving us," their enlistments having expired. He pointed out also that "two hundred [are] unfit for Duty for want of Shoes & Shirts."

Huntington might have added that the food supply was also critical at the front. The men had nothing to eat but "Indian [corn] meal, and not over much of that," for a long period of time. On one occasion during a refugee raid on the American advance post at Halsted's Point, the enemy, "cut open the knapsacks of the guard and strewed the Indian meal about the floor, laughing at the poverty of the Yankee soldiery who had nothing but hog's fodder, as they termed it, to eat."

Despite Huntington's request to have his troops relieved, it would not be until May 14, three days short of an additional month, that a relief detachment would arrive. Sent to relieve Huntington was the New Jersey brigade under Brig. Gen. William Maxwell. On May 15, Maxwell wrote a note to Washington from Connecticut Farms stating that "The troops of my Brigade arrived here yesterday. Coll. [Elias] Dayton . . . has taken command of Elizth. Town and its vicinity."

After considerable wrangling as to where Col. Dayton should make his camp, Rev. Caldwell appealed by letter to Gen. Washington, urging him to order that the camp be made on "Kelly Hill" so as to give better protection to the Elizabethtown residents, which appeal seems to have been granted. This was presumably a hill on the farm of William Kelley, presently in Elizabeth, west of the Elizabeth River, bounded by Williamson Street, Washington Avenue, and Pearl Street.

On May 16, after two and a half months of strenuous service at the front for his Connecticut troops, Huntington wrote Washington a short note that "I expect to march [for Morristown] tomorrow." Upon their arrival in camp, Private Joseph Plumb Martin, one of the Connecticut men, noted in his diary, "We did not reoccupy the huts which we built, but some others that the troops had left." These, presumably, were the huts of the Maryland division, which recently had departed camp for the south.

As Huntington and his men settled into their new quarters, Pvt. Martin said that "We had entertained some hopes that when we left the lines and joined the main army, we should fare a little better, but we found that there was no betterment in the case. For several days after we rejoined the army, we got a little musty bread and a little beef, about every other day but this lasted only a short time and then we got nothing at all."

Then, on May 25, the day that the Committee to Headquarters issued its final report on conditions at Morristown, the rank and file of the 1st Connecticut brigade, not having had food for several days, decided to do what the troops had done back in January during starvation week. They would go out into the country and take food, to keep from starving.

The troops decided, however, that they would first let their officers know what they were about to do. To this end, they wrote an anonymous letter to Colonel Return Meigs, senior Connecticut officer of the brigade living in camp. Upon receipt of the letter, Meigs called his officers together and told them that "a letter without Signature was Found in the Rear of this brigade with complaints of want of provisions, and intimations that if matters were not redress'd immediately, the troops would march into the Country."

"At evening roll call they [the rank and file of the 1st brigade] began to show their dissatisfaction by snapping at the officers and acting contrary to their orders. After their dismissal from the parade, the officers went, as usual, to their quarters, except the adjutant, who happened to remain, giving details for the next day's duty to the orderly sergeants."

Because of the grumbling of the troops and disobedience to their officers, the adjutant called one of the complainers "a mutinous rascal," whereupon the entire 8th Connecticut regiment "fell in and formed" again, without officers. Then the 4th Connecticut, which lay to the left of the 8th, "formed, and came and paraded" with the 8th, also without officers. Pvt. Martin of the 8th said, "We now concluded to go in a body to the other two regiments [the 3rd and 6th] that belonged to our brigade and induce them to join with us . . . We did not wish to have anyone in particular to command, lest he might be singled out for a court-martial."

"By this time our officers had obtained knowledge of our military maneuvering . . . Colonel Meigs of the Sixth Regiment, exerted himself to prevent his men from obtaining their arms until he received a severe wound in his side by a bayonet in the scuffle." Then, eventually, said Martin, "we dispersed to our huts and laid by our arms of our own accord, but the worm of hunger gnawing so keen kept us from being entirely quiet."

Although "Several of the men who appear'd to be principals" were placed under arrest, Col. Meigs made a plea that they should not be harshly punished. He informed Gen. Washington that "Mr. Gamble [James Gamble in charge of the commissary at Morristown] or the Brigade commissary are doubtless to blame—this Brigade is now ten days deficient in Meat, notwithstanding my efforts to have them Supply'd—there cannot possibly be a case where mutiny can be admitted: But that this Brigade has been worse Served with provisions than any other in the Army will I believe appear by Mr. Gambles books."

The Invasion Begins

The day after the incident concerning the Connecticut troops, Gen. Knyphausen, the enemy commander at New York, learned of it. He was told that "great dissatisfaction prevails in the rebel army, and specifically that the Connecticut militia is threatening to go home." This was encouraging news to Knyphausen, but he had received other reports of possible revolts in the American army, yet no revolt had materialized.

Then, on May 29, a day or so later, the frigate *Iris* sailed into New York Harbor, having left Charleston on May 17. The captain of the vessel brought the news of the reduction of Charleston by Gen. Henry Clinton. By the next morning, Knyphausen had hand bills printed to be smuggled into Elizabethtown announcing the fall of Charleston.

Upon arrival of the hand bills in Elizabethtown, Col. Dayton seized and destroyed them, for he believed them to be false propaganda of the enemy, but they were not. Dayton did, however, forward one of the hand bills to Washington with a note referring to the work as "Lying Rivington's account of the reduction of C. Town." More specifically, he meant the work of James Rivington, New York printer and publisher.

Based on the fall of Charlestown and news of disorder in Morristown, Gen. Knyphausen called a council of war to discuss whether this might be the moment to take advantage of these circumstances, which must have demoralized the American forces to the point of giving up their struggle for independence.

At the end of the council, it was decided by Gen. Knyphausen that "as a result of recently received reports, virtually all agreeing that the Army of General Washington is highly disconnected and, at the first opportunity, would largely desert to our side, in addition to various other reasons, I [Knyphausen] was moved (especially through repeated recommendations and remarks by the English Generals) to cross over to Jersey with a considerable part of the army," on Tuesday morning, June 6. One of these English generals was Major General James Robertson, Royal Governor of New York Province, having recently arrived at New York "on the 21st" of March to take that post. The other English general was Major General William Tryon who had been colonial governor of New York Province before entering the British army.

Regarding this decision to invade New Jersey, Gen. Robertson wrote to Lord George Germain, British Secretary of State for Colonial Affairs, as follows: "He [Knyphausen] had intelligence that Washington's Army at Morris Town did not exceed 4000—2200 of these Philadelphia troops who had given evident proofs that they hated Congress and were tired of rebellion. Washington had made a detachment to protect the Chesepeak against Sir H. Clinton; another to protect the County of Albany from [Colonel] Sir John Johnson, who was then on the Mohawk river; and a third to cover the frontiers of Pennsylvania against [Lieutenant Colonel John] Butler and the Indians. The account of the reduction of Charlestown was fresh. The General thought under these circumstances by approaching the enemy to find means of giving advantages to the King's arms, and encreasing the difficulties of the rebels."

The decision to make a move into New Jersey on June 6 was not immediately communicated to the various military units at New York for fear that the information would be carried to Morristown through some intelligence leak. But on June 3, the troops were ordered to set up details in each regiment for the purpose of "making cartridge." This was a sure sign to the troops that there was to be action somewhere.

During the waiting period, the high command at New York made more copies of the notice of the surrender of American troops at Charleston. Upon reaching New Jersey, these would be distributed to the citizenry to weaken their resistance.

On the evening of the 5th, at 5 o'clock, the troops were told to be ready to move out the next morning. They were to take with them "seven days' provision." With the expectation of moving swiftly, they were instructed to bring "no carriages with us, or provision but what the men carryed." During the evening of the 5th, men scurried about to find someone with whom they could leave "money and papers in . . . safe-keeping." But when they found that most everyone whom they approached had been alerted also, they came to the conclusion that the operation was a big one. Almost the entire New York and Staten Island garrisons were to be involved. The force was "7375 men fit for duty."

On the 6th, after all of the troops were aboard ship, Knyphausen went aboard his command vessel, and set sail. Then, moments after Knyphausen's vessel had left its lower New York dock, Knyphausen received a message from Gen. Clinton, carried by Major William Crosbie, adjutant to Clinton. Lieutenant Colonel Johann Friedrich von Cochenhausen, Knyphausen's aide, said that Knyphausen had "hardly set sail when Major Crosbie with his dispatches from General Clinton boarded our ship."

The principal message delivered by Crosbie was that Clinton was bound for the Chesapeake but would proceed from there to New York. Crosbie had planned to arrive much earlier with this important message, but he had been delayed at sea. Upon the approach to New York Harbor "through a mutual ignorance of signals [from ships on station that were guarding the entrance to

New York Harbor, Crosbie's ship was] repeatedly driven off the coast and thereby retarded in her arrival at least a fortnight longer than necessary.'' Col. Cochenhausen said ''if these dispatches had arrived a few hours earlier, the entire expedition would have been called off.''

What appears to have happened upon Maj. Crosbie's arrival aboard was that a conference was called by Gen. Knyphausen, participated in by at least ''Generals Robertson and [Brigadier General Cortland] Skinner.'' It was decided that at this late hour, there was no way of stopping the invasion without seriously endangering the troops already in motion. Particular concern was voiced over the 1st Division, which had instructions to start across the sound from Staten Island to New Jersey at 11 p.m. that night. There was no way of contacting them before that hour.

Further, there appeared to be a good chance that New Jersey would fall with little effort, if the strike were made now. Thus, the force of Gen. Clinton would not be needed, and the invasion should go forward as planned.

It was not until ''5 o'clock'' p.m. that all ''56 sloops'' and schooners of the fleet arrived off Cole's Ferry, near what is now Tompkinsville, Staten Island, at which time they were given orders to proceed ''to Decker's Ferry,'' now Port Richmond, Staten Island.

At Decker's Ferry, the main invasion force was joined by one of the two garrison forces stationed on Staten Island. This contingent consisted of the ''22nd and 57th Regiments, the Regiment Buenau and the 1st and 4th Battalion of the Regiment Skinner, one company of the 17th Infantry Regiment as well as the cavalry detachment stationed on the aforementioned Island.'' These troops were designated the 2nd division of the invasion force; the 3rd, 4th, and 5th divisions were the New York force. The 1st division was already poised on the western end of Staten Island opposite Elizabethtown.

When the men of the 2nd division were aboard ship, the four divisions departed from Decker's Ferry through what is now Kill van Kull toward Elizabethtown, where the troops were to be landed on Elizabethtown Point by small boats from the sloops and schooners. ''Unfavorable wind and tides'' prevented the passage through the kill, and the fleet returned to Decker's Ferry.

This additional delay might not have been of great concern to Gen. Knyphausen if his entire force had been together, which was not the case. The 1st division, far out of contact on the western end of Staten Island, had orders to spearhead the attack, beginning at ''11 o'clock'' p.m. They would be transported across the sound to De Hart's Point in ''40 flatboats'' provided for the crossing.

Because the crossing by the 1st division was to begin within two hours, Gen. Knyphausen, at ''9 o'clock in the evening'' ordered his force ashore at Decker's Ferry, and started the long journey across the top of Staten Island, in a forced march. Knyphausen arrived at ''Garret Post House, opposite Elizabethtown Point'' sometime after midnight. His men were extremely fatigued by the march, and they were much in need of sleep.

The force did get some rest, for it was not until ''half past three in the morning,'' on the 7th, that the first troops were ferried across the sound. It had taken the intervening three hours to bring down to Garret Post House the 40 boats employed by the 1st division in their crossing at De Hart's Point, which was a mile north of Knyphausen's position. Further, the 40 flatboats could carry only part of one division at a time. Thus, there were great delays at the landing. The swampy terrain was another obstacle in their crossing ''the ground being very muddy'' before the troops could reach the water's edge.

The order of embarkation from Staten Island to New Jersey was as follows: ''2nd Division, 3rd Division, 4th Division, 5th Division.'' It was not until ''three in the afternoon'' of the 7th that the crossing had been accomplished. By this time, the 1st division of the invasion force had been in action fifteen hours and had taken a severe mauling by the Americans.

Advance Through Elizabethtown

Knyphausen's 1st division consisted of the ''37th, 38th, Leib and Landgraf'' regiments; the first two regiments were British and the last two Hessian. They carried with them two six-pounders. Their commander was British Brig. Gen. Thomas Stirling, who had opposed American Maj. Gen. Lord Stirling in the January raid on Staten Island.

Thomas Stirling had also participated in an earlier incursion into New Jersey at Elizabethtown. On February 25, 1779, then a lieutenant colonel, he led the British 32nd and 34th regiments in an attempt to capture Governor William Livingston who lived on the northern outskirts of Elizabethtown. On that occasion, ''At 5 o'clock in the morning, the British took possession of the Governor's House,'' but Stirling found the governor was not at home.

Over the past week, Brig. Gen. Stirling's men had had free access to Elizabethtown. American security had completely broken down. On June 2, Col. Dayton of the New Jersey brigade reported to his commander Brig. Gen. Maxwell: ''As there is not any guards at or near Eliz. Town I cannot venture to stay there any longer, matters are not conducted at that place as I could wish. Flags [of truce] arrive [from Staten Island] come up to the town and remain as long as they think proper.''

As Col. Dayton's men withdrew out of Elizabethtown to about what is now Cherry Street and Trotter Lane, Elizabeth, he also called in his outposts at Woodbridge and Rahway. The Newark outpost was also withdrawn, whereupon Gen. Maxwell moved his reserve force up to join it. Maxwell's new position was ''a short distance west of Newark.'' More specifically, as reported by the enemy, he took a position ''at the head of Bound Creek.'' This probably was at Lyons Farms, near what is now Lyons and Elizabeth Avenues, Newark.

Brig. Gen. Stirling was sure that he would have no difficulty in making a landing in New Jersey, and that, probably, there would be hardly a shot fired. In fact, his mission was thought by some to be one merely of ''news carriers, in distributing plentifully Rivington's new hand bills (published by authority) giving an account of the surrender of Charlestown to the British.'' With these hopeful expectations, Brig. Gen. Stirling reviewed his orders, which called for him, after landing, to ''march to Connecticut Farms with his division, and to hold that post until the army should arrive.''

As planned, Brig. Gen. Stirling ''landed at [De] Hart's Point,'' at ''11 o'clock at night [the 6th] while the [main invasion] army was [still] in march,'' across Staten Island.

Stirling's landing at De Hart's was accomplished without incident, and after the force had assembled near the landing, it advanced up what is now New Point Road. Then, at ''12 o'clock'' midnight, the 1st division, with Stirling riding at its head, was fired upon, and Stirling was hit ''in the thigh'' by an American bullet. Stirling's men were greatly surprised to be met by enemy fire. They thought that the Americans had withdrawn from the town, and that the populace would be perfectly submissive.

Gen. Washington, however, had been worried about the complete lack of security at Elizabethtown, and on June 5, had sent a small force there to investigate, and to try to establish some order. The force was Washington's own personal Guard of ''150 men,'' under the command of Maj. Caleb Gibbs. Maj. Gibbs had been relieved of his Guard assignment the day before in order to be sent on this mission.

It was Lieutenant William Colfax, second in command under Gibbs, who was closest to the landing, and who ''gave the enemy the first charge,'' which wounded Brig. Gen. Stirling. Stirling's men returned the fire and ''Mr. Ford . . . received two balls thro his thigh.''

The wounded ''Mr. Ford'' was Timothy Ford, the oldest of

the Jacob Ford children who had been allowed to go along on the mission as a volunteer with his friend Maj. Gibbs. Although Tim Ford's wound was serious it was not as critical as the wound that Lt. Colfax's men had given Brig. Gen. Stirling. Stirling's was so serious that it halted the entire enemy advance, while a roadside conference was held. In the roadside conference it was decided that Brig. Gen. Stirling could not go on, and the command fell to the next senior officer in the 1st division, "Colonel [Friedrich Wilhelm] von Wurmb" of the Hessian Leib regiment. The conference and related matters took about an hour and a half.

It was 1:30 a.m. when the 1st division was in march again, still outside the limits of Elizabethtown. With Col. von Wurmb now in command, "they chased the enemy out of Elizabethtown and pursued him on the road to Springfield." There was no disturbance or encounter in Elizabethtown as the only American troops in the town, had been those of Maj. Gibbs, and they had retired after the first skirmish, to join the "two regiments" under Col. Dayton who were north of the town.

Brig. Gen. Maxwell, who was lying west of Newark, had heard the first shots exchanged between the advance enemy force and Lt. Colfax's detachment. Captain, and Brigade-Major, Aaron Ogden "lying on the ground, on his blanket, in his tent, [also] heard this firing and immediately volunteered his services to General Maxwell to ascertain the cause of it."

Maxwell decided to ride along with Ogden to be on hand should any important decisions have to be made. Fortunately, the delay caused by Brig. Gen. Stirling's injury gave Capt. Ogden and Brig. Gen. Maxwell time to ride the five miles to the position of Col. Dayton, north of Elizabethtown. As Ogden and Maxwell came closer, they could see Dayton's two regiments already "paraded on the hill in the rear of Elizabeth Town river."

When Maxwell arrived at Dayton's side, he learned of the enemy landing, whereupon he immediately ordered the alarm gun to be set off. "The alarm gun, an iron eighteen pounder, was placed on the highest point of what are called the Short Hills in the neighborhood of Springfield."

This large alarm gun could be heard as far away as Morristown, and orders in camp specified that as soon as "the Alarm Gun on the heights above Springfield [was] to be fired; This is to be answered by the Alarm Guns in camp upon which the brigades are to form, on their respective parades and wait orders."

After a short consultation with Dayton, Maxwell decided that because Morristown appeared to be the enemy's objective, Dayton's two regiments should retire only as pressed to do so. This would give Ogden time to return to the other regiments of the brigade with the information that the enemy appeared to have landed in force, and that the most suitable place to put up a defense would be where the whole brigade could be joined together "behind a ravine near Wade Tan yard," at Connecticut Farms. The tanyard was located on the west branch of the Elizabeth River near the present Chestnut Street and the Garden State Parkway, in Union.

The strength of the New Jersey brigade was "741 rank and file fit for duty." Col. von Wurmb's 1st division, in pursuit, had a strength of "1634 men."

While withdrawing to Connecticut Farms Brig. Gen. Maxwell sent messages to New Jersey militia units in the area informing them of his plan to retire to Connecticut Farms, and of his intention to stand there.

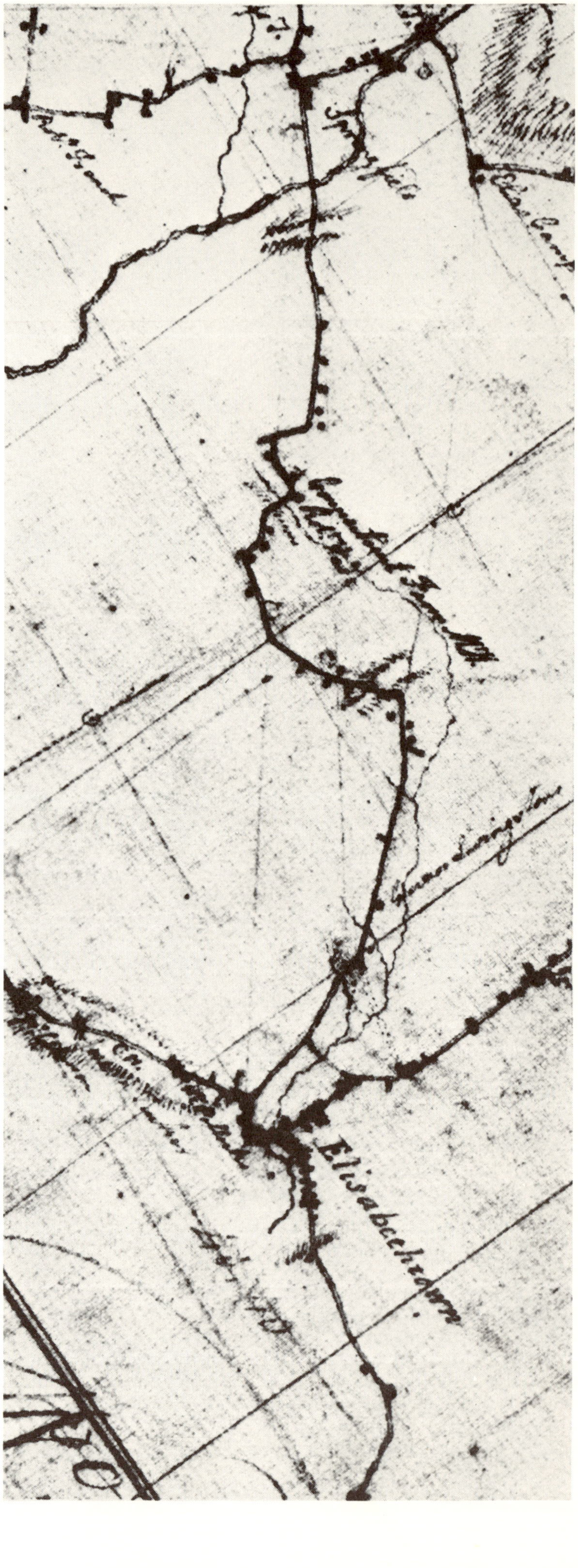

THE BATTLE ROAD—Reproduced here is a section of the Simeon De Witt map #106A, titled Contractions in the Jerseys *(AmM 14/106A), courtesy* The New York Historical Society. *Another map showing the same road is by Robert Erskine, map #75B, titled* Road from Springfield to Elizabethtown. *(AmM 17/75B) This latter map also shows the road as it ran past "Bryant's Tavern" and through Hobart Gap to Chatham. It also gives the names of numerous residents along the length of the road.*

June 7, however, was not an opportune day for the invasion as far as the New Jersey militia was concerned. On the 5th, each regiment stationed in the invasion area had been rotated as part of a "fortnightly" schedule. One half of each regiment served two weeks, then was relieved by the other half of the regiment. Frequently there were lags between the time that men were scheduled to go home and the time that their relief arrived. On occasion, the outgoing militia did not wait to be relieved; they just went home.

These rotating New Jersey militia regiments had been assigned the following positions: The 1st, or Southern, Essex regiment under Colonel Moses Jaques was scheduled to occupy "Elizabethtown." Due to the insecurity in town, they had withdrawn out of town to the north, on the road to Newark, with their left flank anchored against the Newark Meadows.

Farther north of Elizabethtown, the 2nd, or Northern, Essex regiment under Colonel Philip van Cortland occupied "Newark." South of Elizabethtown, on the "west side Raritan" River, in back of what is now Perth Amboy, lay a combined regiment made up of the Western Morris and the 2nd Middlesex regiments under Colonel John Starke and Lieutenant Colonel Benoni Hathaway of Morris, plus Major John Emburg of Middlesex.

"East of Raritan" River, back of what is now South Amboy, was stationed the 1st Middlesex under Lieutenant Colonel Samuel Crow. He owned a mill nearby on the Raritan River, at the foot of what is now Crow's Mill Road, in the village of Fords.

Back of these shore units on the road to Morristown, was stationed Colonel Sylvanus Seeley's Eastern Morris regiment at "Bottle Hill" now Madison. Col. Seeley's regiment was in march to the front soon after it was alerted. It passed through Springfield and, according to Private Ashbel Green, halted "a short distance from Connecticut Farms when Mr. [the Reverend James] Caldwell rode up and addressed us in a very animated manner." One of the things Green remembered that Caldwell said, was, "Your comrades, countrymen, are acting nobly. They have been fighting the British this morning with a bravery which would have done honour to the troops of the Duke of Marlborough," one of the great military commanders of history. After Caldwell's inspirational talk, Seeley's men marched on toward the front.

Total New Jersey militia strength in the area at the time of invasion was approximately 650 men, serving an alternate two weeks of service with another 650 men from the same units. Maj. Gen. Philemon Dickinson was commander of all New Jersey militia, and Maj. Gen. Lord Stirling was in command of both militia and continental forces in and near Elizabethtown. There is no evidence, however, that either Maj. Gen. Lord Stirling or Maj. Gen. Dickinson were with the fighting troops during the first few hours of the invasion.

Brig. Gen. Maxwell appears to have been the senior officer at the front, and one of his first steps was to provide for the security of Gov. William Livingston and his family. As the Elizabethtown wing of his brigade began to retire toward Connecticut Farms, Maxwell, personally, went to Liberty Hall, the governor's home, near what is now North and Morris Avenues, Elizabeth. Upon arrival there, he informed the occupants of the house that the enemy was advancing in that direction. The governor was not at home at the time, but the women of the family appear to have decided to remain in the house, despite the oncoming enemy. "Son William," who might have been taken prisoner had he remained at home, accompanied Maxwell in his retreat toward Connecticut Farms, and he stayed with Maxwell "all the day."

It was not long after Maxwell and young Livingston left Liberty Hall that the women of the Livingston family saw the enemy coming into view. The sun had risen at 4:31 a.m., and it was now about 6 a.m., and broad daylight. Soon Col. Wurmb, the new commander of the enemy 1st division, was seen riding up the lane to the governor's house, accompanied by several others, all on horseback. Upon reaching the house, Col. Wurmb noticed a blooming red rose bush climbing the porch trestle. He also saw a young lady standing on the porch. Upon inquiry, he found that she was the governor's daughter, Susannah, and that her father was not at home, whereupon the colonel admired the roses and "asked leave to pick one," which he did—then he rode away.

Connecticut Farms Stand

While Col. Wurmb was making his stop at Gov. Livingston's house, his column marched up what is now Cherry Street and Morris Avenue, past the Livingston house. At Colonial Avenue, the column, which Col. Wurmb soon rejoined, made a sharp turn to the left over what is now Colonial Avenue, thus skirting the swampy areas of the west branch of the Elizabeth River. With the enemy now firmly in control of Elizabethtown and Elizabethtown Point, refugees from Staten Island began swarming across the sound and moving inland behind the advancing invading column.

By the time the enemy reached Colonial Avenue, the off-duty New Jersey militia, began to gather in well protected spots along the road, to harass the advancing column. Now, there was "constant skirmishing." The Hessians said that after the Americans would fire one or two shots, they "ran off as hard as they could . . . They ran much faster than we. They are a thin long-legged make, most of them without shoes and stockings and without coats."

It was shortly before 8 a.m. when the head of the 1st division of the invaders turned off Colonial Avenue onto what is now Chestnut Avenue. A few minutes later they halted where the road dropped down into a ravine through which ran the west branch of the Elizabeth River. They could see that the hills on both sides of the road overlooking the ravine were places the Americans were sure to occupy.

Cautiously, the scouts of the 1st division descended into the ravine. They were promptly attacked from these hill positions, and were forced to retreat. In pursuit, the Americans "crossed over the defile and drove them to the tavern that was Jeremiah Smith's." In this advanced position, the Americans saw "at least 1500 men" forming in battle order, whereupon the Americans beat a retreat back across the ravine to Brig. Gen. Maxwell's main position.

Maxwell had his troops well placed at Connecticut Farms, although they were much spread out. He said, "I ordered a few small parties to defend the defile near the Farm Meetinghouse," the present site of the Connecticut Farms Presbyterian Church, deploying them on two hills both of which overlooked the defile. "The main body of the brigade had to watch the enemy on the road leading to the right and left toward Springfield." The "right" road to which Maxwell referred followed the present Chestnut Street, which passed below the church in the ravine and proceeded west to the present Caldwell Avenue, where it turned north to the present Elmwood Avenue. The "left" road was Vauxhall Road.

As the New Jersey militia filtered into Connecticut Farms "in small bodies" to report, they were somewhat disorganized. Brig. Gen. Maxwell saw that they were not being properly utilized, so they were all "committed to [Brigade] Major Ogden" of the continental brigade so as to form them into a fighting unit until their regular militia units had reported in sufficient numbers to form.

By 8 a.m., Maxwell had assembled, behind the ravine at Wade's tanyard at Connecticut Farms, his 741 man brigade of New Jersey continentals, plus Maj. Gibbs 150 continentals, and perhaps 300 New Jersey militia totaling about 1,200 men. Earlier he had been informed by Col. Dayton that the enemy force descending upon him was nearly 5,000, actually 7,000 men. He knew that the whole enemy force eventually would be brought to bear upon his Connecticut Farms position. Maxwell also was very much aware that any help from the balance of the American army was at least a day's march away. He realized that his stand at the Farms could not be for long, and he was soon to be confronted with this fact.

By the time Maxwell had finished deploying his troops back of Wade's tanyard, the main invasion force under Gen. Knyphausen had progressed considerably in its difficult crossing from Staten

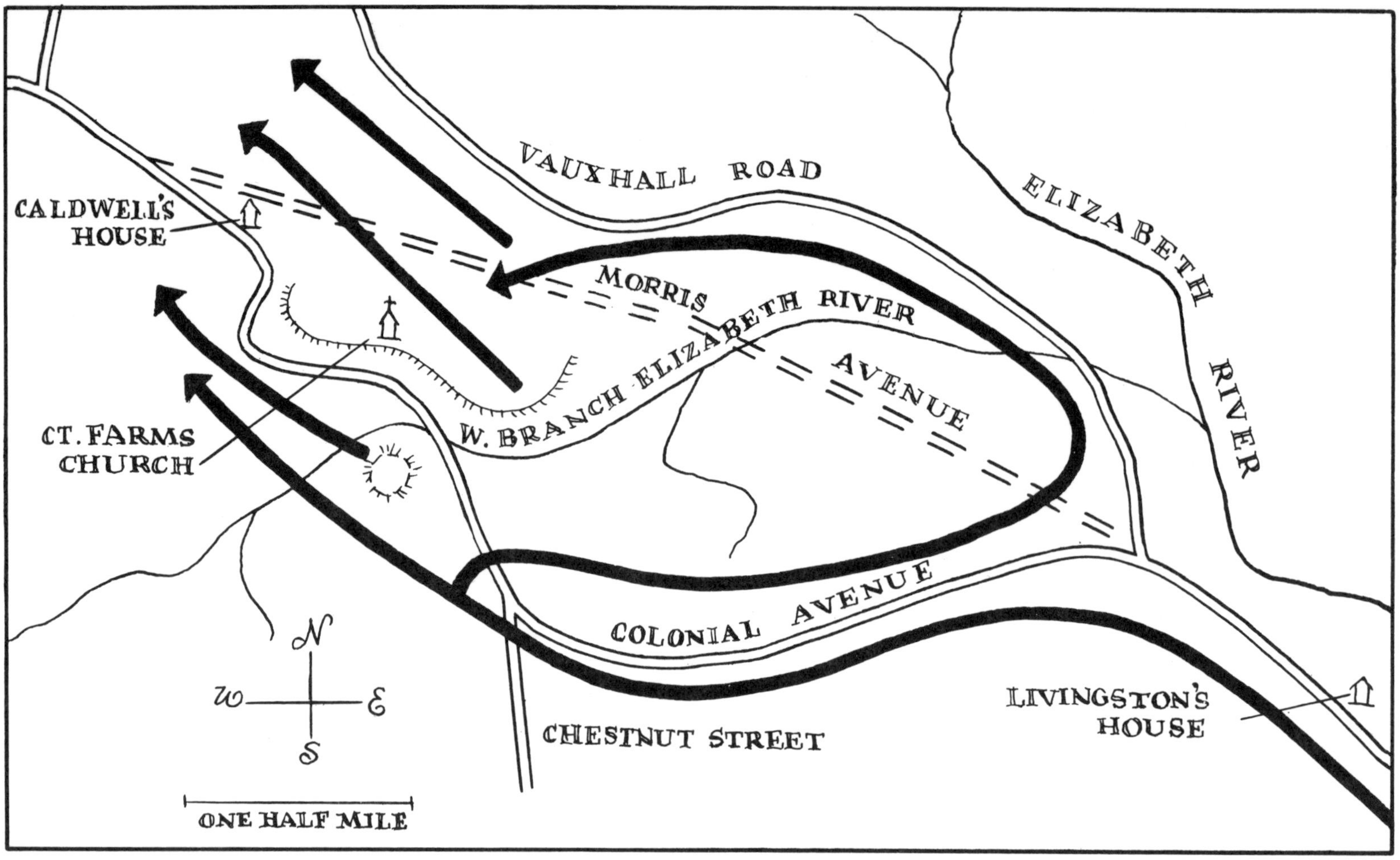

Island to New Jersey. Some of that force already was well along the road to Connecticut Farms. "As soon as the [2nd] division of [Major] General [Edward] Matthew was landed [below Elizabethtown], it took off for the support of the division Sterling" now commanded by Col. Wurmb. When the 3rd division under the command of Maj. Gen. Tryon was landed, two fast moving lightly equipped units of Jaegers were dispatched to the front, on the double. The units were one dismounted company of Hessian and one dismounted company of Anspach Jaegers.

It was "half past eight" a.m. when the Jaegers joined Col. Wurmb's force, and it was a half hour later "at nine o'clock that the entire Corps, [Matthew's division] with the exception of cannons and cavalry, arrived safely" near the Connecticut Farms defile. Maj. Gen. Matthew, upon his arrival, took the over-all command. The two divisions plus the two companies of Jaegers totaled about 3,500 men, which was over twice Brig. Gen. Maxwell's strength.

Fifteen minutes after its arrival, the detachment of Jaegers was ordered to take a position "in front of the column to protect it against enemy fire." The idea was not to make a frontal attack but to work toward the enemy from roadside cover, so as to rout out the sniping positions of the Americans, which were located on the two hills overlooking the defile.

While the Jaegers were making their move, part of Maj. Gen. Matthew's force was sent back toward Elizabethtown to pick up an extension of Vauxhall Road, at a junction now designated approximately Liberty and Morris Avenues, Union. They were to advance up Vauxhall Road and try to cut off some, or all, of the American force defending the defile.

During the Vauxhall Road circling movement, the Jaegers at the defile got within shooting distance of the two hill positions of the Americans, but found it difficult to dislodge them. The Jaegers said that they "met with unaccustomed resistance." The exchange of fire between the Jaegers and the Americans continued for some time, and it appeared that the Jaegers might be turned back. The fighting was so close at one point that the Jaegers were held off "with fixed bayonets." The Jaegers, however, could not compete in this type of close fighting because their rifles were not fitted with bayonets, while muskets of the American continental soldiers were.

Then, just as success seemed to be with the Americans, a message was delivered to both American hill positions that their "left was turned by the enemy on another road." This was the force that had back-tracked over Colonial Avenue in order to take the Vauxhall Road to Connecticut Farms.

Although the Americans were forced to give up their defile positions, they did not make a disorganized retreat. They executed a slow withdrawal, fighting from behind trees, fences, and houses, and even from inside "some houses."

Near the western edge of Connecticut Farms, just east of what is now Elmwood and Morris Avenues, on Elmwood, stood, and still stands, the parsonage of the Connecticut Farms Presbyterian Church. At the time, the parsonage was temporarily occupied by the family of Rev. James Caldwell, the pastor of the 1st Presbyterian Church of Elizabethtown, recently burned.

From a position just east of the parsonage, Brig. Gen. Maxwell tried to make a stand, but he was soon compelled to withdraw. During this withdrawal, the parsonage was within the heaviest fire from both sides. In the melee, the parson's wife, Hannah Caldwell, was shot dead through "the window" of the parsonage.

While this tragedy was taking place, a number of buildings in Connecticut Farms were burned in much the same manner that burnings had taken place on Staten Island, in Elizabethtown, Newark and other places where refugees were permitted to tag along with an invading force. In the case of Connecticut Farms, "the Presbyterian church and 14 dwelling houses and barns" were set afire. The British army claimed that some buildings were burned because they were "hourly occupied by armed men." But such authorized burnings usually turned out to be a signal for revengeful refugees to burn a few buildings for themselves.

The Americans were not able to maintain a stand on the western outskirts of Connecticut Farms, which position had placed Brig. Gen. Maxwell on ground not to his liking. Thus, he ordered his force to retreat "slowly toward the heights toward Springfield." This withdrawal would have been damaging to the rear of Maxwell's continentals had the New Jersey militia and civilians not taken such an active part. "Everyone that had a rifle," for miles around, seemed to have rallied to the cause.

The Jaegers said that the "impenetrable wood on both sides of the road was full of militia who could not be chased out of them." The militia would lie under cover, and suddenly would appear on the edge of the woods in small detachments and fire at the advancing Jaegers who had to stay pretty much to the road.

Regarding the American stand at Connecticut Farms, Brig. Gen. Maxwell said, "Our parties of Continental troops and militia at the defile performed wonders . . . stopping the advance of the enemy near three hours."

Action Before Springfield

At his Morristown Headquarters, about 18 miles from Elizabethtown, General Washington had received a short note from Captain Jonathan Dayton, written near Elizabethtown at "past 1 o'clock Wednesday morning," the 7th, stating "I am directed by Col. [Elias] Dayton to inform your excellency that the enemy landed this night at 12 o'clock, from the best intelligence four or five thousand with field pieces . . . they intend to penetrate into the country."

Washington must have received this message before 4 o'clock a.m., for it was at that hour he issued orders for "The Troops to be held in readiness to march at a moment's warning; Each man to be furnish'd with 40 rounds and two days provisions."

At 7 o'clock, additional orders were given that "The Army will march immediately in the following order: 2nd Connecticut; 1st Connecticut; Stark's; Hand's; 2nd Pennsylvania and 1st Pennsylvania. The Brigade Commissaries are to follow with provisions."

While the troops started in march down the road to Elizabethtown, Washington hurried off a note to the somewhat recovered Maj. Gen. Lord Stirling, over-all American commander in the Elizabethtown area, asking him to "give the alarm as extensively as you can in your quarter and to remain to form them as they collect and march them towards the enemy with direction to skirmish on their left flank . . . I wish your Lordship's particular attention to the Militia."

Washington also wrote to Major Jeremiah Talbot of the 7th Pennsylvania regiment, current commanding officer at Paramus, New Jersey, telling him of the invasion and asking him "to communicate this intelligence to the Militia Officers in the vicinity of your post immediately that they may alarm the Country and that you will march . . . with the detachment under your command and with all the Militia that will join You, for Chatham; keeping the Mountains below you on your left." In these letters to Stirling and Talbot, Washington was depending greatly on the New Jersey militia, for his whole New Jersey force of continental soldiers, as of four days earlier, numbered only "3,760 rank and file."

The letter to Talbot was written at "1/2 after 8" a.m. Washington had now spent over four hours putting his army in motion; still there were things to do and more orders to be given. Yet, Washington knew that he must no longer delay joining his troops. As he departed from the Ford house, sometime after 8 a.m., Mrs. Ford was quite aware of "the hurry and confusion with which the genl. left the house."

Enroute to the front, Washington stopped along the way to consult with various commanders as he passed his men in march. Following these delays, he "reached the heights in the rear of Springfield on Wednesday [that] afternoon," a distance of about nine miles from Headquarters.

Upon arrival at the front, Gen. Washington sought out Brig. Gen. Maxwell to plan further strategy. It was soon decided that Maxwell would try to hold off the enemy at the Rahway River as long as he could, in order to give the main army time to arrive at the strategic heights above Springfield and to organize a defensive line there. During this conference, Washington's troops were still in march, some three to four miles back.

While Maxwell was conferring with Washington, the 3rd enemy division had come up to join their advance troops under Maj. Gen. Matthew. This was the division of Maj. Gen. William Tryon, with Maj. Gen. James Robertson attached. This force consisted of two battalions of Guards, the dismounted Jaegers, and the Guides and Pioneers bringing the total advanced British-Hessian force to about 4,500 men, with Maj. Gen. Matthew still in command.

In the last few hours, Brig. Gen. Maxwell's advance force had increased in strength by militia arrivals to about 1,750 men. It was under these 2½ to 1 odds against him that Maxwell launched an attack on the enemy. In Maxwell's own words, "The whole brigade, with the militia, advanced their right, left, and front with the greatest rapidity, and drove their advance to the main body." Maxwell said, "this was the closest action I have seen this war."

Maxwell did have one advantage. In addition to knowing the ground better than the enemy did, the terrain favored him. The road here passed through heavy woods, except for small clearings adjacent to farmhouses. This would not permit the enemy to bring a large force up to the front to form in battle order. They must do their fighting with a relatively small body of men.

Because the Jaegers were taking such a beating on their front from the continentals and on their flanks from militia, it was necessary for the Jaegers to call for reinforcements. The reinforcements, that were sent to assist the Jaegers had just arrived with the 3rd division. They were the "two Light Infantry and two Grenadier companies of the Guards." Seeing the new troops coming to assist them, the Jaegers "yelled Hurrah," as they had little ammunition left.

The Americans saw the new troops join the fight, and they started to withdraw, whereupon the Jaegers took advantage of the situation and "advanced in fast speed about 200 steps before the English could merge into their line under a heavy fire." The Americans were forced to retreat all the way to the Rahway River, and to cross the river before the Hessians slackened their pace. In the words of Brig. Gen. Maxwell, we were literally "pushed over the bridge at Springfield."

When Maxwell's force got over the Rahway River, his men formed, ready to resist a crossing either at the bridge or through the stream, which was wadable in places. The line Maxwell formed extended about "1/2 English miles."

As the last of the Americans crossed over the bridge, two American artillery pieces located "pretty near the bridge, behind a small eminence" began firing at the Hessians and British Guards who were coming down the road. One of the cannon was "an old iron 4 pound field piece," belonging to the militia. The other piece was a "three pounder" manned by the Hunterdon County militia, under Captain Yard. John Burrows of this outfit said "our company and another of artillery" did considerable damage to the enemy on that occasion.

Burrows continued, "The road they [the advancing Jaegers and British Guards] came was straight and open for three fourths of a mile, and we had fair play at them the whole way until they came to the bridge." The road itself descended "for about half a mile, [in] a gentle slope till it reaches the bridge." The road leading to the bridge was roughly the present Morris Avenue. On the American side of the bridge there was a small hill, which crests at about what is now Warner Avenue, Springfield. This was the "small eminence

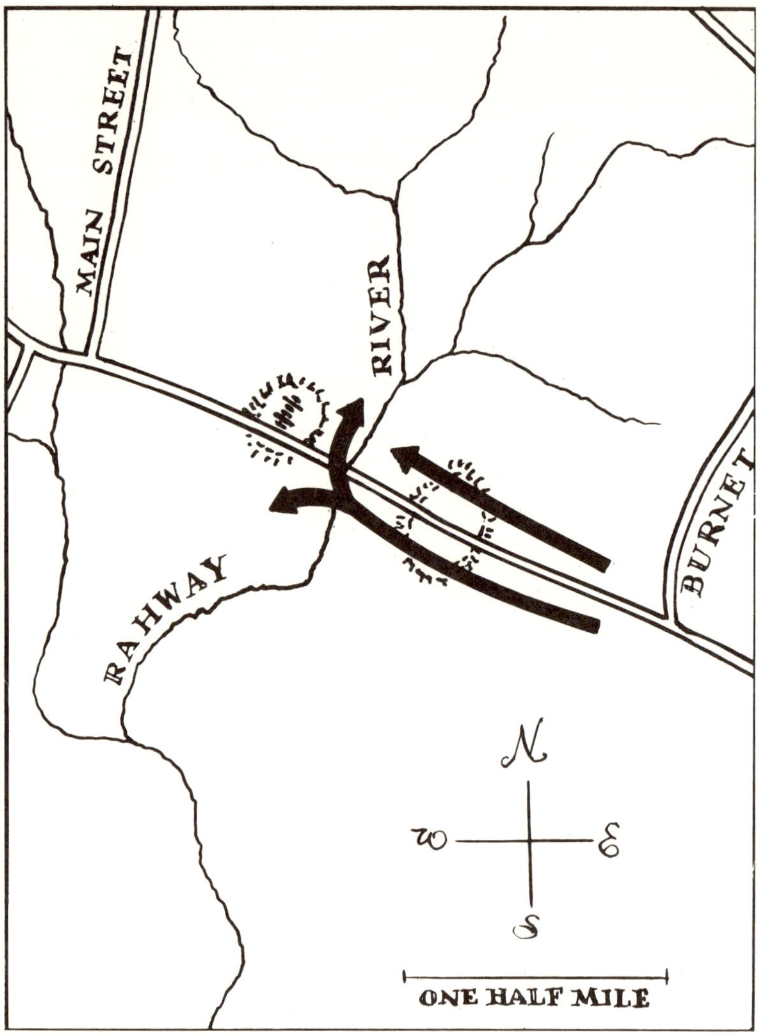

. . . pretty near the bridge" from which position artilleryman Burrows could see right down the road "straight and open for three quarters of a mile" giving him "fair play at them the whole way until they came to the bridge." Burrows said the enemy "were twice on the bridge, but were beaten back, and considering, as we had to judge of their conduct, that they would buy their victory too dear, from the advantage we had of them, they gathered up their dead and wounded, and retreated."

Actually, the enemy advance was halted by Gen. Knyphausen himself who had just arrived at the front with the 3rd division, and he had seen the entire encounter where the New Jersey militia cannon were so effective. Knyphausen's cannon had not yet come up to the front, causing him to give "orders to halt" until the cannon arrived. He gave additional orders that his troops should stay close enough to "defend the bridge" in case the Americans tried to dismantle it. The main British-Hessian force, then took a position on "the heights between Connecticut Farms and Springfield . . . waiting for the Cannon and Baggage." It was Gen. Knyphausen's plan for his force that "the next day it would advance through Springfield and occupy the Short Hills."

At "4 o'clock [p.m., Major General Carl Wilhelm von] Hackenberg arrived . . . with the 4th division consisting of the Regiments Anspach and Bose . . . also bringing six cannon along." The 43rd regiment of this division had been left at Elizabethtown to maintain communications with Staten Island.

There were still three hours and a half before sunset, and four hours before dark. It was therefore decided "after General Hackenberg's arrival, to conquer the pass near Springfield and to advance a few more miles in order to occupy more advantageous positions than those presently had."

As Gen. Knyphausen, now in field command, was about to move out to take the Short Hills, Gen. Washington, now also in field command, was just deploying his army to defend the Short Hills. Washington placed his forces as follows: "The first line" was formed just west of the junction of what is now Springfield Avenue and Morris Avenue, straddling Morris Avenue; "The second line" was formed just west of Hobart Gap Road, on both sides of Morris Avenue, as shown on one of General Lafayette's maps made by Lieutenant Colonel Jean-Baptiste De Gouvion.

Commanders of the lines and brigades were designated in General Orders as follows: "The First line composed of the Pennsylvania division on the right commanded by Major General Greene [now relieved of his quartermaster duties.] The Connecticut division on the left commanded by Major General the Marquis La Fayette. The 2nd line composed of Hand's and Stark's Brigades, commanded by Major General Baron de Steuben."

Retreat to Elizabethtown

Just as Gen. Knyphausen was about to give the order to advance to attack Gen. Washington's new positions, Maj. Crosbie arrived at the front with a new message from Gen. Clinton. It said that "Genl. Clinton was not bound for the Chesapeak [as had been expected] but in a few days would be at Sandy Hook."

At about the time Gen. Knyphausen was receiving this latest message from Gen. Clinton, a deserter from the American lines was being interrogated by Knyphausen aides. From this source, it was learned that "Washington had got time to occupy with his force the strong post of Short hills." It was learned further from the deserter that Washington had "detached General [Lord] Stirling to cut off, if possible, the communication of the British army with the water," namely, Staten Island Sound.

The information secured from the deserter was confirmed through the interrogation of five prisoners brought in that day. They did not have all the details, but they confirmed enough to verify that the deserter's statements were substantially true.

When this body of information was presented to Gen. Knyphausen, it was decided to return to Elizabethtown. Halting orders were then sent back to Major General Friedrich Wilhelm von Lossberg. He was in march up the road from Elizabethtown bringing the 5th division, consisting of the Donop regiment, some cavalry detachments, plus a number of cannon and baggage. The orders were that he was "to await the return of the army at Livingston House," the home of Governor Livingston, on the present Morris Avenue, Elizabeth.

Then, "about ten o'clock the whole [invasion] army got in motion, and moved off. It was exceedingly dark, and there was such strict silence observed, that one regiment could not perceive the next regiment going off." Lieutenant George Matthew noted that "It was the darkest night I can remember in my life, with the most heavy rain, thunder, and lightning known in this country for many years." It was just "sunrise," 4:30 a.m., when Knyphausen marched through Elizabethtown. It had been a very difficult retreat because of the elements, but there had been no contact with the Americans during the entire night.

The day had been a resounding victory for the Americans. Brig. Gen. Maxwell noted "Our [continental] loss was one ensign killed, and three lieutenants wounded, seven privates killed, twenty-eight wounded and five missing. The militia lost several [killed] and had a number wounded." Gen. Washington was very gratified with the performance of the troops, and he visited the wounded and consoled them.

Captain Isaac Reeves of the Essex County militia had been wounded severely in the day's fight. Reeves was "carried in a horse litter from the field to Stephen Parkhurst's mill. General Washington . . . saw the wounded officer, dismounted and examined his wounds."

Enemy losses on this day were much more severe. Maxwell said, "We had good reason to believe, from the number of dead left

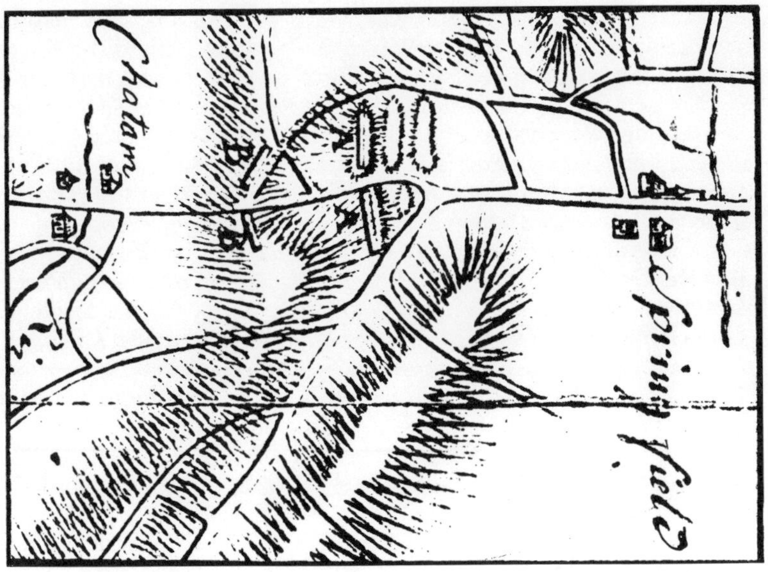

SPRINGFIELD TO CHATHAM JUNE 21, 1780—This is a section of a map made by Lt. Col. Jean-Baptiste de Gouvion who was on the staff of Maj. Gen. Lafayette. The map accompanied a battle account dated "at Camp, Short Hills, 21 June, 1780." Neither the map nor the battle account are signed, but Peter J. Guthorn, a student of Gouvion's work, has identified it as that of Gouvion. The map and account are in the Archives De La Guerre, Vincennes, France, Service Historique de l' Armie Section Ancienne. (Al-3732 piece 80) The map text identifies American positions as follows: (A) Premiere ligne, (B) Second ligne. The Springfield Presbyterian Church is shown on the northeast corner of present Main Street and Morris Avenue. Compare this map with a later situation map covering much the same area and showing street and road identifications.

on the ground, and from the information of many of the inhabitants where they had their dead and wounded, that they lost three times the number we did." One American report said, "the enemy's loss is near 300 in their attack at the bridge, numbers of them are daily found in the woods." Maxwell said, "47 of the enemy dead were found the next day scattered through the woods and fields, besides those whom they themselves had buried and [or] carried off."

Enemy Corporal Stephen Popp who was on the scene, said "it took three boats to carry the wounded to New York." In addition to the enemy dead and wounded, the Americans took "about 40 prisoners."

Brig. Gen. Maxwell, summed up the day's activity: "Never did troops, either continental or militia, behave better than ours did. Every one that had an opportunity (which they mostly all had) vied with each other who could serve the country most."

Chapter VI

WAITING FOR CLINTON

Fight Below Elizabethtown

A summary of Gen. Knyphausen's intelligence, as he completed his withdrawal to Elizabethtown, was that Gen. Washington was planning to hit Knyphausen's force very strongly, if and when he tried to cross the sound, back to Staten Island. Knyphausen decided, therefore, that he would deploy his troops below Elizabethtown until matters stabilized.

In Knyphausen's new defensive positions, the British 22nd regiment occupied the advanced post on the road to Elizabethtown, at the junction of present New Point Road and First Avenue. The Hessian troops were placed below the 22nd regiment, straddling the routes to the two points. The balance of the force lay still closer to Elizabethtown Point, along the east side of the road to the point.

At daybreak on the 8th, Gen. Knyphausen used the 40 flat boats of the 1st division to "ship the Hessian Jaegers back to Staten Island" for they were out of ammunition. They had used it all the day before. "The cavalry, the wagons, etc." were also shipped back to Staten Island, after the Jaegers crossed.

At about 8 o'clock a.m., the Americans made their appearance at Elizabethtown. The force was the Morris County New Jersey militia under Col. Sylvanus Seeley. They had been ordered to advance, cautiously. Seeley said that they followed the enemy retreat the night before, and had advanced "to Thompson's Mills [on the west branch of the Elizabeth River just below Connecticut Farms] whare we lay all night." After Seeley's men resumed their pursuit in the morning, they came across "a guard in the woods back of Deacon Ogden's hous and at the forks of the road," near Elizabethtown. Seeley was extremely familiar with the Elizabethtown terrain. He had been stationed there with his regiment until "the latter end of the year 1779," less than six months past.

Also advancing cautiously on the enemy were Maj. Caleb Gibbs and his detachment, which had begun the action the day before. Maj. Gibbs had written Gen. Washington a note from "Vauxhall at the Bridge [at] 6 o'clock a.m. 8th June," informing the general that I plan to "march off toward the enemy's right, if I can find them." Col. Philip van Cortland's 2nd Essex militia regiment, would also move toward Elizabethtown and be on hand to fight, as would Col. Moses Jaques's 1st Essex militia regiment.

To strengthen this advanced force, Gen. Washington, early in the morning of the 8th, ordered "Major Generals Greene, La Fayette and Steuben's divisions each give a battalion to form a detachment which is to be commanded by Brigadier General [Edward] Hand, Greene's gives 120 files, La Fayette's 80 files, Steuben's 100 files" making a total of 300 men. These men were to march immediately to the front. Upon their arrival, the total advanced force would number close to 1,000 men.

Back of this force, according to orders, "Maxwell's brigade will preserve the post it held last evening [between Springfield and Connecticut Farms] reposing to-day and acting as a covering party." Both Brig. Gen. Maxwell and Brig. Gen. Hand would be under the field command of Maj. Gen. Lord Stirling who had been technically in charge of the advance troops on the 7th but had not been on hand to get into the action.

Maj. Gen. Lord Stirling, was likewise extremely familiar with the area. Instructions to Lord Stirling this day were that he "must act chiefly in the woods, as this mode will not only be best to harass the enemy, but will be best adapted to security, especially against horse of which the enemy are said to have a considerable body." Stirling was further instructed, in a departure from usual procedure, that the continental troops are "to be employed to-day . . . in conjunction with the Militia." Ordinarily, continental and militia operated under separate commands.

Under these circumstances, Maj. Gibbs's continental detachment, which was on the enemy's right, would be working directly "in conjunction with" Col. Phillip van Cortland's militia regiment, also on the enemy's right. Senior officer, Col. van Cortland, who would command this wing, had served as a militia colonel since 1776, and was a very capable and respected officer.

Col. Seeley said that "after sum time," probably around 9 a.m., he was "joined by Lord Stirling's troops," more specifically, Brig. Gen. Hand's 300 men plus Col. Jaques's 1st Essex militia.

At about 9 a.m., Col. van Cortland, with Maj. Gibbs, came over to Lord Stirling's position, located below Gov. Livingston's house. Here they held a conference to decide the time, place and manner of attack as outlined by Gen. Washington.

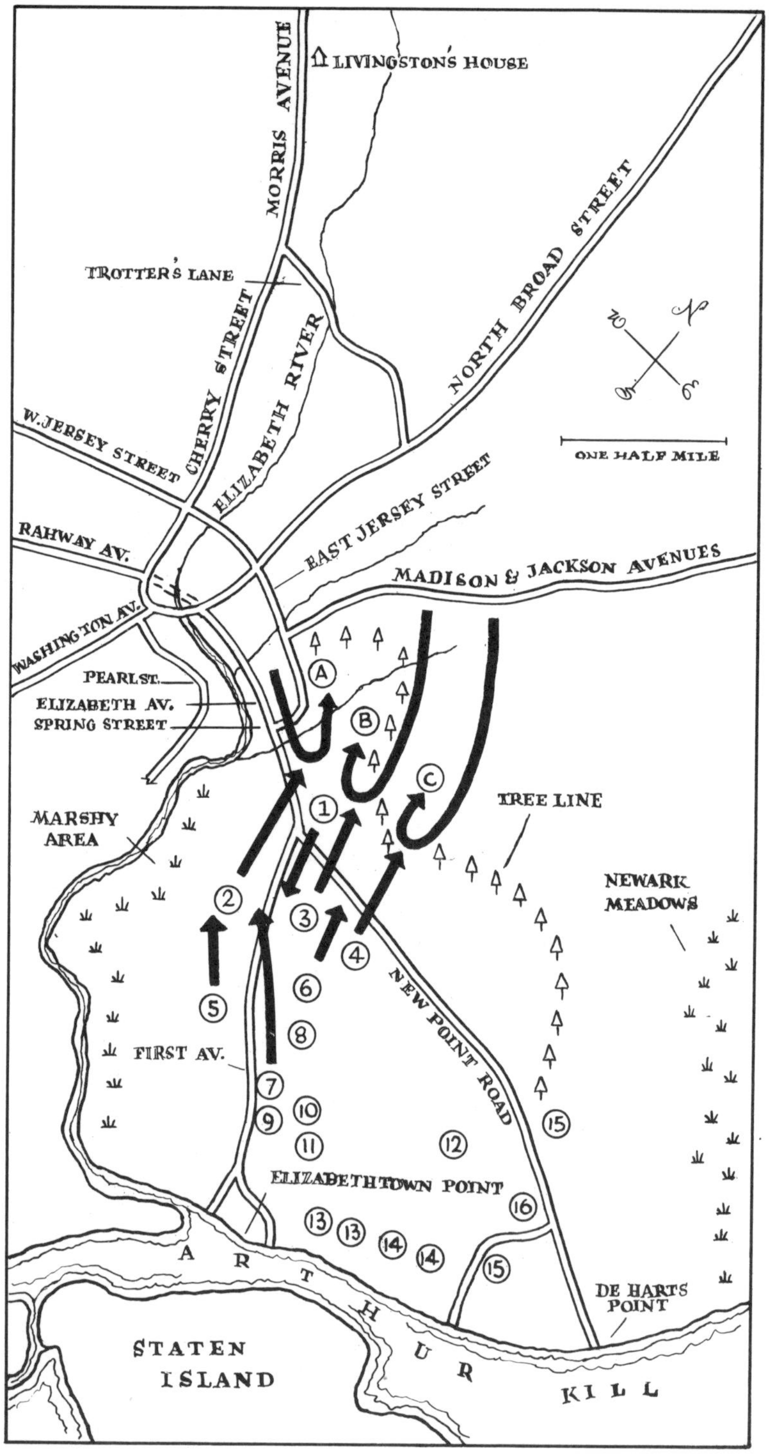

ACTION BELOW ELIZABETHTOWN JUNE 8, 1780—(A) Hand and Jaques, (B) Seeley, (C) van Cortland and Gibbs, (1) 22nd, (2) Anspach, (3) Bose, (4) Donop, (5) Buenau, (6) Leib, (7) Landgraf, (8) 38th, (9) 43rd, (10) 37th, (11) 17th foot, (12) Skinner's N. J. Vols. (13) Guards, (14) Br. Cav., (15) Hess. Cav., (16) 57th.

At "10 o'clock in the morning," Lord Stirling launched his attack. According to Col. Seeley, it was an "advance in three colloms, one on the main road [which was Gen. Hand's wing], the Continental troops of Col. Cortland [along with Maj. Gibbs] on the left, and myself [Col. Seeley] in the center."

In the first skirmish between the 22nd British regiment and van Cortland's left wing, the 22nd was a little over anxious "and had twice fired without hitting" anyone; then they withdrew. As the 22nd regiment pulled back, the "Buenau and Anspack regiments" were ordered to advance against Hand's right wing, the Anspack regiment taking the lead and the Buenau regiment acting as reserve.

Simultaneously, said Ensign Krafft of the von Donop regiment, "Bose's and our regiment had to advance." The Bose regiment moved against Seeley's center position and the von Donop regiment against van Cortland's left wing. The Leib and Landgraf regiments advanced to fill the positions vacated by the advancing Bose and von Donop regiments. As the Bose regiment moved forward, Seeley said that one of his platoons "fell back a little, but after being ordered to com up, came up and stood there ground well."

The men of the von Donop regiment, who were now attacking the van Cortland left wing, were having fire-power troubles, as the 22nd had had. They found that they were generally in range for the Americans but the Americans were out of range for them. As a result, the von Donop regiment had several wounded "by rifle shots, which was surprising considering the distance." This would suggest that many of the militia were firing long range hunting rifles rather than the usual smooth bore muskets carried by most men on both sides.

In addition to the American range advantage, the Hessians noted that the Americans "are excellent marksmen," and "we did not dare to let ourselves be seen standing upright." The Americans remained in the bushes, firing from behind them, and the Hessians could not even see them. The Hessians said, "We have not yet learned to meet them the same way."

Eventually, the Hessians were compelled to bring up a number of field pieces. When these cannon started firing into the bushes and woods, "General Hand ordered a retreat [of all three wings], which was performed in good order."

The retreat was ordered even though the enemy bombardment was rather ineffectual. Pvt. Green noted that "Their balls struck the trees among which we were standing, some yards above our heads; and I heard of a man or two being either killed, or dangerously wounded by the falling of some of these balls on their heads from the trees which had arrested their course . . . It was a special mercy that they overshot us, otherwise the carnage must have been horrible. The ground trembled under us at every step, and . . . no thunder storm I have ever witnessed, either in loudness of sound or the shaking of the earth, equalled what I saw and felt."

The Americans retired "about half a mile" where Col. Seeley said "we lay on ower armes untill evening and then returned to the north end of town and staid all night."

It had been an extremely successful day for the Americans. The enemy had suffered many casualties. Further, the New Jersey militia had taken "about 20 prisoners" in the woods during the first encounter, and they proved to give very valuable intelligence relative to the strength and intentions of the Knyphausen force.

The Hessians were also receiving their measure of intelligence. During the course of the evening, an American deserter came in and said that "the New Jersey Brigade [was] at Connecticut Farms and that the now very large militia was advancing on Elizabethtown and was standing at both his [Knyphausen's] flanks" ready to attack the next morning as they had done that day.

This caused Gen. Knyphausen to abandon a plan to return to Staten Island as soon as the front settled down. To attempt a crossing in 40 small boats would be too risky, with the Americans standing on both of his flanks. Under these circumstances, it was "deemed best to maintain the post at Elizabethtown point till the arrival of Sir Henry Clinton."

Fight in Elizabethtown

During the afternoon of the 8th, when Gen. Washington learned of the success of Lord Stirling's force, and "having been informed that part of the English had retreated to Staten Island, and that the rest were in confusion at the Point, [Washington] ordered his army to advance," more specifically, to move closer to the enemy. To accomplish this, Brig. Gen. Maxwell was ordered to change from his position between Springfield and Connecticut Farms to a position below Connecticut Farms. The first line was ordered to move from Short Hills to "Connecticut Farms" and the second line from Hobart Gap to "Springfield Heights."

On this night of June 8/9, after the move, Gen. Washington made his headquarters "at a House where the Roads fork on this [the east] side of Springfield . . . The House I stay at [he wrote in a note to Lord Stirling] is Mr. [Timothy] Whitehead's."

During the night, Gen. Washington learned that the "information he had received had been exaggerated." The enemy had not retreated in any great strength to Staten Island, and they were not in confusion. Therefore, the next "morning at six o'clock [the 1st line was ordered] to resume the Short hills position," and, presumably, the second line resumed its former Hobart Gap position at the same time. This would prevent the possibility of a surprise flanking movement by the enemy to gain the pass through the Short Hills. Upon his return to earlier positions, Washington set up a new alarm system. "The firing of two pieces of cannon from the centre of the Second line will announce the advance of the enemy."

While Gen. Washington had been moving forward with his troops on the afternoon of the 8th, Gen. Knyphausen was questioning his men who had been in action against Lord Stirling so as to determine why they had been so easily handled by the Americans. He soon found that it was principally a matter of their inability to get the enemy within range. Yet, the Americans could easily reach them.

If the same type of action were to take place tomorrow, Knyphausen's only solution would be to get the Jaegers back from Staten Island. They were the only troops in his force equipped with rifles. Thus, "toward evening the cavalry received orders to join the army again as did also the Jaegers," both units then being on Staten Island.

When the Jaegers received the order to return to New Jersey, they were in the midst of making cartridges to replace the supply they had used up on the previous day. They had not completed the task, so a collection of finished cartridges was taken from all of the Jaegers, and it was found that they had enough for 60 men. Thus, "60 Jaegers were given the collected ammunition of the Corps and were sent across [to Jersey] to occupy the outpost in front of the enemy." The balance of the Jaegers were to follow when prepared. In the morning, the baggage and cavalry also recrossed to Jersey along with some artillery.

On the 9th, it was relatively quiet while Gen. Washington was correcting his position, and while Gen. Knyphausen was deploying his troops to defend Elizabethtown Point more effectively. By the morning of the 10th, Knyphausen had completed his defenses, including the redeployment of the entire Jaeger Corps and the cavalry.

The Jaegers, freshly supplied with ammunition, were sent to occupy a position close to Elizabethtown. They were positioned at about what is now Elizabeth Avenue and South Street. The 22nd regiment took its old position at the Junction of First Avenue and New Point Road. The cavalry bivouacked near the 22nd, to be in ready support of either the Jaegers or the 22nd. The main body of the enemy lay in a line from the Newark Meadows to the Elizabeth River. The line from east to west ran mainly between Fifth and Sixth Streets in present Elizabeth. Positions of units along this line were from right to left as follows: "Guards, Two batts. New Jersey Volunteers, 22nd, 37th, 43rd, 57th, 38th, Du Corps [Leib], Landgrave, Donop, Bose, and 1st batt. Anspach," a line "2216 yards" long.

The two main armies now had taken defensive positions about eight miles apart, and they appeared content to allow each of their advance forces to fight for control of Elizabethtown. Gen. Knyphausen's advance was just below Elizabethtown. Gen. Washington's advance under Lord Stirling was in the town. Stirling, however, was just leaving his command of the American advance.

On the 9th, Gen. Washington ordered that "Major General Lord Stirling is to take command of the second line and Major General Baron Steuben [then commander of the second line] to take command of the Troops in advance consisting of General Maxwell's brigade, Major Gibbs's detachment and such Militia as are at present advanced." The two militia regiments of "Webster and Chamberlain" would be under continental general, "Maxwell," while three militia regiments, "Philips's, Cortland's & Jaques's" would be under militia general, Nathaniel "Heard."

The militia were now reporting in great numbers. One observer noted that on the morning of the 9th he saw "2000 of them below the mountains, and more flocking down continually." Among them were "all those from Hunterdon, and Coll. [William] Scudder's of Middlesex, Coll. [John] Neilsons [of Middlesex]— Those of Somerset, Essex and Morris being already here," at Springfield, or in more advanced positions.

It was now a few days after the death of Mrs. Caldwell, and the news had spread rapidly throughout the countryside that Hannah Caldwell had been deliberately murdered by the enemy in reprisal for the Patriot activities of her husband. Details of the circulating story got into print in the local Chatham newspaper, *The New-Jersey Journal*. The article said that when the enemy came, "Mr. Caldwell could not remove his property, nor all his family. His amiable wife, with a babe of eight months, and one of three years old, with the housekeeper and the little maid, were left . . . The babe was in the arms of the housekeeper, the other child the mother held by the hand, all sitting upon the side of the bed, when one of the barbarians advancing round the house . . . fired two balls into the amiable lady, so well directed that they ended her life in a moment."

Some years later, there was an admission. A New Jersey militiaman, Private Frazee Craig, of Captain Amos Morses's company, of Colonel Jaques's Essex County regiments, testified that he was "at the Farms [Connecticut Farms] when Mrs. Caldwell was shot by one of Capt. [John] Craig's men," also of Col. Jaques's regiment. The shooting by an American, if indeed, he did it, surely was accidental.

But emotions were running high after Hannah Caldwell's death, and no one seemed to think of nor care to ask about witnesses. The populace was aroused. They had a likely culprit with a motive, and the militia turned out in unprecedented numbers. The continental soldiers also seemed to catch the spirit of revenge, and Maj. Gen. Steuben, who was now the front line commander, must have sensed the feeling of the men as he took over the front line command.

Maj. Gen. Steuben made his headquarters at Rev. James "Caldwell's former house . . . on the hill." This house was located in present Elizabeth, near Pearl and Race Streets, on the West bank of the Elizabeth River.

Even before going to his quarters, Steuben began visiting all of his defenses and all of his troops, including militia units. It was while on this tour of inspection that one of the privates of militia saw Steuben for the first time, although he had heard much about him. Private Green said, "He rode up to our encampment, and requested to see our commanding officer. And never before or since, have I had such an impression of the ancient fabled god of war, as when I then looked on the Baron—he seemed to me to be a perfect personification of Mars. The trapping of his horse, the enormous holsters of his pistols, his large size, and his strikingly martial aspect, all seemed to favour the idea."

On the 10th, Steuben made his first move against the advance troops of the enemy. He employed the same hit-from-cover tactics used over the past few days. The Hessians said that all day there "were constant short attacks."

Finally, the cavalry supporting the Hessians rushed the American advance troops whereupon the Americans withdrew "for about one mile and a half beyond [north of] the town," forcing

Steuben to abandon his headquarters. The cavalry took two prisoners; the balance of the Americans disappeared into the thick bush cover, which could not be penetrated by the horse troops. From the two captured prisoners, it was learned that the Americans were drawn up in strength at the house of Gov. "Livingston and were from there sending their patrols" out to harass the Hessian pickets. After this encounter, the Jaegers "moved farther into town."

On the 12th, Lieutenant Colonel William Smith with Spencer's regiment of New Jersey continentals, maneuvered his troops into a position where "after the exchange of a few shots . . . [they] obtained possession of the western part of the Town. The enemy remains on the opposite side of the creek," namely the Elizabeth River.

During the night, both Hessians and Americans "were withdrawn" from their part of the town so as not to be caught off guard. In the morning, they returned to their positions on opposite sides of the Elizabeth River. The Hessians said that throughout the night "no one was allowed to undress." It is presumed that the Americans were equally alert.

On the 12th, the Hessians spotted, at a distance, the first American cavalry to be seen. It was a small detachment, estimated at "about 100 infantry and 50 cavalry." This was the cavalry troop of Maj. Henry Lee, which recently had been sent south to join Maj. Gen. Lincoln but, when the enemy came to New Jersey, had been summoned to return. The infantry was the 7th Pennsylvania regiment, commanded by Major James Parr. Temporarily, this unit had been assigned to Maj. Lee, because Lee's dismounted cavalry had been sent south by boat, and could not be called back.

On the 13th, Maj. Lee, advanced to a position north of Elizabethtown on what is now North Broad Street, where they annoyed the Hessians all day, even though it had been raining hard. In the evening, however, Lee was attacked by the enemy cavalry. On the 14th and 15th, Elizabethtown continued to be a no-man's-land. Both sides entered the town during the day, engaged each other wherever possible, then retired at night.

On the 16th, a "floating bridge to Staten Island was completed" by Gen. Knyphausen's engineers. It was laid on top of the decks of 19 flat boats; the span was "228 yards." On the day the bridge was completed, General Knyphausen had intelligence that General Washington "is said to prepare for an attack on the British army before General Clinton could unite with it."

One of the first to use the new bridge was Vice "Admiral [Marriot] Arbuthnot [who] came to Jersey and brought the news of the arrival within a few days of the troops from Charleston." Adm. Arbuthnot had arrived in his flagship the *Europa,* coming from Charleston. He made better time than the fleet of transports and other vessels that carried Gen. Clinton and his army.

On the day Arbuthnot came to Jersey, an incident took place on the eastern outskirts of Elizabethtown, which netted the Americans several captives and a wealth of intelligence. According to Hessian reports, "in the morning Lieutenant [William] Sherlock of the 43rd [British] regiment, made an advance patrol with six men of his piquet . . . [and] he and his men were taken prisoner by Major Lee's Dragoons."

The Americans saw it a different way. They said Lt. Sherlock with his group were robbing a henroost when captured. Sherlock had already committed the act and was about to return to his station when he was captured with the "fowls in hand."

From Sherlock and his six men, each being questioned separately it was learned that the British were dangerously weak. They had brought with them "no tents except for the officers." To deceive the Americans, they had put their blankets up on sticks during the day to appear "like tents at a distance." They also learned that "None of the British have any Knapsacks or any kind of baggage with them—except one shirt . . . [and] had not more than eight or ten Waggons upon the front except artillery waggons."

On the day that Lt. Sherlock was captured, Brig. Gen. Irvine of the Pennsylvania line reported the incident in a letter to his wife, and he followed the account by admitting that the Americans also were without tents. He wrote, "We have now been thirteen days at this place [in the Short Hills] without tents or baggage."

On the 17th, official Hessian reports said, "nothing special; all is quiet." There were, however, enemy troop arrivals in New Jersey on this day. "The Regiment [battalion] Beyreuth joined the army and was posted to reserve behind the center," of the line. The other Anspach-Beyreuth battalion was already in the line.

Major General James Pattison, New York commandant, noted that "The two Battns. of the Anspach-[Beyreuth] Regiment having been sent from hence to Elizabeth Town Point, leaves this Garrison [New York] so exceedingly Weak as renders it impossible to Mount the Guards that are absolutely necessary." In New York there was only the 76th regiment numbering "531 fit for duty and the Provincial Loyal Americans numbering 187 fit for duty," together with some Royal artillery. In New Jersey as of the 18th there were "7375 men."

In the afternoon of Saturday, the 17th, John Stillwell who was on watch duty at "Garrets Hill," back of the present Belford, New Jersey, overlooking the entrance to New York Bay, saw what he thought was a fleet of ships coming in. He watched for some time through his glass, then he recorded in his log "4 o'clock appeared a fleet of 31 sloops standing from the southward . . . 5 o'clock came 19 sails more."

Stillwell hurried off a report to militia Brigadier General David Forman, at Freehold, New Jersey. Brig. Gen. Forman, in turn, rushed the news to Gen. Washington informing him of the arrival of "Sir Henry Clinton . . . from the Southward."

Clinton Changes Plans

Under the escort of Adm. Arbuthnot's squadron, Gen. Clinton had left Charleston on June 8, not knowing that Gen. Knyphausen had invaded New Jersey. With Clinton on his return north were the "light infantry, the British and Hessian grenadiers, the 42nd Regiment, the Hessian Jaeger detachment under Major von Wurmb, and the infantry of the Queen's Rangers," consisting of "about 4500" men.

A few days before Clinton left Charleston, he had sent a message north, telling Knyphausen of his revised intentions. The message, as previously noted, was that "Sir H. Clinton was not bound for Chesapeak, but in a few days would be at Sandy Hook."

Enroute to New York, General Clinton developed plans for action, which he had dispatched north on June 11. They were sent on board the *Europa* with Admiral Arbuthnot. These instructions were in the hands of "Adjutant General [John Andre] with such further order as I [Clinton] judged requisite for conducting my designs with the proper secrecy and expedition."

These plans consisted of "a sudden unexpected move, [to] seize upon their [Washington's] grand depot of military stores at Morristown and capture or disperse the forces that covered them." Clinton added that immediately upon arrival he would throw his entire force ashore "at Amboy." He would then march up the Raritan River to Middle Brook, just beyond Bound Brook, then up Middle Brook "to Mordecai's Gap," and through the First and Second Watchung Mountains to Morristown.

In a coordinated movement, Knyphausen would cross "to Elizabeth Town Point the instant the fleet from Charleston arrived at Sandy Hook." Knyphausen's line of march would be "to Chatham," and thence to Morristown.

Gen. Clinton said that as he was nearing the end of his voyage north, "I had the mortification to hear by a frigate that joined us on our approach to the coast that Generals Knyphausen and Robertson had already entered the Jersies with a considerable part of the New York force."

Immediately upon Gen. Clinton's arrival at Staten Island,

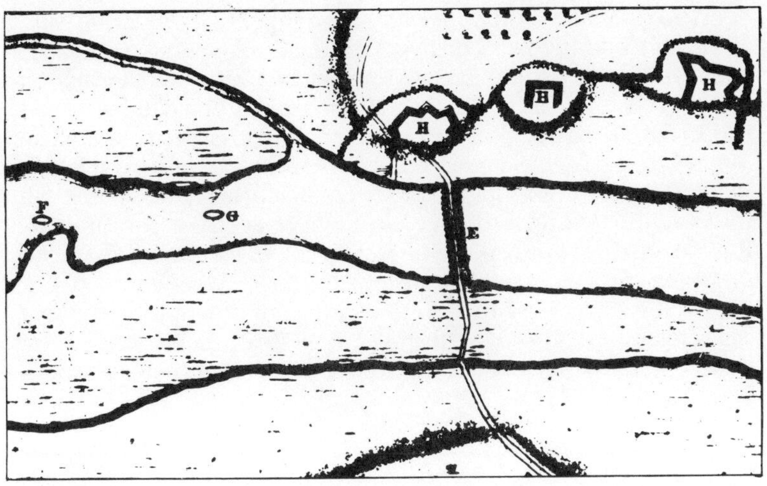

PONTOON BRIDGE ACROSS STATEN ISLAND SOUND—This is a section of a printed map in the William Faden Atlas of Battles of the American Revolution *in the* Geography and Map Division, Library of Congress. *The map is by Lt. John Hills of the British 23d regt. (BrM 57/16) The map is titled* Sketch of the Positions of the British Forces at Elizabeth Town Point . . . . *Text material applicable to this map section is as follows: (E) Bridge of Sloops for the Passage of the Army, (F) Gun boat, (G) A Boom, (H) Works erected to cover the Passage of the Army to Staten Island on 23d June, 1780. Lt. Hills, at the time attached to the artillery or the engineers, was wounded while sketching the map. See* John Hills, Assistant Engineer *by Peter J. Guthorn, Portolan Press, Brielle, N.J., 1976. For a more detailed drawing of the pontoon bridge see (Brun 467.)*

Gen. Knyphausen delivered a report to Clinton via Knyphausen's aide de camp, Captain George Beckwith. Whether the message was verbal, or in writing, is not known. Clinton did, however, write down the substance of the message at the end of which he noted "The above memoranda of General Knyphausen's operations were delivered me by Capt. Beckwith."

Beckwith reported that "Washington's army [was] weakened by detachments to the southern provinces, and by the march of the [New] York Brigade to the Northward, said against the Indians, [thereby his force] was reduced to 3,000 men . . . with a large Train of Artillery without horses to remove them; the Troops much dissatisfied and anxious for an Opportunity of deserting, the militia of the country dispirited and tired of the War."

Despite this alarming information that Knyphausen was already in New Jersey, Clinton decided to continue with the plan of a two-pronged attack on Morristown.

During the same meeting at which Capt. Beckwith gave his report on the status of Gen. Washington's army, Beckwith delivered to Gen. Clinton two letters from American Maj. Gen. Benedict Arnold, written at Morristown on the 12th. The letters, in code, had been smuggled out of Morristown. They were addressed to either Capt. Beckwith or Maj. Andre.

Upon Beckwith's receipt of these two letters, they were decoded by Reverend Jonathan Odell, a loyalist preacher of Burlington, New Jersey, who had become a chaplain with the Pennsylvania Loyalist troops at New York. All of these involved men, by previous arrangement, had been assigned code names. Odell's was James Osborne, Andre's was John Anderson, and Beckwith's was G. B. Ring. Arnold's code name was Mr. Moore.

Benedict Arnold's first letter of the 12th, informed Clinton that "Six French Ships of the Line, several Frigates and a number of Transports with six thousand Troops are to be expected at Rhode Island in two or three weeks to act under General Washington." Arnold had been told this by Washington while Arnold was a dinner guest of Washington, at Morristown.

Benedict Arnold's second letter written at 10 p.m. on June 12, informed Clinton that West Point was very weakly defended. "Only 1500 men" held the garrison. In the fort there was little flour and none to be had but from Pennsylvania. Arnold added that he thought "it would be a good Stroke to get between General Washington and West Point."

Benedict Arnold had no way of knowing that Clinton's two-pronged attack toward Morristown was now in motion. Clinton's troops already had been debarked at Staten Island and "some of the troops are advanced on Both the roads leading to Amboy as far as within five miles of the ferry on west end of the island."

Although not known to Benedict Arnold, this was no great surprise to Washington. A few days earlier it had been noted by John Mercereau, one of Washington's spies, that the British had begun "sounding about the mouth of the Raritan River and sett up some stakes."

Maj. Gen. Philemon Dickinson of the New Jersey militia received confirming reports. His information was that "the main body [which had landed from Charleston] were marching toward Amboy . . . to the Blazing Stars." These were Old Blazing Star and New Blazing Star ferries from Staten Island to New Jersey, with their New Jersey termini at what is now Carteret. Further, "a number of boats, were come around into Prince's Bay," now Prince Bay, Staten Island, to ferry the army across.

Major Clarkson Edgar of the 1st Middlesex militia had brought Maj. Gen. Dickinson this intelligence, and Maj. Edgar was ordered to take "half his battalion and some horsemen" to the landing place, and to form a line of resistance, until other forces could be brought up.

Dickinson also took steps to deprive the enemy of provisions, should they land at Amboy. He ordered "the cattle removed" from the general area. This frightened the populace and the Patriot inhabitants began removing their household effects to the back country.

As Clinton's forces moved toward Amboy, Clinton received a third letter from Benedict Arnold. It was dated June 16, and it was written from Fishkill, New York. The letter informed Clinton that Arnold had just visited West Point, and he found it more poorly defended than represented in his letter of June 12. Arnold even outlined how an attack could be made. He pointed out that the British could "land three miles below and have a good road to bring up heavy Cannon to Rocky Hill," which was defenseless on the back and it could be taken with a few men. Arnold then pointed out that Rocky Hill commands all the other works at West Point.

This last letter from Arnold gave Clinton the information that caused him to call off his Mordecai Gap thrust into New Jersey and to direct his force toward the capture of West Point. His new design would be to have Knyphausen continue with the plan to move toward Morristown via Chatham, which would force Washington to stay nearby to protect Morristown, while Clinton went "up the North River, and by landing on its western bank, [could] rapidly strike between the enemy and his object," that is, to strike between Washington's army and West Point.

To implement this revised plan, Clinton went to New Jersey on the 19th, where he "arrived at 10 o'clock" in the morning. After going over all of the details of the plan with Knyphausen, Clinton reviewed the troops in the afternoon. Then, he departed for Staten Island where he "took his residence at Mr. Banker's," which was near "Decker's Ferry," now Port Richmond.

From his Staten Island Headquarters, on the 19th, Clinton said, "I . . . directed all the troops I had brought with me [except the Queen's Rangers] to be reembarked as quickly as possible," for transport up the Hudson. The force totaled 3,807 men, based on an official embarkation list made on December 23, 1779, when departing for Charleston.

It was only a matter of a few hours from the time Clinton outlined his new plan to Knyphausen, that American Maj. Henry Lee, through his spy setup, was able to warn Maj. Gen. Steuben that he had good information that the current object of Gen. Clinton was to capture West Point. Maj. Lee was so sure of his information that he ventured the prediction that the Americans would "hear of Gen. Clinton's being before West point in less than 48 hours." Then Lee added, with complete confidence in his source of information, "this wind is very fair," that is, it is favorable for Clinton to run up the North River.

Steuben immediately passed Lee's intelligence on to Washington, and upon receipt of same, Washington expressed concern over such conflicting intelligence. Both Mercereau and Dickinson had told Washington that the entire Clinton force was converging on the Amboy crossing to New Jersey. Now, within a few hours, Lee had intelligence that West Point was Clinton's objective. Amid all of this confusion, Washington directed Lieutenant Colonel Richard Meade, his aide, to "send some person into New York," a spy, to clarify the situation.

West Point Dilemma

Although Gen. Washington was much concerned when he learned from Maj. Lee that Gen. Clinton's Charleston fleet was headed for West Point, he was not altogether unprepared for such a move. As early as June 10, Washington had written to Maj. Gen. Robert Howe, commander at West Point, that there is a "suspicion of something being intended against that post." He warned Howe that Gen. Henry Clinton was momentarily expected from Charleston and will probably push "immediately up the North River."

To guard against such an event, Washington, on the 10th, ordered Brig. Gen. James Clinton's New York brigade to "return with the utmost expedition to West Point, and to put yourself under the command of Genl. Howe." Brig. Gen. Clinton was in northern New York, and he would be able to drop down to West Point without delay.

On the 15th, General Washington had shown additional concern for West Point when he wrote to Maj. Gen. Alexander McDougall who was recouperating at Fishkill, New York: "My apprehensions are up for West Point. [General Henry] Clinton is every moment expected, and may push up the North River. I shall be happy to have the Aid of your abilities at the post, and am to desire you will immediately on receipt of this repair thither. The Garrison consists of five Brigades which will afford you a command." McDougall, a New Yorker, had commanded the posts in the New York Highlands for much of the early part of the war.

When Washington heard on the 18th that Gen. Henry Clinton had finally returned from Charleston, he took immediate steps to "supply a large number of Waggons to move the Army and its Baggage and Stores, and to forward provisions to the North River," should it be necessary.

On the 19th, Washington learned that "Six of the Enemy's Ships, one a frigate, run up the North River in sight of Verplanks point on the 18th, but they have fallen down again." Washington was now convinced that there was some sort of attack in motion against West Point, but he was extremely confused by reports from Dickinson and Mercereau that the Charleston force was marching for Amboy.

Could the British be planning a three-pronged attack—one via Mordecai's Gap, one via Chatham, and another up the Hudson River. Washington would have to wait almost two days to learn that the Mordecai's Gap offensive had been abandoned in favor of a thrust up the Hudson.

Despite all of these rumors, the Knyphausen force in New Jersey was still poised opposite Maj. Gen. Steuben who now commanded the American front line. And it was lucky for Steuben that the Knyphausen force made no attack on the 19th, for there was great confusion this day in the American front line.

As of the morning of the 19th, there were "1168 rank and file" militia on the line, but by nightfall Steuben reported that "I do not think I have 500 militia here." One half of each of the militia regiments of "Colonels Cortland, Phillips, Jaques, and Scudder" had, on the 19th, completed its fortnightly duty and was to be replaced by the other units.

When the reliefs did not arrive on the appointed hour, the old troops simply left the lines vacant. Steuben had been aware of the rotation system, but he did not expect the old troops to leave before replacements arrived, and he was much annoyed.

On the 20th, Washington was quite certain that the Mordecai Gap offensive was off, and that the North River attack was on, but he was still unwilling to move troops. He did, however, order a select group of officers to repair to Morristown to take the officers' heavy baggage from the huts and to place the baggage "in the Farmer's houses, in the Vicinity of the Huts."

On the 20th, Maj. Gen. Steuben also became convinced that the West Point attack was on, and he wrote to Gen. Washington, "I think my presence is necessary at the No[rth] River where many arrangements are necessary."

Steuben's wishes were granted on the 21st, when Washington issued orders that, as a replacement, "Major General Greene will for the present Command the advance Corps of the Army consisting of Maxwell's and Stark's brigades, the Light Horse and Militia."

In after orders on the 21st, Gen. Washington made his move. He ordered that "The Troops under Command of Major General Arthur St. Clair and the Connecticut Line are to march tomorrow morning at three o'clock," for West Point. St. Clair's troops consisted of the 1st and 2nd Pennsylvania brigades and Hand's brigade. The Connecticut line consisted of the 1st and 2nd Connecticut brigades. These troops totaled 2,556 rank and file. Maj. Gen. St. Clair was in overall command.

St. Clair's force got under way at daybreak on the 22nd, with instructions to "halt on some good ground at or near Rockaway bridge where the troops will remain until further orders." From the wording of this order, it would appear that Washington still had some doubts as to the enemy's intention.

To keep an eye on movements of the enemy on the Hudson below West Point, Gen. Washington ordered Col. Stephen Moylan to place a commissioned officer and six of his dragoons at King's Ferry, and from there to send a message each day to the general, who would be somewhere enroute to the Hudson. The method was to "dispatch a Dragoon every morning with a written report of any appearance upon the Water."

On June 4, Moylan had been ordered to move his regiment from their Connecticut winter quarters to West Point. Then, on the 10th, they were ordered to join the main army at Springfield because, as Washington noted, "the enemy have a good many cavalry and we have none here." Pursuant to these orders, Moylan was enroute to Springfield when he was ordered to stop at King's Ferry.

Washington did not leave with his troops at daybreak on the 22nd, but stayed in Springfield for a few hours where he wrote several letters, and gave praise "of the Conduct and Bravery of the officers and Men of Maxwell's brigade in annoying the Enemy in their incursion of the 7th inst." Washington also noted that "the behavior of the [New Jersey] militia has been such as to do them signal Honor and entitled them to the warmest approbation. There never since the commencement of the Contest appeared a more general ardor."

After praising his troops, Gen. Washington returned to his headquarters at Jacob Briant's Tavern, where he paid the innkeeper "eight hundred dollars . . . for Sundrys during his stay." He then mounted his horse, and rode north to join his troops in march toward West Point, leaving the New Jersey command to Maj. Gen. Greene.

The New Jersey front had been quiet for two days when

Washington left, but within minutes of his departure, there was action by the enemy. "A patrol pushed forward as far as Livingston's house." They were met by the New Jersey militia and some of the enemy were captured.

From the captured prisoners, the Americans learned that the Queen's Rangers had crossed the pontoon bridge to reinforce Gen. Knyphausen. The mounted section of the Queen's Rangers was already in New Jersey, and the move to send over their foot soldiers was merely to reunite the foot and mounted sections of this very effective corps, but the information appeared significant to the Americans.

Following the receipt of this information, Maj. Gen. Greene received intelligence that the enemy would be marching against him at any moment. Greene's informant was a "Mr. P." The man had come to headquarters and had asked to see Gen. Washington. Mr. P. informed the headquarters guard that he had been in Gen. Washington's employ, and he wished to give the General intelligence on the enemy. Mr. P. was told that Washington was not there, whereupon he asked to see the next ranking officer.

On being admitted to see Maj. Gen. Greene, Mr. P. told Greene that he was in fact "a double spy" and that he had information from the enemy headquarters that they were about to march toward Morristown. Gen. Greene immediately alerted all his troops, and he sent Col. Dayton down into the lines to see if he could gain additional intelligence.

By 10 p.m., having no news of any enemy advance, Greene was becoming suspicious that Mr. P. was lying, and that he was perhaps trying to keep Greene's force in place while the enemy would attack his flank. Throughout the long night, Mr. P., who was being held at headquarters, insisted that he was in the employ of Washington, and that he was "willing to forfeit his life if everything he tells is not strictly true."

Chapter VII

THE SECOND INVASION

Connecticut Farms Recaptured

"At 3 o'clock in the morning" the next day, June 23, as predicted by Mr. P., the Knyphausen force marched from their positions below Elizabethtown. They advanced in two columns. The first column, under the Command of Maj. Gen. Matthew, consisted of the "Queens Rangers, Guards, Regt. Landgraf, 1st and 4th Batl. Skinners." Matthew also had with him "Diemar's Hussars and the Staten Island Dragoons."

Matthew's column took to the road with "the Queens Rangers at its head." The 1st and 4th regiments of Skinner's brigade of New Jersey Loyalists "flanked the march." All wagons were left behind, and the advance was described as "rapid and compact."

The second column got in march as soon as the road was clear, which was "at 4 o'clock." It was commanded by Maj. Gen. Tryon and consisted of the "Jaegers, 37th, 38th, Leib, Bose, and 57th regiments." Riding with this column was Gen. Knyphausen, plus "a detachment of the 17th dragoon regiment," to act as dispatch riders for Knyphausen.

According to official returns made five days before the march, Matthew's column totaled "2313 men and Tryon's 2430 men." To these figures should be added the men of several artillery units, bringing the grand total of the Knyphausen force to nearly 5,000 men.

Staying behind at Elizabethtown Point to defend the pontoon bridge to Staten Island, as well as to man other defenses in case of a flanking counterattack, was a force under Maj. Gen. Robertson. It consisted of "The Piquets of the army, the 22nd and 43rd Regiments, the Regiments Anspach, Donop and Buenau and the company of the 17th Infantry Regiment." His strength was "2745 men," plus some of the artillery.

The Queen's Rangers, followed by the two regiments of Guards, marched through Elizabethtown without meeting any resistance. After crossing to the western side of the Elizabeth River, they expected to be confronted by the enemy who had held that side of the river much of the time over the past few days. To their surprise, there was no enemy in sight.

As the column marched up what is now Cherry Street, Lieutenant Colonel Cosmo Gordon took it upon himself to make a social call. He stayed with his regiment of Guards "till they were within a quarter of a mile of Livingston's house." At this point, Lt. Col. Gordon "proposed to [Lieutenant] Colonel [Chappele] Norton to canter on in front to see the Ladies at the Rebel Governor's house." "After five minutes conversation . . . they made their bow and rejoined the column that was then passing nearly opposite," up Morris Avenue. Upon rejoining his troops, Gordon was seen "with a flower in his hat" presumably from the Livingston gardens.

It is interesting to note that "Lieut. Colonels Gordon and Norton" had been at nearby Amboy, the second week in March, just 3 months past. They had been attending a meeting of commissioners for the exchange of prisoners together with a team of American commissioners that included Alexander Hamilton, who was a very dear friend of the Livingstons.

It was now "about four o'clock a.m. or a little after," and Maj. Gen. Matthew's column had been in march about an hour. Then, just as Col. Gordon was rejoining his unit, "the enemy vanguard was met near Governor Livingston's house."

The contact apparently was made in the "fields of the back part of the house of the rebel Governor Livingston" by one of Col. Skinner's two Loyalist regiments who were acting as flankers for the main column. The Americans who were encountered probably were the pickets of Col. Jaques's Essex County New Jersey militia who were retiring in front of the enemy advance, but had halted just long enough to give a shot.

As Maj. Gen. Matthew's column moved up the road toward Connecticut Farms, it was harassed by additional "small parties [which] fell back" after firing a shot or two from ambush.

The main body of the invasion force did not make a halt until it reached the outskirts of Connecticut Farms. Here the Americans had planned to make their first stand in regimental strength, at "a strong pass."

Col. Elias Dayton had deployed his New Jersey continental regiment and some militia on two elevations overlooking the road that dipped down into a deep gulley formed by the west branch of Elizabeth River. These were the same two hills so effectively defended just the week before.

It was Col. Skinner's Loyalist flankers who received the first shot as they descended into the hollow to cross the bridge. For a short distance, they advanced while exchanging fire with the troops posted on the two hills; but Skinner's men were soon forced to fall back on their main column.

Maj. Gen. Matthew, in command of the advance column, could not see the Americans on the two hills, but he knew from their fire that they were there. Brig. Gen. Maxwell's men were placed nicely under cover, on their "right by a thicket and on the left by an orchard."

There was considerable delay at this point until it was decided that the Queen's Rangers would attempt to force the pass. When prepared, "Lt. Col. [John Graves] Simcoe closed the companies of the Rangers, and directed them to rush down the hollow road in column without firing, and then by wheeling to the right, to ascend to the orchard and divide the enemy's parties."

The Rangers rush down the hill and over the bridge was so rapid that the Americans had time to fire but one or two rounds. "Capt. Stevenson who led with the riflemen and light infantry company [of the Rangers] obtained the ground on their flank . . .

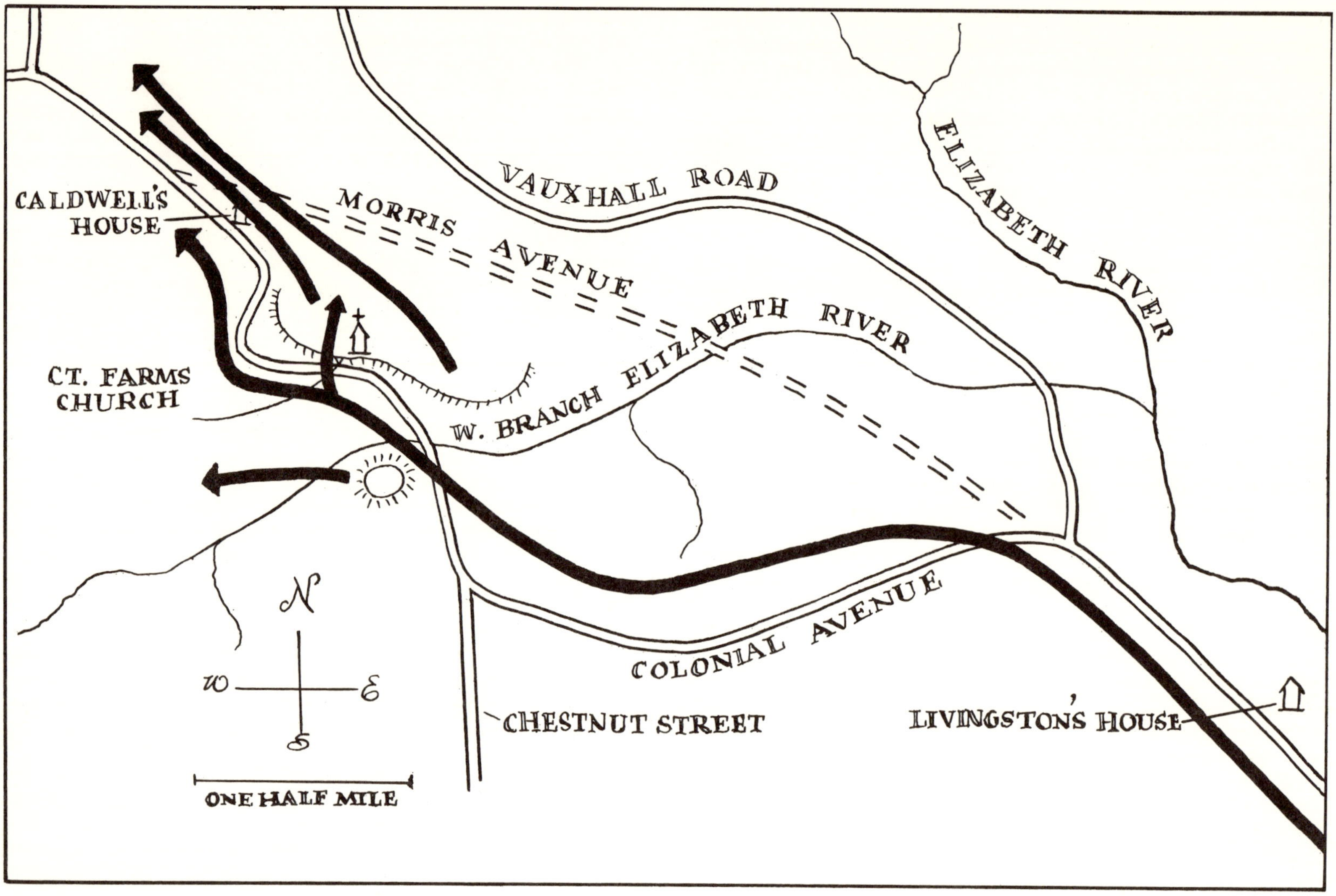

making several prisoners."

Seeing that they were about to be surrounded, the Americans in the orchard withdrew as the Rangers "pursued closely on the right, where the ridge continued, and which commanded the road, virtually, becoming a flanking party to the line of march" of the main Matthew column.

As soon as the Queen's Rangers saw that most of the enemy in the orchard had avoided the trap, they slowed pace to let their main force proceed down the hill and over the bridge. This gave Col. Dayton time to reorganize his regiment and to rejoin the other regiments of Brig. Gen. Maxwell's New Jersey brigade, standing by in reserve on the western outskirts of Connecticut Farms.

It had not been the American plan for Maxwell to make a stand between Connecticut Farms and Springfield. After holding as long as he could at the Connecticut Farms defile, his brigade was to withdraw slowly to a position behind the Rahway River, where he would be joined by the balance of the American force.

It was "six o'clock" in the morning when news of the advance of the enemy had reached the American camp in the Short Hills, and a general alarm was sounded. The alarm consisted of the firing of cannon after which "the drums throughout . . . camp beat to arms, announcing the approach of the enemy."

The men, as they responded to the drums, seemed to be looking forward to the fight. One officer of Stark's brigade noted that "animation and composure seem to prevade every countenance . . . every arm is nerved for defense."

For several days they had been expecting the call; now it was here. Nathan Beers of Webb's Connecticut regiments said that as soon as the alarm was sounded, "Jackson's and our battalion marched immediately for Springfield." They were followed by the other regiments of Stark's brigade and the militia.

Maj. Gen. Nathanael Greene and his aides rode with Brig. Gen. John Stark, at the head of Stark's column. Upon arrival at Springfield, Gens. Greene and Stark were met by Gen. Maxwell, and the deployment of the entire force was rapidly put in motion. Some troops were already in designated position at the Rahway River when the three generals met.

The Rahway River was an excellent natural barrier behind which a strong defense could be erected, although it was fordable in many places. The "entire front was covered by the river and several swamps." Only two roads crossed the Rahway along the front. One was Vauxhall Road and the other Springfield Road, now, roughly, Morris Avenue.

"Major Lee with his dragoons and the pickets, commanded by Capt. Walker [probably George Walker of Capt. Nixon's Middlesex light horse] was posted at the Little's [Littell's?] Bridge on the Vauxhall road." This bridge spanned the East Branch of the Rahway.

Maj. Lee was already in position, and according to plan, after the Jersey brigade's retirement from Connecticut Farms, "Col. Ogden was detached to support him." Also supporting Maj. Lee were "Capt. [now Major] Gibbs and Col. van Cortland." They had been active on the enemy's right flank since the 8th of the month.

On the Springfield Road, "Col. [Israel] Angell with his [Rhode Island] regiment, and several small detachments, and one piece of artillery, was posted to secure the bridge in front of the town" of Springfield. Supporting Col. Angell's right flank were the militia regiments of "Col. [Frederick] Frelinghausen [Frelinghuysen] and Col. [John] Webster." Maj. Gen. Dickinson, commanding all New Jersey militia, was with this body of troops.

Behind Col. Angell, on the Springfield Road, "Col. [Israel] Shreve's regiment was drawn up at the second bridge to cover the retreat of those posted at the first" should that be necessary. Spencer's regiment, under Lt. Col. Smith, was also stationed here, with Col. Shreve in overall command at the bridge. This was the bridge crossing over Van Winckle's Creek near what is now Flemer and Morris Avenues, Springfield.

The second "line formed half a mile west of Springfield Meeting house," which would be at the present junction of Short Hills and Morris Avenues. This line consisted of, "1 Jersey [Dayton's], Jackson's and our [Webb's] Battalion with 2 Pieces of artillery under Capt. Johnston."

"The remainder of General Maxwell's and Stark's brigades were drawn up on the high ground at the mill," meaning the heights above Springfield near the junction of Hobart Avenue and Old Short Hills Road. This "remainder" consisted of the New Jersey militia regiments of "Cols. Starke, Seeley, van Dyke, Nielson, and Taylor."

It could have been during Col. Dayton's withdrawal to his new position "half a mile west of Springfield Meeting house," that Dayton's regiment was met by Rev. James Caldwell. The regiment had held off the enemy for two hours at Connecticut Farms, and their ammunition was surely almost, if not completely gone. It was under these circumstances, in the undocumented words of historian Washington Irving, in his *Life of George Washington,* published in 1855, that Rev. Caldwell, "Finding the men in want of wadding, he galloped to the Presbyterian church and brought thence a quantity of Watts psalm and hymn books, which he distributed for the purpose among the soldiers. Now, cried he, 'put Watts into them boys.' "

By "8 o'clock" a.m., Greene's entire force was in position, which was approximately the same hour that Knyphausen arrived with the second column of his army at the junction of the Springfield Road and what is now Burnet Avenue. Here, Knyphausen found his first column under Matthew, already drawn up and waiting. Greene's and Knyphausen's forces were now approximately the same strength.

Rahway Bridges Stormed

Upon Knyphausen's arrival at the front, "The following disposition was made: General Matthew with his division was to try to cross the Rahway about one mile and a half upstream of the Springfield bridge." This was familiar territory to Matthew and several of his subordinate officers. Matthew had commanded all British forces north of the Raritan River during the British occupation of New Jersey in late 1776 and early 1777.

Brig. Gen. Cortland Skinner, commander of the Loyalist troops under Matthew, was in home country, having resided in Perth Amboy before escaping to Staten Island as a refugee. Most of Skinner's subordinate officers were natives of New Jersey including Lieutenant Colonel Joseph Barton who was "well acquainted with the road" upon which Matthew's column was marching.

When Matthew's column was ready, it advanced over roughly Burnet Avenue and Vauxhall Road for about a mile when, "between the hours of nine and ten in the morning, the column of Maj. Gen. Matthew received orders to halt in the road . . . in which Lt. Col. Barton's corps were engaged with the Rebels." More specifically, the place was at "Vauxhall" near what is now Hilton Avenue and Vauxhall Road.

When the Matthew column stopped in the road, Barton's Loyalists went into an orchard to root-out the harassing New Jersey militia. The fire was coming from the Essex militia regiment of Col. Jaques, the first troops to encounter Matthew's force as it left Elizabethtown. Here, at Vauxhall, Jaques had found a convenient place to do more damage.

As Barton's men approached the buildings of the owner of the orchard, Jaques's men gave them some very accurate fire. One American soldier said that to avoid being shot down, one of Barton's men, after firing one shot, took refuge "inside a back house loading his gun, and an American officer followed him in and ran his espadone [broadsword] through the soldier.

Jaques had been instructed not to engage the enemy. He was to find suitable cover—fire a few rounds—then retreat. Jaques had not placed his whole regiment in this orchard. He had them spread all along the road in "small parties . . . scattered up and down in the fields and woods, which shelved at a considerable distance from the Newark hills."

At length, Matthew worked his column forward to a position overlooking the bridge, which crossed the East Branch of the Rahway. Upon arrival there, it had been Matthew's plan to set up cannon to cover an attack on the bridge. When in position, Matthew would give Knyphausen the "signal by firing a cannon." It would be Matthew's first cannon shot, and it would be the sign for simultaneous attacks on the upper and lower bridges over the Rahway.

After considerable reconnoitering, Matthew placed 2-six pounders on a rise of land overlooking the bridge crossing. Then, at "11 o'clock" Matthew fired his first shot to signal that he had begun his attack on the upper bridge.

There were several additional shots from Matthew's cannon to make the Americans disperse. Then, as they had done at the Connecticut Farms bridge earlier in the day, "Lt. Col. Simcoe advanced towards the bridge in column." After rushing across the bridge, they began "forming the line, and extending it to the left," along what is now Millburn Avenue.

American after-reports said that "the bridge was disputed with great obstinacy, and the enemy must have received very considerable injury," as it poured across the bridge. Maj. Lee, in his well protected position on the ridge, which overlooked the bridge and road, had a big advantage. At length, however, Lee was driven from his position, by the British "fording the river [upstream] and gaining the point of the hill" from which Lee was delivering his damaging fire.

Maj. Lee could not have hoped to, nor did he have instructions to defend the bridge. He had with him only his small cavalry unit, and currently only "fifty infantry." His instructions were to do as much damage as possible, then withdraw.

It had taken Matthew about two hours to move his column approximately a mile and a half. Knyphausen had been waiting all this time under cover of a hill overlooking the approaches to the Springfield Road bridge crossing. During this wait, Gen. Knyphausen's flankers had been sent out, but were driven back by the New Jersey militia under Maj. Gen. Dickinson.

After Matthew had fired his first signal cannon at 11 o'clock, Knyphausen began his assault on the Springfield Road bridge over the Rahway River. His first order was to put into action the "six cannon" he had installed on the hill overlooking the east bank of the River at what is now about Alvin Place.

As soon as Knyphausen's guns began firing, the Americans replied with their one cannon attached to Col. Angell's regiment. The one cannon, and Angell's regiment, "were posted on the heights so that his approximate center defended the bridge, which leads to the town" of Springfield. This must have been at about what is now Warner Avenue, Springfield, the same position occupied by American cannon on the 7th.

After a softening-up process of several cannon shots, the Knyphausen force moved out from behind its hill position and proceeded "on the Springfield road with a very heavy column" of about 2,000 men.

Col. Angell had only "160 rank and file" with him on his hill, plus the detachment of artillery commanded by "Captain-Lieutenant [Thomas] Thompson" of Colonel John Lamb's regiment of artillery. As in the defense of the upper bridge by Maj. Lee, there was no intention that Col. Angell should make a stand at the bridge. His instructions were to do as much damage as possible from his advantageous position, then get out.

As the Knyphausen column advanced, it was almost a repeat

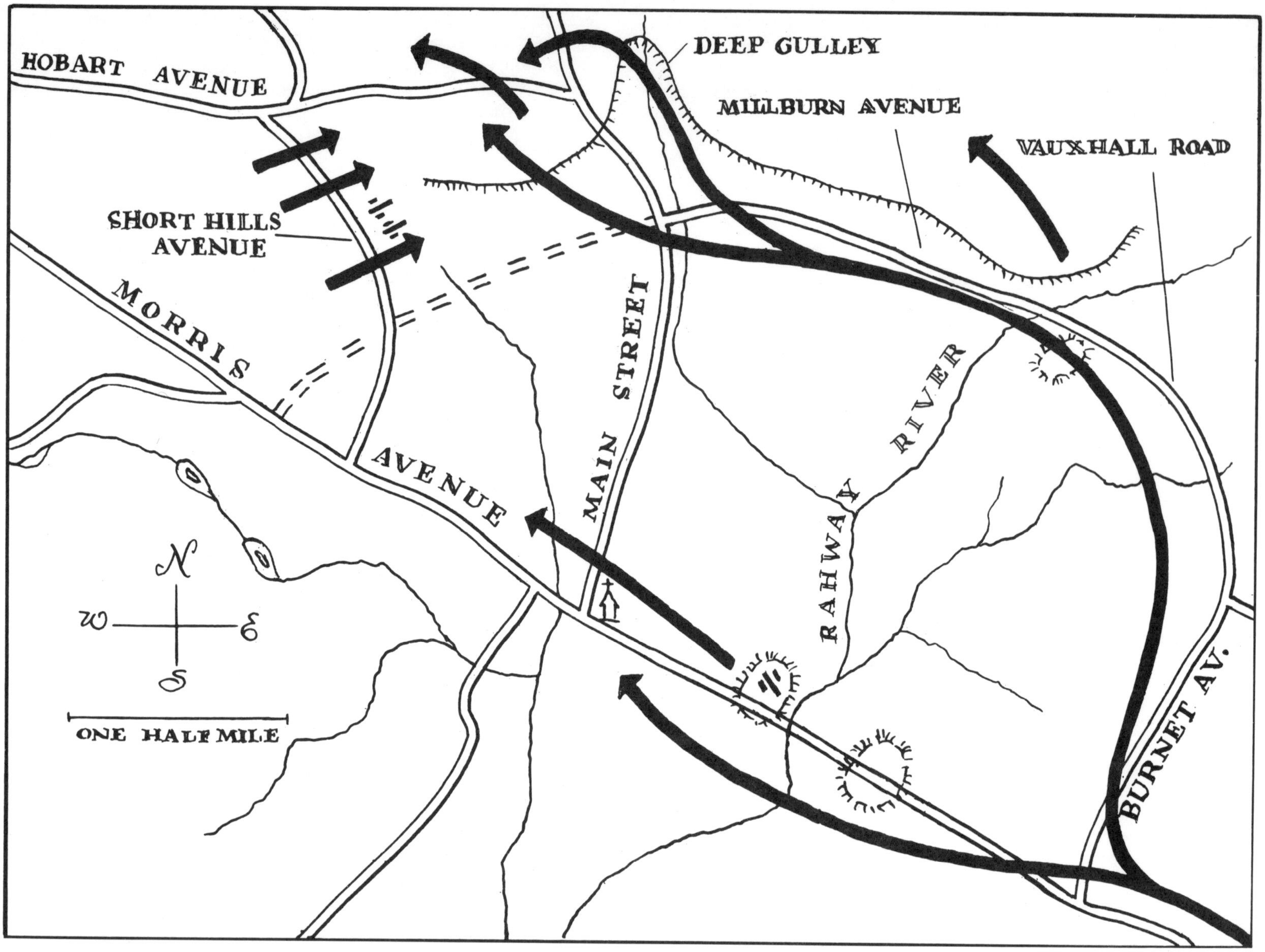

performance of the action on the 7th when the British and Hessians came down that road "that was straight and open for three-fourths of a mile, and we [the Americans] had fair play at them the whole way until they came to the bridge." Thompson's cannon was very effective against the advancing "solid column." It pointed right down the road and the piece merely had to be lowered or elevated to hit any part of the column.

Seeing the damage that the cannon was doing to the column, Gen. Knyphausen, as he approached the bridge, deployed his force as follows: "The Jaeger corps was in front on the right and left of the bridge, Leib regiment supported the right wing and the 37th the left one. The 57th covered the cannon" which had been limbered so they could advance with the troops.

When the force got near the bridge, they fell under the rifle fire of Angell's men but "the 37th rushed the bridge and crossed it." "The planks of the bridge had been removed, but the beams which supported them remained [allowing the enemy to cross] on the naked beams."

The Jaegers did not wait to cross the Bridge. Most of them began "wading through the water up to their bellys . . . exposed to a heavy fire." As the Jaegers were getting to the opposite bank and were forming, Captain Stephen Olney "asked [Lieutenant] Colonel Jeremiah Olney [of Angell's regiment] to let me take my platoon and engage them." Getting permission, Capt. Olney "marched a few rods into an orchard of large trees, and thought it prudent to place several men behind each tree believing they would fire more accurately and be less exposed."

Olney's men were having great success as Olney kept "moving about from one to the other . . . directing them to take good aim." As Olney dodged from tree to tree and man to man, he said the Jaegers came on steadily and firing, some of the balls coming so close that their wind would "shake the hair of my head."

Each one of Olney's men got in "five or six" shots from their tree positions before Hessians got within "twenty yards" of them. About that time, Olney saw the "right of the [Angell's] regiment on the retreat" being pursued by the troops that had crossed the bridge; so he decided to get out.

Olney did not retreat far, but took a position slightly to the rear, where there was "a small hill covered with wood." Here Olney continued his sniping at the advancing Jaegers. Then, Olney was hit by a Jaeger rifle ball. His wound was in the left arm, and he bound it with his handkerchief.

What had happened down at the bridge was, that following the 37th regiment, the "57th [had] advanced over the bridge," including the cannon, after planks were relaid. They did not try to storm Angell's hill position, but moved around the hill as if to outflank Angell. Seeing this situation, Angell gathered up his casualties, which numbered "6 killed and 32 wounded," and they withdrew down the back of the hill to safety.

In addition to Colonel Angell's regimental losses, "Captain Lieutenant Thompson of artillery . . . received a most formidable wound, a cannon-ball having passed through both his thighs near the knee joint . . . He expired in a few hours." How many men in Thompson's detachment, beside himself, were killed or wounded, is not known.

Angell's small detachment of 160 rank and file plus Thompson's artillery detachment had done their job well. They had held off an army of 2,000 for nearly "forty minutes."

Springfield Village Taken

In calling for a retreat of his regiment, Col. Angell had been aware that there was fighting off to his left toward the Vauxhall Road, but he could not see the action. Neither could Capt. Olney see it, until Olney had retreated some distance back from where he was injured.

Olney noted that "we had not passed the road [now Main Street, Springfield] more than five or six rods when I discovered a fresh column of the enemy advancing to attack us in the rear." That is, he could see the column of Maj. Gen. Matthew marching over what is now Millburn Avenue, east of Main Street, Springfield.

They marched in "three ranks . . . at 18 Inches intervals." The column consisted of the following: In the lead, was the 1st battalion of Guards marching in divisions "followed close in divisions by the second" battalion. More exactly, they were marching "in divisions by companies following each other in succession." There were "six battalion companies" forming three divisions in each battalion. Thus, it became a much-extended column.

To add to the invader's difficulties, it is probable that in this hilly country the flanking companies of Skinner's battalion were forced to stay in the road and to march single file on each side of the main column.

The column made an ideal target for the troops under Col. van Cortland and Maj. Gibbs who were lying in well protected hill positions strung out along the road. Col. van Cortland could see the British column coming down the road, and it was his plan to let the head of the column march by, and then to strike at the middle and the end of the column. When they had marched a sufficient distance, Col. Cortland gave the command to fire, and there was much confusion. It "was towards the rear, the heaviest fire was."

At the head of the column, and in temporary command of the 1st battalion of British Guards, was Lt. Col. Cosmo Gordon. Their regular commander, Lieutenant Colonel John Howard, had just turned over command to Gordon so that Howard could "go to Colonel Simcoe," commander of the Queen's Rangers, next behind the two battalion of Guards. Col. Howard expected to find Maj. Gen. Matthew there, and from him, he would be able to get further orders. It was about "12 o'clock noon" when Col. Howard left for the rear, and it was shortly thereafter that Col. van Cortland began his action. Lt. Col. Gordon did not stop the march of his battalion when the shooting started, but he continued his advance, in order "to gain the heights" of Springfield.

As Gordon proceeded along Millburn Avenue, he came to the second bridge. Soon the Americans saw the British force deploy to the left and right of the bridge, whereupon the Americans decided to withdraw to the heights of Springfield, a more defensible position. There was some contact in "the orchards" below the heights, before the Americans withdrew.

The force that was defending the second bridge was the New Jersey continental regiment of Col. Ogden. He had been dispatched to support Maj. Lee at the first bridge over the east branch of the Rahway, but after its fall, he had retired behind the second bridge.

What is now Millburn Avenue did not then continue west beyond Main Street. Just beyond the second bridge the road turned up what is now Old Short Hill Road, where it forked at Hobart Avenue, with Hobart being the left fork. It was near the fork in the road, on the heights of Springfield that the Americans took their new position. They did not line-up in battle order, but were "drawn up in small bodies by echelon, so as to concentrate their fire upon the road."

By this time, Lt. Col. Simcoe's Queen's Rangers had by-passed the 2nd Guards, the 2nd Guards having halted to back up Skinner's flanking companies who were sent into the hills to rout-out van Cortland's scattered parties.

Lt. Cols. Simcoe and Gordon soon went into a roadside conference, and it was decided to send a "sergeant's party" up the gulley of a brook lying just east of what is now Brookside Avenue. The banks of the stream formed a very pronounced ravine from the bottom of which a party could not be seen by the Americans. A thicket covered the comparatively level ground above the gulley and to the east of the stream.

As the sergeant's party proceeded up the gulley, they were covered "by the riflemen whom Lt. Shaw had well disposed" in the thicket overlooking the gulley. This prevented the Americans from advancing close enough to the gulley to fire down upon the sergeant's party.

As the men moved up the gulley, Lt. Shaw advanced cautiously in the same direction until he reached a point near the present Glen Avenue, where he joined with the gulley force, and together they moved up the back of Springfield heights. Lt. Shaw was slightly wounded in the action. The Americans on the heights "immediately fell back," upon the discovery that they had been outflanked.

When it could be seen that the gulley detachment controlled the heights, the rest of the British force, having waited down by the bridge, proceeded toward the heights "the flanking companies excepted." Most of the flanking companies were still engaged with Col. van Cortland's force, some distance back.

As the British approached the heights, "the Queen's Rangers . . . [were] closely following the Guards." When the 1st battalion of Guards reached the heights, Lt. Col. Gordon "formed them facing outwards towards the enemy, and ordered them to halt, recommending to his men to be on their arms under the shade of the bushes; it being about noon [probably near 1 p.m.] and excessively hot."

Under these circumstances, with the enemy out of sight, Gordon went to reconnoiter. As he moved along Hobart Avenue a short way, he came to a clearing where he could see some distance ahead. There, with a spy glass, he saw "three columns of the enemy with four pieces of cannon." They were "at a house which might be about 300 yards distance." Lt. Col. Stewart of the Guards also took a look with the glass, but he came to the conclusion there were but "three pieces of cannon" down there.

Actually, there were only two pieces of cannon with the American force, which consisted of "1 Jersey [Dayton's] Jackson's and our [Webb's] Battalion with two Pieces of artillery under the command of Capt. Johnston."

Soon the Americans began firing at the Guards "with one or two pieces of cannon." One "cannon ball struck the fence directly by his [Gordon's] side." Gordon then returned to his battalion and ordered "the left of the battalion to fall back, so as to form an oblique front to the enemy."

Even while Gordon was deploying his men "another ball from the enemy . . . killed two Queen's Rangers," nearby. At this point, the British decided they could advance no farther until the Royal Artillery's two cannon could be brought up to offset the American pieces. Thus, they arranged themselves in a semi-defensive position, temporarily.

As the British Guards and Queen's Rangers lay on top of the heights of Springfield, one of the officers of the Guards noted that "the village of Springfield was on his left." He had heard the action down in the village for the past hour.

Down there Col. Angell, under heavy pressure, had been forced "to retire over the second bridge," which spanned Van Winckle's Creek near Main Street in Springfield village. Lt. Col. Smith, with Spencer's New Jersey continental regiment, had been posted here along with Col. Shreve's New Jersey continentals, to cover Col. Angell's retreat. Smith's main body of men was "in an orchard about the center of town." He also had "thrown a small party into a stone house upon his left flank."

In Smith's secure positions behind the bridge, covered by an orchard, with a stone house acting as a virtual fort near the bridge, "the enemy was warmly received." Smith's defense of the bridge was so effective that the enemy "lost a considerable number of men" here.

Eventually the enemy was able to ford Van Winckle's Creek in various places, and Smith and Shreve decided that they must retire to a position "about a quarter of a mile . . . where the troops rallied." When the stone house was reached by the enemy, "they burnt the house from whence the rebels fired."

The delays encountered by Matthew's Vauxhall Road division had prevented Matthew from successfully executing a flanking movement to capture a large part of the American force before it could reach safe ground back of Hobart Gap. When Knyphausen realized this, he ordered Matthew's division to join his division at Springfield.

As the British Guards came down from the heights of Springfield over Main Street, they noted that they were "passing the burned church at Springfield." This would indicate that the Springfield Church was set afire by one o'clock in the afternoon, or before.

As to the burning of the Springfield church, it was filled with American military supplies, held there under the supervision of Rev. Caldwell. Thus, to the British, it was considered a military objective. A booklet published by the First Presbyterian Church of Springfield, in 1899, titled *Then and Now,* confirms this. The booklet states that "as early as 1778, it was so taken up with public stores, that the congregation abandoned it for the time being, and fitted up a garret of the old parsonage as a temporary place of worship."

In Springfield, it was Knyphausen's intention "to halt for two or three hours to refresh the troops" before taking up the action again. To make this rest period secure, "the Jaegers were posted in front on meadow land" to the "left" of the road. The Guards took a post "beyond the town of Springfield on the right." The Queen's Rangers, also in an advanced position, "lay in an orchard full of deep hollows," occupying the road and positions immediately adjacent to it. Knyphausen placed "a battalion of Gen. Skinner's [on] his right flank."

Soon after Gen. Knyphausen had arranged his troops, American Maj. Gen. Greene took a "post upon the first range of hills [near Hobart Gap] in the rear of Bryant's [Jacob Briant's] tavern where the roads are brought so near to a point, [present Morris and Hobart Avenues], that succour might readily be given from one [road] to the other." By being at the point of roads, Greene said "This enabled me to detach Col. [Samuel] Webb's regiment commanded by Lieut. Col. [Ebenezer] Huntington, and Col. [Henry] Jackson's regiment with one piece of artillery, which entirely checked the advance of the enemy on our left and secured the pass," via the present Short Hills and Highland Avenues.

To the south of the present Morris Avenue, Greene dispatched "his militia and light troops in great numbers . . . as close to the front as intervening thickets could shelter them." It was from this American force, placed south of the road, that the most harassment came to the British.

Lt. Col. Simcoe noted that "On their right [the Americans' right] ran a rivulet, forming small and swampy islets, covered with thickets" along what is now approximately Bryant Avenue and Lyon Place, Springfield. From this favorable cover, the Americans were particularly annoying to the Queen's Rangers, and several of the Rangers were wounded.

At American headquarters, while this long range cannonading and picket exchange was going on, Maj. Gen. Greene decided to take time to write to Gen. Washington who was at Rockaway Bridge, enroute toward West Point. Greene outlined to Washington the events of the day, so far. He informed him that the enemy are "directing their force against this pass [Hobart Gap], which I am determined to dispute so far as I am capable."

West Point Thrust

Maj. Gen. Greene's report to Gen. Washington on the progress of the battle was reasonably encouraging, certainly not discouraging. As Greene was dispatching this letter, Washington was just receiving Greene's of the 20th, three days earlier. This letter informed Washington that through a spy, a Mr. P., intelligence had been received that "three thousand [troops from Charleston] are to embark from Kings ferry, if the wind and tide favor their designs [are to move up the Hudson]. The residue of the Army [the force of Gen. Knyphausen] are to march towards Kings Ferry by Newark and Slauter dam a little above Aquakanunck," now Passaic.

To meet this possible threat, Washington moved part of his army back from Rockaway Bridge to Whippany, which was a distance of "five or six miles." Before departing Rockaway Bridge, Washington ordered that another part of his force, "the 1st and 2nd Pennsylvania and Hand's Brigades march by the Left [up the west side of the Pompton River] tomorrow morning 5 o'Clock for Pumpton Plains," in the direction of West Point.

The spy, Mr. P., had given quite accurate information on Gen. Clinton's intended Hudson River thrust, but matters were not going altogether on schedule for Clinton. On the 22nd, "all the troops on Staten Island except the 42nd Regiment and the Queen's Rangers," had gone aboard boats, prepared to move up the Hudson or North River the next morning. Clinton's force was then "cantoned near Richmond."

But when Gen. Clinton asked Adm. Arbuthnot for naval support for his incursion up the Hudson, Arbuthnot demurred. Arbuthnot reminded Clinton of the intelligence received from the American, Benedict Arnold, regarding the impending arrival of the French fleet.

Although Arnold's information was to the effect that the destination of the French fleet was Rhode Island, Arbuthnot wanted to make sure he would not get bottled up in the Hudson. Consequently, soon after receiving this information, Arbuthnot had set about making plans "to put his fleet under sailing orders," which would take them out into the open sea.

On the 23rd, as scheduled, and without Arbuthnot's protection, the troops that had come from Charleston sailed from Staten Island aboard transports. The transports moved up the Hudson as far north as Phillipsburg, now North Tarrytown, New York, where they anchored. The troops did not debark here, but remained aboard ship.

Considering Adm. Arbuthnot's reluctance to run the risk of being bottled up in the Hudson with his fighting ships, Gen. Clinton advanced "in person to Haverstraw Bay" in order to reconnoiter the area. He wanted to determine whether the task could be done quickly, and if so, whether he might be able to convince Adm. Arbuthnot that the operation could be accomplished before the arrival of the French, thus, with Arbuthnot's help.

Under these circumstances of delay and uncertainty, Clinton had decided on the 23rd, before leaving Staten Island, that he would order the Knyphausen force, after proceeding some distance into the country in order to hold the Americans in position, to "return . . . to Elizabethtown" and to repass to Staten Island the next morning. The orders probably were not a direct command to return. They undoubtedly provided some alternative should Knyphausen meet with unusual success in his advance, which, at that early hour on the 23rd, Clinton had no way of knowing.

Clinton's messenger carrying the orders for Knyphausen to return to Elizabethtown and then to Staten Island reached Knyphausen near 2 p.m., the 23rd. There was a conference with ranking officers, all of whom were at that moment in Springfield.

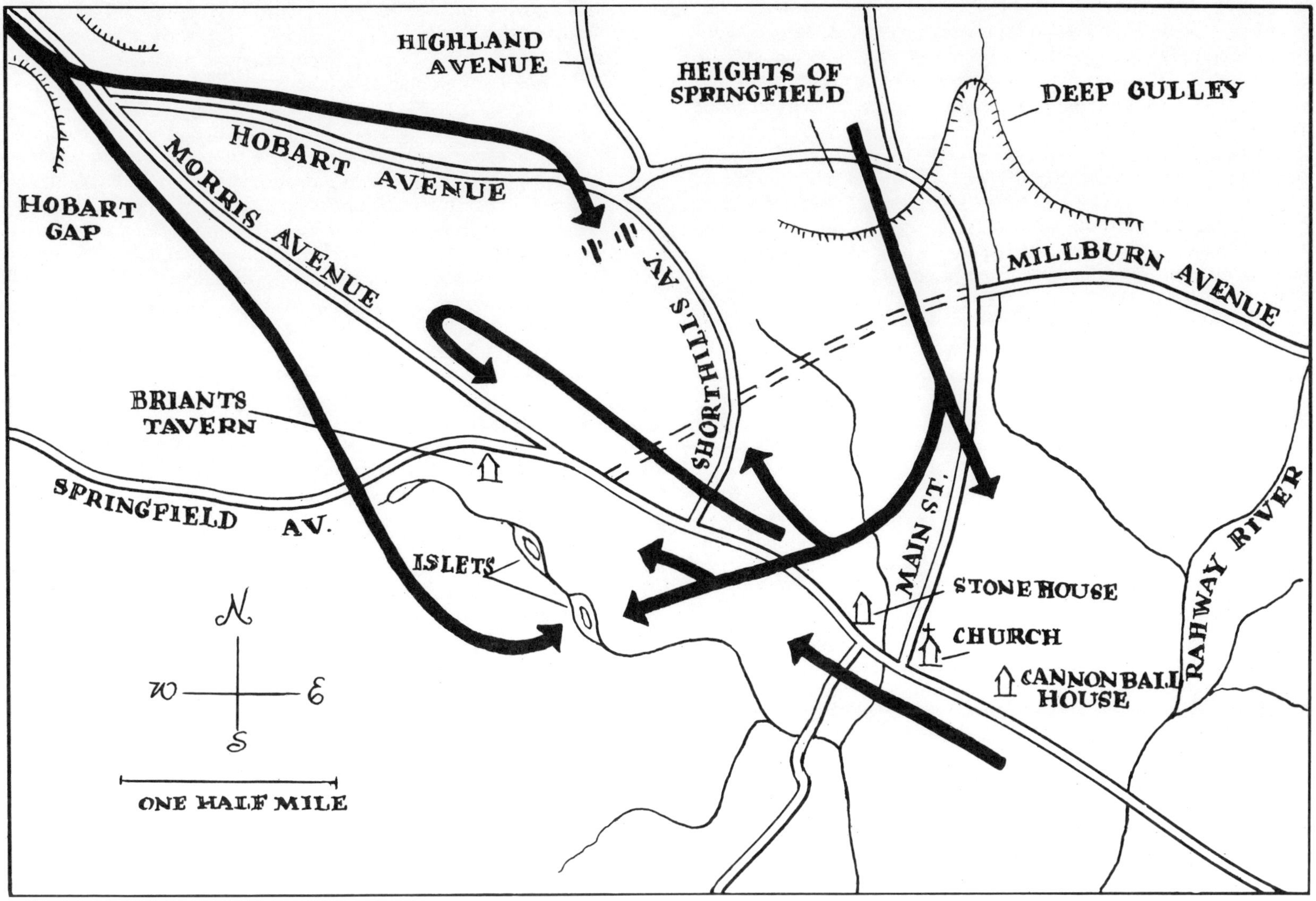

The decision coming out of the meeting was to withdraw.

During this period of delay, several houses in Springfield had been set on fire. In total, "nineteen dwelling houses" were burned. Only "two houses" in town were left standing. According to the British high command, all of the Springfield houses that were burned, except the stone house used as a fort, was the work of "some refugees."

It took about an hour for Knyphausen to put the command to withdraw into operation. Thus, it was "3 o'clock p.m. when they passed the Rahway in two columns and marched back to Elizabethtown." This would suggest that Matthew's division took the Millburn Avenue, Vauxhall Road route, and may have proceeded over Vauxhall's continuation, roughly Joanna Way. Knyphausen's division took the main road. "The right was closed by the Yagers, that on the left by the [Queen's] Rangers." That is, these two units covered the rear of each column.

Immediately upon learning of the enemy's retreat, American "Capt. Davis, with a detachment of 120 men, several small parties, with a large body of militia, fell upon their rear and flanks." Stark's brigade was also ordered "to pursue the retreating enemy but . . . could not overtake them." They did, however, discover "several fresh graves and found fifteen dead bodies." These were along Vauxhall Road.

The militia and continentals under Col. van Cortland and Col. Jaques had remained near their last positions on Vauxhall Road. Thus, when the enemy was seen coming back, they gave them the same treatment they had received on their way out. Private Esek Ryno in Col. Jaques's Essex militia regiment said that he alone "fired 48 rounds at the enemy at Springfield, [and] on the retreat of the enemy towards the Farms and towards Elizabethtown."

The pressure on the force retreating along the main Springfield road was also damaging. There was "constant firing." In some instances, the effect was so telling that the enemy was forced to retreat at "a full trot." Occasionally, the end of the retreating column was cut off and in one such maneuver, the militia "took fifteen prisoners."

The American pressure had been so effective that when the Knyphausen force reached a position about a mile and a half from Elizabethtown the Jaegers had to be replaced in their rear guard duty. They "were relieved by the 37th regiment."

The whole invasion force arrived back at the Elizabethtown camp at 7 o'clock p.m., whereupon the baggage began to cross the floating bridge to Staten Island, followed by the artillery, the cavalry, the infantry, the piquets of the army, and the Queen's Rangers. "The Regiment von Donop formed the rear guard and occupied the position which formed the bridgehead." All of the troops were over the bridge by midnight, and "between 12 and 1 o'clock the bridge was destroyed and the Regt. von Donop . . . was brought over [to Staten Island] in flatboats."

It was "moon-light" during the crossing, which was of great assistance to the Knyphausen force; but soon after their landing on Staten Island "a heavy thunder storm" came up. It was quite distressing, and made it impossible for the troops to get any rest.

Early in the morning, the 24th, the Knyphausen force "marched to Ryerson's Ferry," now St. George. Here they "embarked in available sloops and schooners and sailed up the North River to Philipsburg," where they found the Charleston force at anchor, waiting for word from Clinton as to his decision regarding the campaign against West Point.

Clinton had hoped to find that when he reached Haverstraw, that as a result of Knyphausen's advance, Washington would have pulled back far enough toward Morristown for him to land on the west bank and move inland to get between Washington's force and West Point.

When Clinton arrived at Haverstraw, he found that Washington "by marching his army wide of the [Hudson] river contrived to place every part of it beyond our reach." By this, Clinton meant that upon arrival he received intelligence that Brigadier General Jedediah Huntington who was leading the advance of General Washington's force, was so far advanced toward West Point and so far inland that Gen. Clinton could not execute his plan effectively. Huntington was at "Horns Yappo seven miles from Suffrans." Youpoh was two miles north of the present Oakland, New Jersey.

Finally, Clinton decided that, with the knowledge of the impending arrival of the French fleet, coupled with the fact that the Americans were staying so far inland in their march north, "I could not in prudence think of engaging in an operation which was likely to be drawn out to any length."

Between the 23rd and the 26th, while Gen. Clinton remained at Haverstraw, a few of his transports had come up-river and were laying off shore. Then, on the 27th, "about 8 o'clock this morning, 14 transports, with several smaller vessels, went down the river," and landed their troops at Philipsburg.

Thus, the Revolutionary War in the north, which had been waged furiously for four years, quietly came to an end.

The war would continue in the south for almost another two years, ending in American victory at Yorktown. The story, however, might have been different. On June 23, had Clinton's 3,807 men marched through Mordecai's Gap and Knyphausen's 5,000 men marched through Hobart Gap according to Clinton's plan, they might well have overpowered Washington's 3,760 continentals, plus militia. Fate, however, intervened, and Clinton's plan was scotched for Benedict Arnold's plan to turn over West Point to the British. This operation failed mainly because Arnold's intelligence of the coming of the French frightened British Admiral Arbuthnot into putting out to sea. In a manner, then, it might be argued that Benedict Arnold, in his treason, became the unwitting savior of the young United States of America.

BIBLIOGRAPHY

Short
Title

Am. Curiosities—*American Historical and Literary Curiosities . . .* John Jay Smith, ed., Philadelphia, 1861.

AmM—Peter J. Guthorn, *American Maps and Map Makers of the Revolution,* Monmouth Beach, 1966.

Angell—Edward Field, ed., *Diary of Colonel Israel Angell . . . 1778-1781,* 1899.

Assembly Votes—*New Jersey Legislature, General Assembly, Minutes of Votes and Proceedings, Aug. 27, 1776—June 7, 1777,* Trenton.

Baur—Bernhard A. Uhlendorf ed. and trans., *Revolution in America . . . Adjutant General Major Baurmeister of the Hessian Forces,* New Brunswick, 1957.

Beers—Deacon Nathan Beers Journal, Library of Congress, Manuscript Division, Washington.

Blaine ltr. bk.—Ephraim Blaine letter book 1780-83. Photo copy in Morristown National Historical Park Library.

Bogart—*The John Bogart Letters . . . 1776-1782,* Rutgers College Publication, Second Series, New Brunswick, 1914.

Br.—Samuel S. Smith, *The Battle of Brandywine,* Monmouth Beach, 1976.

BrM—Peter J. Guthorn, *British Maps of the American Revolution,* Monmouth Beach, 1972.

Burnett—Edmund C. Burnett, ed., *Letters of Members of the Continental Congress,* Washington, 1963 edition.

Caldwell—A. L. [Dr. Arthur L.] Johnson, compiler, *Certain Facts Relating to the Tragic Death of Hannah Caldwell,* Elizabeth, 1934. Based on September 4, 1780 statement of James Caldwell, printed 1780 in pamphlet form.

Chastellux—Howard C. Rice Jr. ed., *Travels in North America . . . by Marquis De Chastellux,* Williamsburg, 1963.

Clinton—William B. Willcox, ed., *The American Rebellion, Sir Henry Clinton's Narrative. . . .* New Haven, 1954.

CO—Colonial Office Records, Public Record Office, London.

Condit—Genealogical Notices of Various New Jersey Families Collected by Lewis Condit from Applications for Pension and other sources. Pension application testimony taken before Judge Condit in New Jersey during the years 1833 and 1834. New Jersey Historical Society, Manuscripts Collection, Newark. Published in PNJHS/NS/V, VI, VII, VIII, IX, X.

Conn. Men—Henry P. Johnston, ed., *Records of Connecticut Men in the . . . War of the Revolution 1775-1783,* Hartford, 1889.

CP—Clinton Papers, William L. Clements Library, Ann Arbor.

Felcone—Joseph J. Felcone, *Abstracts of New Jersey Manuscripts in the Sol Feinstone Collection of the American Revolution,* David Library of the Revolution, Washington Crossing, Pa., 1976.

Fisher Jnl.—W. B. Lapham, ed., *Elijah Fisher's Journal,* Augusta, 1880.

Force—Peter Force Miscellany, Library of Congress, Manuscript Division, Washington.

Gouvion—Account of Events in New Jersey June 7-25, 1780, with map, Lieutenant Colonel Jean-Baptiste De Gouvion, transcribed by F. Ch. Rice, Feb. 1967, translated by Eveline Merlin, 1971. Original in Archives de la Guerre, Vincennes, France.

Green—Joseph H. Jones, *The Life of Ashbel Green V.D.M.,* New York, 1849.

Greene Corres.—Correspondence of General Nathanael Greene, American Philosophical Society Library, Philadelphia.

Hatfield—Abraham Hatfield, *The Descendants of Matthias Hatfield,* New York, 1954.

Hawkins O. B.—Sergeant Major John H. Hawkins Orderly Books #1 & #2 for Moses Hazen's regiment, Hand's brigade. Pennsylvania Historical Society, Manuscript Division, Philadelphia.

Headquarters O.B.—Headquarters [Morristown] Orderly Book 1779-80, New York Historical Society, Manuscript Division, New York.

Hist. Mag.—*The Historical Magazine,* New York and London.

Hopper deposition—Deposition of Mary Hopper, widow of Captain John A. Hopper, to the House of Representatives, 1838. Transcript in the possession of a descendant, Fred W. Bogert.

Hoskins—Barbara E. Hoskins et al, *Washington Valley an Information History . . .,* Ann Arbor, 1960.

HSD—Historical Society of Delaware, Manuscripts Collection, Wilmington.

Irvine Papers—William Irvine Papers, Historical Society of Pennsylvania, Manuscripts Collection, Philadelphia.

Jones—E. A. Jones, *The Loyalists of New Jersey . . .,* New Jersey Historical Society, Newark, 1927.

Jung.—Von Jungkenn Papers, William L. Clements Library, Ann Arbor.

Kalb—Friedrich Kapp, *Life of John Kalb,* New York, 1870.

KP—*The [Stephen] Kemble Papers,* New York Historical Society, New York, 1884-1885.

Krafft—*Journal of Lieutenant John Charles Philip von Krafft 1776-1784,* Collections of New York Historical Society, New York, 1882.

Lafayette—J. Bennett Nolan, *Lafayette in America Day by Day*, 1934.

Lauber—Almon W. Lauber, ed., *Orderly Books of the Fourth New York Regiment . . . with the Diaries of Samuel Tallmadge 1780-1782 and John Barr 1779-1782*, Albany, 1932.

Local cit.—Local citation.

LP—William Livingston Papers, New York Historical Society, Manuscripts Collection, New York.

Mackenzie—Mackenzie Papers, William L. Clements Library, Ann Arbor.

Martin—Joseph Plumb Martin, George F. Scheer, ed., *Private Yankee Doodle*, New York, 1962. First published as *A Narrative of Some of the Adventures, Dangers, and Sufferings of a Revolutionary Soldier*, Hollowell, Me., 1830.

MC&H—*Military Collector and Historian*, The Company of Military Historians.

McDougall—Alexander McDougall Papers, New York Historical Society, Manuscripts Collection, New York.

M. C. Records—Morris County Records, Morristown.

MNHP—Morristown National Historical Park, Manuscripts Collection, Morristown.

MPL—Morristown Public Library, Manuscripts Collection, Morristown.

M.T. Presby. Minutes—*Printed Minutes of the Trustees and Parish*, Morristown Presbyterian Church, Morristown.

Muench.—Friedrich von Muenchhausen, Ernst Kipping, trans., *At General Howe's Side*, Monmouth Beach, 1974.

Narrative—James Moody, *Lieutenant James Moody's Narrative* . . . New York, 1968 edition. First published in London 1783.

NJA—*New Jersey Archives*, Trenton.

NJH—*New Jersey History*, New Jersey Historical Society, Newark.

NJ Laws—William Paterson, *Laws of New Jersey*, New Brunswick, 1800 edition.

NJSA—New Jersey State Archives, State Library, Trenton.

NY Col. Doc.—E. B. O'Callaghan, ed., *Documents Relative to the Colonial History of the State of New York*, Albany.

NYHS—New York Historical Society, Manuscripts Collection, New York.

Ogden—Aaron Ogden, *Autobiography of Colonel Aaron Ogden*. Printed in *Proceedings of the New Jersey Historical Society*, Newark, 1892.

Olney—*Journal of Captain Stephen Olney*. Excerpts printed in *Biography of Revolutionary Heroes* by Mrs. [Catherine] Williams, Providence, 1839.

Pa. Mag.—*Pennsylvania Magazine of History and Biography*, Pennsylvania Historical Society, Philadelphia.

Pattison—*Official Letters of Major General James Pattison*, New York Historical Society, New York, 1875.

PCC—Papers of the Continental Congress 1774-1789, National Archives, Washington.

PNJHS—*Proceedings of the New Jersey Historical Society*, Newark.

Popp—Joseph G. Rosengarten, ed., *Stephan Popp Journal 1777-1783*. Published in *Pennsylvania Magazine of History and Biography*, April and July 1902. Original in Library Bayreuth, Germany.

Pr.—Samuel S. Smith, *The Battle of Princeton*, Monmouth Beach, 1967.

Princeton Maps—Princeton University Maps Collection, Princeton.

Princeton Mss.—Princeton University, Manuscripts Collection, Princeton.

Randolph—Benjamin Randolph Pocket Almanacs 1775, 1776, 1778, 1780, Pennsylvania Historical Society, Manuscripts Collection, Philadelphia.

Reed Papers—Joseph Reed Papers, New York Historical Society, Manuscripts Collection, New York.

RIHS—Rhode Island Historical Society, Manuscripts Collection, Providence.

Rivington—*Rivington's Royal Gazette*, New York.

Rodney Diary—*Letters to and from Caesar Rodney 1756-1784*, Philadelphia, 1933.

Rolls—Revolutionary War Rolls, Micro Copy 246, National Archives, Washington.

Scammell—Adjutant General Alexander Scammell, Orderly Book 1780, New Jersey Historical Society, Manuscripts Collection, Newark.

Seeley Jnl.—Sylvanus Seeley Journal, Morristown National Historical Park Library, Morristown.

Simcoe—Lieutenant Colonel J. G. Simcoe, *Simcoe's Military Journal*, New York, 1844.

Spy map—Plan of Gen. Washington's Winter Cantonment & Environs, M. P. G. 1015/325. In New York Gov. William Tryon's of 26 Feb. 1780, No. 89. Removed from CO5/1110, Public Record Office, London.

Staff Rept.—Hessian General Staff Report on events in New Jersey, June 6-23, 1780. Translated by Dr. Gerhard O. W. Mueller, and published in Millburn, New Jersey, *Item*, January 31, 1963. Original in Hessian State Archives, Marburg, Germany.

Sullivan Expd.—*Journals of the Military Expedition of Major General John Sullivan against the Six Nations of Indians in 1779* . . . Auburn, 1887.

Thacher—James Thacher M. D., *Military Journal of the American Revolution*, Hartford, 1862. Earlier editions published 1823, 1827, 1854.

Trial—*The Trial of Lieutenant Colonel Cosmo Gordon*, London, 1781. *The Trial of Colonel Cosmo Gordon*, London, 1783.

Trussell—John B. B. Trussell Jr., *The Pennsylvania Line Regimental Organization and Operations, 1776-1783*, Harrisburg, 1977.

Uhlendorf—Bernhard A. Uhlendorf, *The Siege of Charleston*, Ann Arbor, 1938.

Wayne Mss.—Wayne Manuscripts, Historical Society of Pennsylvania, Manuscripts Collection, Philadelphia.

WP—Washington Papers, Library of Congress, Manuscript Division, Washington.

WW—John C. Fitzpatrick, ed., *The Writings of Washington*, Washington.

REFERENCES

"There never was . . ."	McDougall 2.80 Reel III

Chapter I

MORRISTOWN ENCAMPMENT

"Those who have . . ."	Kalb 183

Winter Deployment

"From present appearances . . ."	WW 17:98
"the West Indies"	WW 17:108
"3,500 rank and . . ."	PCC M 247 Roll 167
"8,433 rank and . . ."	WP 12.18.79 ret.
"sixty or eighty . . ."	Chastellux 1:115
"two churches and . . ."	BrM 80/18
"alum and awls"	2 NJA 4:269
"give the highest . . ."	ibid
"the double purposes . . ."	WW 17:101
"preserve us from . . ."	WW 17:111
"I very well . . ."	WW 17:101

"The Virginia Division . . ."	WP Gre/- 11.16.79
"by water to . . ."	ibid
"to cover the . . ."	WW 17:301
"Congress having directed . . ."	WW 17:133
"November 23"	WW 17:175
"proceed with the . . ."	WW 17:301
"three regiments"	WW 18:14 note
"Danbury"	WP Sta/GW 11.28.79
"Kings ferry, Suffrans and . . ."	WW 17:186
"at Danbury"	WW 18:103
"orders generally from . . ."	WW 17:478
"an eye on . . ."	WW 17:209
"Paramus"	Felcone 2131
"Moylans, Sheldons and . . ."	WW 17:210
"Fifteen Massachusetts Regiments"	WW 18:13
"1st, 2d, 3d . . ."	WW 17:202
"Incamped near the . . ."	WW 17:210
"furnish garrisons for . . ."	ibid
"in the neighbourhood . . ."	WW 17:87
"Paulus Hook"	WW 17:307
"Scotch Plains"	Sullivan Expd. 114
"the country from . . ."	WW 17:256
"Burlington"	WW 17:189, 211
"Sandy Hook"	WW 17:422 note

Settling-in

"Reports worthy of . . ."	WW 17:206
"I have determined . . ."	WW 17:206, 207
"Sufferan's [and] Pompton"	WW 17:209
"Lieutenant Colonel [William] . . ."	WW 17:212
"125 men"	ibid
"the whole of . . ."	WW 17:239
"The logs and . . ."	WW 17:251
"arrives at the . . ."	WW 17:256
"the fleet has . . ."	WW 17:312
"the second division . . ."	WW 17:327
"88"	Uhlendorf opp. 108
"the [British and . . ."	Uhlendorf 21
"7,258 [regulars . . ."	Uhlendorf opp. 108
"6,613 British and . . ."	Mackenzie 6.15.80 ret.
"8,433 rank and . . ."	WP 12.18.79 ret.
"detach the Massachusetts . . ."	WW 17:329
"for leave of . . ."	WP Way/GW 1.7.80
"We had a . . ."	NYHS Irv/Ree 12.12.79
"owing to the . . ."	WW 17:92
"the deficiency of . . ."	WW 17:300
"Willetts & [Colonel . . ."	Greene Corres. Abe/Gre 11.23.79
"near Hanover"	Pa. Mag. 28:23
"The First Maryland . . ."	ibid
"The Division will . . ."	Conn. Men 134
"a severe storm"	Pa. Mag. 28:23
"Great part of . . ."	ibid
"in a day . . ."	WW 17:206
"Pumpton"	Angell 101
"on the 14th . . ."	Thacher 180
"17 to Eyre's . . ."	Sullivan Expd. 114
"Ayer's Forge"	NJH LXXXVI #3 (fall 1968) 135-157
"about three miles"	WW 17:216
"the ground you . . ."	Greene Corres. Abe/Gre 10.23.79
"laying out ground . . ."	ibid
"the Troops as . . ."	ibid
"The ground is . . ."	PCC Gre/StC et al 12.1.79
"All regimental officers . . ."	WW 17:214
"Generals St Clair, De Kalb . . ."	PCC Gre/StC et al 12.1.79
"Maxwell's and Hand's . . ."	WW 17:265
"on the frozen . . ."	Thacher 180
"baggage [including tents] . . ."	ibid
"except, if good . . ."	Conn. Men 135
"November 25 . . . The . . ."	Pa. Mag. 28:23
"experienced one of . . ."	Thacher 185
"the storm continues . . ."	Lauber 817
"the snow set . . ."	WW 17:372
"the sufferings of . . ."	Thacher 185
"22.1 degrees"	2 NJA 4:156
"A number of . . ."	MC&H XXX/3/116
"Kembles"	AmM 14/106A; WW 17: opp.256
"Wick's"	ibid
"Lazaliers"	ibid
"about a mile . . ."	Pa. Mag. 28:23; Spy map
"Roberts"	Hoskins; AmM 17/104D
"Jonathan Ogden"	Hoskins
"Jacob Arnold"	Spy map; Princeton Mss. Gre/Arn 12.16.79; Hoskins
"Dr. Jabez Campfield"	Local cit.
"extremely concerned to . . ."	WW 17:300
"We have at . . ."	WW 17:437
"There are in . . ."	WW 17:426
"expressed his wishes . . ."	WW 17:202
"some alarming Symptoms . . ."	WW 17:122
"to retire from . . ."	ibid
"health"	WW 17:490
"I have not . . ."	WP Sti/GW 3.19.80
"Philada."	WW 17:299
"Being entirely in . . ."	Kalb 183
"A hat costs . . ."	ibid

Chapter II

ENDLESS BURDENS

Soaring Inflation

"four for one"	WW 17:413
"upwards of 30"	ibid
"Our public Horses . . ."	Burnett 5:98
"to increase the . . ."	WW 17:231
"the indefatigable indeavours . . ."	ibid
"I have done . . ."	Blaine ltr.bk.1.29.80
"The purchasers here . . ."	WP Fli/GW 1.3.80
"Wheat pr bushel . . ."	NJSA Lew/Fur 1.27.80
"for the regulation . . ."	Burnett 5:4
"suspended the operation . . ."	2NJA 4:236
"Provisions and other . . ."	Kalb 184

London Trade

"They came by . . ."	WP Stc/GW 2.7.80
"It lays with . . ."	Burnett 5:98
"give protection to . . ."	WW 17:256
"Sandy Hook"	2NJA 4:134, 154
"cutting off the . . ."	WW 17:359
"that there are . . ."	WP Max/GW 5.24.80
"The detestable and . . ."	WW 17:301
"take the most . . ."	WW 17:392
"Besides the Guards . . ."	WP Kal/GW 3.11.80
"There are a . . ."	WP Bur/Hun 4.9.80

Starving Soldiers

"five or six . . ." WW 17:273
"no provisions for . . ." Beers
"Poor Fellows! They . . ." MNHP Gre/Fur 1.4.80
"We were absolutely . . ." Martin 172
"Gangs of Soldiers . . ." Lauber 231
"Have been at . . ." WW 17:358
"and I have . . ." WW 17:358
"January 2 violent . . ." Seely Jnl.
"impress till you . . ." WW 17:361
"certificates specifying the . . ." WW 17:365
"a prey to . . ." Headquarters O. B. 1.28.80
"Unless the speediest . . ." Burnett 5:62
"We are still . . ." Reed Papers 4.18.80

Lagging Enlistments

"1st of Sepr" WW 17:337
"January 969, February . . ." PCC Roll 46:39:51,52
"It is recommended . . ." Burnett 5:33
"two hundred" WW 17:128
"force at this . . ." WW 18:166
"twelve hundred whose . . ." ibid

Revengeful Refugees

"granting full Liberty . . ." WW 7:62
"Such as go . . ." WW 7:142
"An Act for . . ." NJ Laws 40
"Sussex County" Jones 143
"obtained from their . . ." Narrative 13
"took with him . . ." Narrative 14
"gave too good . . ." NY Col. Doc. VIII 794
"Every thing of . . ." WW 17:390

Chapter III

MORRISTOWN CAMP LIFE

In the Huts

"each Company be . . ." WW 18:349
"at which time . . ." Hawkins O.B. 1.28.80
"Genl Clinton's brigade . . ." Headquarters O.B. 1.29.80
"Every Monday Wednesday . . ." WW 18:350
"In the present . . ." WW 17:473
"The old and . . ." WW 17:473
"Main Guard at . . ." Headquarters O.B. 12.7.79
"every two days" ibid
"Capt, Sub. 3 . . ." ibid 12.22.79
"the Court House . . ." WW 24:92
"continental building" M.T. Presby Minutes II
"on the parsonage . . ." ibid
"A serjeant Corporal and . . ." WW 17:241
"at Suckesuma [was] . . ." ibid
"Whippany River" Spy map
"Veal Town" Headquarters O.B. 2.12.80
"Fatigue at Orderly . . ." ibid 12.27.79
"Sub., 2 Sergts . . ." ibid
"new orderly room" ibid 1.21.80
"To keep no . . ." WW 17:226
"Easton" WW 17:117
"General Hospital [was] . . ." 2 NJA 4:288,289
"at Morristown" ibid
"Princeton, Trenton [and] . . ." ibid
"A Trusty Sergt . . ." Headquarters O.B. 12.7.79
"guard house" ibid 2.1.80
"Police Captain" ibid
"men's huts at . . ." ibid 12.29.79
"aney Soldier are . . ." Lauber 231
"exemplary punishment" WW 10:276
"Strictly forbids aney . . ." Lauber 221
"a company of . . ." Thacher 187
"The culprit being . . ." ibid 186
"Deserting with his . . ." WW 17:343
"No provision is . . ." Hawkins O.B. 1.2.80
"to hut with . . ." WW 17:214
"One Field officer . . ." WW 17:113
"Dined with Colonel . . ." Thacher 195
"Dancing assemblies" Am. Curiosities Pl.22
"Elizabethtown" Pa. Mag. 64:193 et. seq.
"an equal quota . . ." Am. Curiosities Pl.22
"General Washington and . . ." Thacher 192
"All fatigue and . . ." WW 18:120
"ushered in with . . ." 2 NJA 4:322

At Headquarters

"Colonel Ford's regiment . . ." WP Wil/GW 12.8.76
"was seized with . . ." PNJHS (NS)X (1925)178
"Arnold's Tavern" Loc. cit.
"Buried Col. Ford . . ." Rodney Diary
"her way up" WW 8:11
"Mr. Randolph in . . ." ibid
"my house" Randolph
"Stephen Johnes and . . ." Princeton Mss. Randolph Gen.
"Frances Gualdo" MPL Mss. Ford Gen.
"Anna" M.C. Rec. Wills D:374
"Morris Town" WW 7:55
"Mr. Randolph" WW 8:46
"ensign" Headquarters O.B. 4.27.80
"resumes the duties . . ." ibid 4.10.80
"eleven enlisted men's . . ." AmM 13:105
"I have been . . ." WW 17:423,424
"I have been . . ." NJSA Lew/Fur 1.27.80
"Tim Ford . . . and . . ." Bogart 21
"a couple of . . ." ibid 26
"31st." Fisher Jnl 13
"Wm Livingston" BrM 104
"Deborah Olney" Pa. Mag. 65:362, et seq.
"in a closed . . ." RIHS Wm. Allen/Theo. Foster
"blue and buff" Hawkins O. B. 4.17.80
"blue and yellow" ibid
"Colo. Johnston, Cortland, Ogden . . ." Headquarters O.B. 4.17.80
"was crowded with . . ." Thacher 192
"met with his . . ." Headquarters O.B. 4.25.80
"seized the day . . ." WW 18:316
"at head-quarters" Thacher 192, WW 17:316
"a Reprimand from . . ." Headquarters O.B. 4.6.80
"On May 10" Lafayette 105
"Rhode Island" CP 6.12.80

Chapter IV

WINTER OPERATIONS

Staten Island

"750 men" WW 17:380
"Crane's Mills" WP Irv/GW 1.1.80
"convenient both to . . ." ibid
"about 200 men . . ." WP Inquiry 1.30.80
"different movements into . . ." CP Knyp. Jnl.

"Perhamus . . . Hackensac . . . Newark . . ."	ibid
"the night of . . ."	ibid
"the Sound appears . . ."	WP Irv/GW 1.8.80
"provided the state . . ."	WW 17:379
"the detachment of . . ."	WW 17:380
"Col. [Josias] Hall"	Irvine Papers II:116
"tremendeous snow-storm"	Thacher 185
"about five hundred . . ."	Thacher 188; Lauber 817
"pretence of going . . ."	Thacher 188
"Caps and mittings"	Headquarters O.B. 1.22.80
"at five o'clock"	Irvine Papers II:116
"at Halsteds point"	ibid
"at the Old . . ."	ibid
"share with the . . ."	WW 17:390
"found in Arms . . ."	ibid
"if any Officer . . ."	Irvine Papers II:116
"vast multitude who . . ."	WP Cal/GW 1.19.80
"1800 men"	2 NJA 4:467
"our Troops returned . . ."	Lauber 817
"The enemy having . . ."	WP Sti/GW 1.16.80
"observed them advancing . . ."	CO 5/100:3619 Sti/Kny
"the Revels began . . ."	ibid
"200 men . . . and . . ."	ibid
"took a Serjeant . . ."	ibid
"The house [Decker's] . . ."	WP Sti/GW1.16.80
"the inhabitents of . . ."	Seely Jnl.
"our Troops returned . . ."	Lauber 817
"striping women of . . ."	WP Cam/Cal 1.25.80

Elizabethtown-Newark

"While the troops . . ."	WP Sti/GW 1.16.80
"Many of them . . ."	ibid
"all persons possessed . . ."	2 NJA 4:157
"Retailer of Sedition . . ."	2 NJA 4:440
"as relief to . . ."	WW 17:380
"drawing a line . . ."	WP Inquiry 1.30.80
"at De Harts and . . ."	WP StC/GW 1.28.80
"11 men"	WP Inquiry 1.30.80
"Morris Hatfield was . . ."	WP Haz/GW 1.26.80
"he saw his . . ."	ibid
"John Hetfield and . . ."	Hatfield,76,79,84
"Cornelius Hatfield"	Hatfield 46
"managed the farm . . ."	ibid
"Cornelius Hetfield, Job . . ."	2 NJA 4:166
"120 men . . . with . . ."	2 NJA 4:151
"Trembley's Point"	2 NJA 4:166
"relief marches today"	WW 17:441
"990 [would] parade . . ."	Hawkins O. B. 1.24.80
"guides led me . . ."	CP Bus/C1 1.26.80
"it was impossible . . ."	ibid
"July 1779"	Hatfield 47
"burning a church . . ."	WP Cal/GW 1.30.80
"if Mr. Stirling . . ."	WW 17:476
"the Flank Companies . . ."	CO 5/100/3619 Lum/Kny
"passing the Hackinsack . . ."	ibid
"The Detachment after . . ."	ibid
"all of the officers . . ."	CP Bus/C1 1.26.80
"a few Very . . ."	ibid
"Mr. B. [elcher] Smith . . ."	2 NJA 4:149
"Staten Island plunder"	2 NJA 4:519
"About 12 of . . ."	CO 5/100:3619 Lum/Kny
"Robert Neil [and] . . ."	Mackenzie ret. 1.26.80
"an acting commissary"	2 NJA 4:181, 239-241
"one Walker a . . ."	2 NJA 4:188

Unstable Front

"the cause of . . ."	WW 17:455
"A small Party . . ."	WP StC/GW 1.31.80
"march by very . . ."	Simcoe 131
"The snow prevented . . ."	Simcoe 132
"Col. Star with . . ."	WP StC/GW 2.4.80
"The Body of . . ."	WP StC/GW 2.7.80
"Capt. [Israel] Carle . . ."	Force 6.19.80 ret.
"The enemy made . . ."	WP StC/GW 2.11.80
"Finding the snow . . ."	ibid
"the guards at . . ."	ibid
"A number of . . ."	ibid
"The Enemy made . . ."	WP StC/GW 2.20.80
"about twenty head . . ."	ibid
"uninterrupted and unvarying . . ."	Kalb 183
"The passage of . . ."	2 NJA 4:468
"eleven feet thick"	Baur.337
"horse passed on . . ."	WP StC/GW 1.22.80
"extremely apprehensive that . . ."	WP StC/GW 2.23.80

Paramus-Hoppertown

"February 29"	WW 18:60
"many disaffected people"	WW 17:301
"Major Christopher Stuart"	WP Stu/GW 3.25.80
"John A. Hopper . . ."	Hopper deposition
"300 men"	CP How/Mat 3.24.80
"300 men"	ibid
"as soon as . . ."	WP Stu/GW 3.25.80
"Sixty four Prisoners"	CP McP/Kny 3.24.80; 2 NJA 4:252
"burnt the Court-house . . ."	2 NJA 4:276
"Majr. [Thomas Langhorne] . . ."	Headquarters O. B. 4.4.80
"Majr. Anderson"	ibid
"150 men"	NYHS Irvine ltr. 4.18.80
"300 Hessians"	CP Spencer rept. 4.15.80
"105 men"	ibid
"provisions, ammunition and . . ."	Hopper deposition
"an hour after . . ."	CP Spencer rept. 4.15.80
"Seeing it impossible . . ."	ibid
"he was wounded . . ."	ibid
"Two Captains, three . . ."	ibid
"The enemy . . . surprised . . ."	Hopper deposition

Chapter V

RIPE FOR INVASION

Melancholy Spring

"a Cold backward . . ."	PNJHS 52 (1934) 237,238
"Our treasury is . . ."	McDougall Gre/McD 4.15.80
"Maryland division . . . with . . ."	WW 18:270
"Ten Ships and . . ."	WW 18:226
"late incursion of . . ."	WW 18:442
"There never . . . since . . ."	Burnett 5:90
"until the 28th"	PCC 46:38:1
"at my quarters"	WW 18:316
"That the commissaries . . ."	Burnett 5:165,166
"one hundred and . . ."	CP Knyp. ltr. 2.24.80
"The Army is . . ."	CP Cunn. Intell. 2.26.80
"Tis too melancholy . . ."	NYHS Irvine ltr. 4.18.80

The Last Straw

"The Connecticut Line . . ."	WP Hun/GW 4.17.80
"Two hundred [are] . . ."	ibid
"Indian [corn] meal . . ."	Martin 181

"cut open the . . ."	Martin 179
"The troops of . . ."	WP Max/GW 5.15.80
"Kelly Hill"	WP Cal/GW 5.18.80
"I expect to . . ."	WP Hun/GW 5.15.80
"We did not . . ."	Martin 182
"We had entertained . . ."	ibid
"a letter without . . ."	WP Mei/GW 5.26.80
"At evening roll . . ."	Martin 183
"a mutinous rascal"	ibid
"fell in and . . ."	ibid
"formed, and came . . ."	ibid
"We now concluded . . ."	ibid
"By this time . . ."	Martin 183,184
"we dispersed to . . ."	Martin 186
"Several of the . . ."	WP Mei/GW 5.26.80
"Mr. Gamble [James . . ."	ibid

The Invasion Begins

"great dissatisfaction prevails . . ."	Jung. 3:34
"Lying Rivington's account . . ."	WP Day/GW 5.30.80
"as a result . . ."	Staff Rept.
"on the 21st"	WW 18:170
"He [Knyphausen] had . . ."	NY Col. Doc. VIII:793
"making cartridge"	Krafft 111
"seven days' provision"	Baur.353
"no carriage with . . ."	NY Col. Doc. VIII:793
"money and papers . . ."	Krafft 111
"7375 men fit . . ."	CP 6.18.80 ret.
"to Cole's Ferry"	Jung. 7:13
"hardly set sail . . ."	Jung. 3:34
"through a mutual . . ."	Clinton 192
"if these dispatches . . ."	Jung. 3:34
"Generals Robertson and . . ."	Baur. 353
"5 o'clock"	Jung. 7:13
"56 sloops"	Jung. 7:14
"to Decker's Ferry"	Jung. 7:13
"22nd and 57th . . ."	Staff Rept.
"Unfavorable winds and . . ."	Jung. 7:13
"11 o'clock p.m."	ibid
"40 flatboats"	ibid
"9 o'clock in . . ."	Staff Rept.
"Garret Post House . . ."	ibid
"half past three . . ."	Jung. 7:13
"the ground being . . ."	Krafft 112
"2nd Division, 4th . . ."	Jung. 7:13
"three in the . . ."	ibid

Advance Through Elizabethtown

"37th,38th, Leib . . ."	ibid
"At 5 o'clock . . ."	Rivington 3.10.79
"As there is . . ."	WP 137:68
"a short distance . . ."	Ogden 24
"at the head . . ."	CP 6.18.80 memo.
"news carriers, in . . ."	2 NJA 4:441
"march to Connecticut . . ."	Jung. 7:13
"landed at [De] . . ."	Staff Rept.
"11 o'clock at . . ."	Jung. 7:13
"12 o'clock"	ibid
"in the thigh"	WW 19:10
"150 men"	WP 140:66 verso
"gave the enemy . . ."	WP Gib/GW 6.8.80
"Mr. Ford . . . received . . ."	ibid
"Colonel [Friedrich Wilhelm] . . ."	Jung. 7:14
"they chased the . . ."	ibid
"two regiments"	Ogden 24
"lying on the . . ."	Ogden 25
"paraded on the . . ."	ibid
"The alarm gun . . ."	Green 96
"the Alarm Gun . . ."	WW 18:147
"behind the ravine . . ."	Ogden 25
"741 rank and . . ."	WP ret. 6.3.80
"1634 men"	CP 6.18.80 memo.
"fortnightly"	WP 137:31
"Elizabethtown"	ibid
"Newark"	ibid
"west side Raritan"	ibid
"East of Raritan"	ibid
"Bottle Hill"	ibid
"a short distance . . ."	Green 108,109
"Your comrades countrymen . . ."	ibid
"Son William"	Hist. Mag. III:211
"all the day"	ibid
"asked leave to . . ."	2 NJA 4:498

Connecticut Farm Stand

"constant skirmishing"	Jung. 7:13
"ran off as . . ."	Hist. Mag. I:104
"crossed over the . . ."	Hist. Mag. III:211
"at least 1500 . . ."	ibid
"I ordered a . . ."	ibid
"The main body . . ."	ibid
"in small bodies"	ibid
"committed to Major . . ."	Ogden 26
"As soon as . . ."	Jung. 7:14
"half past eight"	Jung. 7:13
"at nine o'clock . . ."	ibid
"in front of . . ."	ibid
"met with unaccustomed . . ."	Baur. 354
"with fixed bayonets"	ibid
"left was turned . . ."	Ogden 26
"some houses"	Jung. 7:14
"the window"	Caldwell 11
"The Presbyterian church . . ."	2 NJA 4:415
"hourly occupied by . . ."	Rivington 6.21.80
"slowly toward the . . ."	Hist. Mag. III:211
"Everyone that had . . ."	Jung. 3:34
"impenetrable wood on . . ."	Jung. 7:14
"Our parties of . . ."	Hist. Mag. III:211

Action Before Springfield

"past 1 o'clock . . ."	WP Day/GW 6.[7].80
"I am directed . . ."	ibid
"The Troops to . . ."	WW 18:486
"The Army will . . ."	ibid
"give the alarm . . ."	WW 18:488
"to communicate this . . ."	WW 18:487,488
"3,760 rank and . . ."	WP ret. 6.3.80
"½ after 8"	WW 18:487
"the hurry and . . ."	WP Ford/GW 7.21.80
"reached the heights . . ."	WW 18:493
"The whole brigade . . ."	Hist. Mag. III:211
"this was the . . ."	ibid
"two Light Infantry . . ."	Jung. 7:13
"yelled Hurrah"	ibid
"advanced in fast . . ."	Jung. 7:14
"pushed over the . . ."	Hist. Mag. III:211
"1/2 English miles"	Jung. 7:14
"pretty near the . . ."	Pa. Mag. 34:425
"an old iron . . ."	2 NJA 4:417
"three pounder"	Force 6.19.80 ret.
"our company and . . ."	Pa. Mag. 34:425
"The road they . . ."	ibid

"for about a . . ."	Green 117
"we were twice . . ."	Pa. Mag. 34:425
"orders to halt"	Jung. 7:13
"defend the bridge"	Jung. 7:14
"the heights between . . ."	CP 6.18.80 memo.
"the next day . . ."	Jung. 7:13
"4 o'clock [p.m. . . ."	Staff Rept.
"after General Hackenberg's . . ."	ibid
"The first line"	Gouvion
"The second line"	ibid
"The first line . . ."	WW 18:487

Retreat to Elizabethtown

"General Clinton was . . ."	NY Col. Doc. VIII:793, CP Andre memo. 6.18.80
"Washington had got . . ."	ibid
"detached General [Lord] . . ."	Jung. 7:13
"to await the . . ."	Staff Rept.
"about 10 o'clock . . ."	Hist. Mag. I:104
"It was the . . ."	Hist. Mag. I:105
"sunrise"	Jung. 7:14
"our [Continental] loss . . ."	Hist. Mag. III:211
"carried in a . . ."	PNJHS (NS) VII:29
"We had good . . ."	Hist. Mag. III:211
"the enemy's loss . . ."	2 NJA 4:448
"47 of the . . ."	Hist. Mag. III:211
"it took three . . ."	Popp 13
"about 40 prisoners"	WW 19:10
"Never did troops . . ."	Hist. Mag. III:211

Chapter VI

WAITING FOR CLINTON

Fight Below Elizabethtown

"ship the Hessians . . ."	Staff Rept.
"The cavalry, the . . ."	ibid
"to Thompson's Mills . . ."	Seeley Jnl.
"a guard in . . ."	ibid
"the latter end . . ."	2 NJA 4:403
"Vauxhall at the . . ."	WP Gib/GW 6.8.80
"march off toward . . ."	ibid
"Major Generals Greene . . ."	WW 18:489
"Maxwell's brigade [of . . ."	WW 18:490
"must act chiefly . . ."	ibid
"to be employed . . ."	ibid
"after sum time"	Seeley Jnl.
"joined by Lord . . ."	ibid
"10 o'clock in . . ."	Jung. 7:14
"advance in three . . ."	Seeley Jnl.
"and had twice . . ."	Krafft 112
"Buneau and Anspack . . ."	Jung. 7:13
"Bose's and our . . ."	Krafft 112
"fell back a . . ."	Seeley Jnl.
"by rifle shots . . ."	Krafft 112,113
"are excellent marksmen"	Baur. 355
"we did not . . ."	Krafft 113
"We have not . . ."	Baur. 355
"General Hand ordered . . ."	Seeley Jnl.
"Their balls struck . . ."	Green 112
"about half a . . ."	Seeley Jnl.
"we lay on . . ."	ibid
"about 20 prisoners"	ibid
"the New Jersey . . ."	Staff Rept.
"deemed best to . . ."	ibid

Fight in Elizabethtown

"having been informed . . ."	Gouvion
"Connecticut Farms"	WW 18:490
"Springfield Heights"	Beers
"at a House . . ."	WW 18:491
"information he had . . ."	Gouvion
"morning at six . . ."	ibid
"The firing of . . ."	Scammell 147
"toward evening . . . the . . ."	Jung. 7:13
"60 Jaegers were . . ."	Jung. 7:13
"Guards, Two batts . . ."	Mackenzie 6.18.80
"2216 yards"	ibid
"Major General Lord . . ."	WW 18:492
"Webster and Chamberlain"	Felcone 1423
"2000 of them . . ."	2 NJA 4:417
"all those from . . ."	LP 6.10.80
"Mr. Caldwell could . . ."	2 NJA 4:422
"at the Farms . . ."	Condit 30
"Caldwell's former house . . ."	WP Mea/GW 6.23.80
"He rode up . . ."	Green 109
"were constant short . . ."	Krafft 113
"for about a . . ."	Staff Rept.
"Livingston and were . . ."	ibid
"the Regiment von . . ."	Jung. 3:34
"after the exchange . . ."	WP Smi/Ste [6.12.80]
"were withdrawn"	Jung. 7:14
"no one was . . ."	Krafft 113,114
"about 100 infantry . . ."	Jung. 7:14
"floating bridge to . . ."	Staff Rept.
"228 yards"	Brun 467
"Washington . . . is said . . ."	Jung. 7:14
"Admiral [Marriot] Arbuthnot . . ."	Jung. 7:13
"in the morning . . ."	Staff Rept.
"fowls in hand"	2 NJA 4:476
"no tents except . . ."	WP Intell. 6.16.80
"like tents at . . ."	ibid
"None of the . . ."	ibid
"We have now . . ."	Hist. Mag. VII #3:81
"nothing special; all . . ."	Jung. 7:13
"The Regiment [battalion] . . ."	Staff Rept.
"The two Battns . . ."	Pattison 403
"531 fit for . . ."	CP 6.15.80 ret.
"7375 men"	CP 6.18.80 ret.
"Garrets Hill"	WP For/GW 6.17.80
"4 o'clock appeared . . ."	ibid
"Sir Henry Clinton . . ."	WW 19:26

Clinton Changes Plans

"light infantry, the . . ."	Baur. 351
"about 4500"	Clinton 191 note
"Sir H. Clinton . . ."	NY Col. Doc. VIII:793
"Adjutant General [John . . ."	Clinton 191
"a sudden unexpected . . ."	Clinton 190
"at Amboy"	Clinton 191
"to Mordecai's Gap"	ibid
"to Elizabeth Town . . ."	ibid
"to Chatham"	ibid
"I had the . . ."	Clinton 192
"The above memoranda . . ."	CP 6.18.80 memo.
"Washington's army [was] . . ."	ibid
"Six French Ships . . ."	CP 6.12.80
"Only 1500 men"	CP 6.15.80
"it would be . . ."	ibid
"some of the . . ."	WP Mer/GW 6.20.80
"sounding about the . . ."	ibid
"the main body . . ."	WP Dic/GW 6.20.80

"a number of . . ."	ibid
"half his battalion . . ."	ibid
"the cattle removed"	ibid
"land three miles . . ."	CP 6.16.80
"up the North . . ."	Clinton 193
"arrived at 10 . . ."	Jung. 7:14
"took his residence . . ."	WP AR/GW 6.24.80
"near Decker's Ferry"	Staff Rept.
"I . . . directed all . . ."	Clinton 193
"hear of Gen. . . ."	WP Lee/Ste 6.19.80
"this wind is . . ."	ibid
"send some person . . ."	WP Mea/GW 6.20.80

West Point Dilemma

"suspicion of something . . ."	WW 18:494
"immediately up the . . ."	WW 18:495
"return with the . . ."	WW 18:496
"My apprehensions are . . ."	WW 19:12,13
"supply a large . . ."	WW 19:27
"Six of the . . ."	WW 19:38
"1168 rank and . . ."	Force 6.19.80 ret.
"I do not . . ."	WP Ste/GW 6.20.80
"Colonels Cortland, Phillips, . . ."	Force 6.19.80 ret.
"in the Farmer's . . ."	WW 19:33
"I think my . . ."	WP Ste/GW 6.20.80
"Major General Greene . . ."	WW 19:50
"The Troops under . . ."	WW 19:51
"halt on some . . ."	WW 19:52
"dispatch a Dragoon . . ."	WW 19:47
"the enemy have . . ."	WW 18:495
"of the Conduct . . ."	WW 19:54,55
"the behavior of . . ."	WW 19:55
"eight hundred dollars . . ."	WW 19:54 note
"A patrol pushed . . ."	Staff Rept.
"Mr. P."	WP Gre/GW 6.22.80
"a double spy"	ibid
"willing to forfeit . . ."	ibid

Chapter VII

THE SECOND INVASION

Connecticut Farms Recaptured

"At 3 o'clock . . ."	Jung. 7:14
"Queen's Rangers, Guards . . ."	ibid
"Diemar's Hussars and . . ."	Staff Rept.
"the Queens Rangers at . . ."	Simcoe 143
"flanked the march . . ."	ibid
"rapid and compact . . ."	2 NJA 4:481
"at 4 o'clock"	Jung. 7:13
"Jaegers, 37th, 38th . . ."	Jung. 7:14
"a detachment of . . ."	Staff Rept.
"2313 men and . . ."	CP 6.18.80 ret.
"The Piquets of . . ."	Staff Rept.
"2745 men"	CP 6.18.80 ret.
"till they were . . ."	Trial 1781:10
"proposed to [Lieutenant . . ."	ibid
"Lieut. Colonels Gordon . . ."	2 NJA 4:227
"After five minutes . . ."	Trial 1781:10
"about 4 o'clock . . ."	ibid
"with a flower . . ."	Trial 1783:109,110
"the enemy vanguard . . ."	Jung. 7:14
"fields of the . . ."	Rivington 6.29.80
"small parties [which . . ."	Simcoe 143
"a strong pass"	Jung. 7:13
"right by a . . ."	Simcoe 143
"Lt. Col. [John . . ."	Simcoe 143,144
"Capt. Stevenson who . . ."	Simcoe 144
"pursued closely on . . ."	ibid
"six o'clock"	Beers
"the drums throughout . . ."	Thacher 200,201
"animation and composure . . ."	Thacher 201
"Jackson's and our . . ."	Beers
"entire front was . . ."	Jung. 7:13
"Major Lee with . . ."	2 NJA 4:481
"Col. Ogden was . . ."	ibid
"Capt. [now Major] . . ."	WP 140:66 verso
"Col. [Israel] Angell . . ."	2 NJA 4:481
"Col. [Frederick] Frelinghausen . . ."	WP 140:66 verso
"Colo. [Israel] Shreve's . . ."	2 NJA 4:481
"line formed half . . ."	Beers
"1 Jersey [Dayton's] . . ."	ibid
"The remainder of . . ."	2 NJA 4:481
"Cols. Starke, Seeley . . ."	WP 140:66 verso
"8 o'clock"	Staff Rept.

Rahway Bridges Stormed

"The following disposition . . ."	Staff Rept.
"very well acquainted . . ."	Trial 1783:101
"between the hours . . ."	Trial 1783:5,69
"Vauxhall"	Trial 1783:122
"inside a backhouse . . ."	PNJHS (NS) VI:93
"Small parties . . ."	Simcoe 144
"signal by firing . . ."	Jung. 7:13
"11 o'clock"	Staff Rept.
"Lt. Col. Simcoe . . ."	Simcoe 145
"forming the line . . ."	ibid
"the bridge was . . ."	2 NJA 4:481
"fording the river . . ."	ibid
"fifty infantry"	WP Lee/GW 6.23.80
"six cannon"	Staff Rept.
"were posted on . . ."	Jung. 7:13
"on the Springfield . . ."	Beers
"160 rank and . . ."	Olney 254
"Captain Lieutenant [Thomas] . . ."	2 NJA 4:482
"that was straight . . ."	Pa. Mag. 34:425
"solid column"	Green 117
"the 37th rushed . . ."	Jung. 7:13
"The planks of . . ."	Green 117
"wading through the . . ."	Jung. 7:13
"asked [Lieutenant] Colonel . . ."	Olney 253
"marched a few . . ."	ibid
"moving about from . . ."	ibid
"shake the hair . . ."	ibid
"five or six"	ibid
"twenty yards"	ibid
"right of the . . ."	ibid
"57th [had] advanced . . ."	Jung. 7:14
"6 killed and . . ."	WP Gre/GW 6.24.80
"Captain Lieutenant Thompson . . ."	Thacher 202
"forty minutes"	WW 19:66

Springfield Village Taken

"we had not . . ."	Olney 253
"three ranks [or . . ."	KP 1:371
"followed close in . . ."	Trial 1781:11
"in divisions by . . ."	Trial 1783:14
"six battalion companies"	Trial 1783:10
"was towards the . . ."	Trial 1781:12
"go to Colonel . . ."	Trial 1781:61

"12 o'clock noon"	Trial 1781:13
"to gain the . . ."	Trial 1781:12
"the orchards"	Trial 1781:11
"drawn up in . . ."	Simcoe 145
"sergeant's party"	Trial 1783:17
"deep gulley covered . . ."	Simcoe 145
"by the riflemen . . ."	ibid
"immediately fell back"	ibid
"the flanking companies . . ."	Trial 1781:19
"the Queen's Rangers . . ."	Trial 1783:60
"formed them facing . . ."	Trial 1781:11
"three columns of . . ."	Trial 1781:20
"at a house . . ."	Trial 1783:117
"three pieces of . . ."	Trial 1781:53
"1 Jersey [Dayton's] . . ."	Beers
"with one or . . ."	Trial 1783:117
"cannon ball struck . . ."	ibid
"the left of . . ."	Trial 1781:20
"another ball from . . ."	Trial 1783:118
"the village of . . ."	Trial 1783:23
"in an orchard . . ."	MNHP: L. Morris 6.24.80
"thrown a small . . ."	ibid
"the enemy was . . ."	2 NJA 4:481
"lost a considerable . . ."	MNHP: L. Morris 6.24.80
"about a quarter . . ."	ibid
"they burnt the . . ."	NY Col. Doc. VIII:794
"passing the burned . . ."	Trial 1781:14
"to halt for . . ."	Simcoe 145
"the Jaegers were . . ."	Jung. 7:13
"left"	Simcoe 146
"beyond the town . . ."	Trial 1781:11
"lay in an . . ."	Simcoe 145
"a battalion of . . ."	Simcoe 146
"post upon the . . ."	2 NJA 4:482
"This enabled me . . ."	ibid
"his militia and . . ."	Simcoe 146
"a house from . . ."	NY Col. Doc. VIII:794
"On their right . . ."	Simcoe 146
"directed their force . . ."	WP Gre/GW 6.23.80

West Point Thrust

"three thousand [troops . . ."	WP Gre/GW 6.22.80
"five or six . . ."	WW 19:64
"the 1st and . . ."	WW 19:62
"all the troops . . ."	Baur. 355
"cantoned near Richmond"	Jung. 7:14
"to put his . . ."	Clinton 194
"in person to . . ."	WW 19:65 note
"return . . . to Elizabethtown"	Clinton 194
"nineteen dwelling houses"	2 NJA 4:461
"two houses"	WW 19:70
"some refugees"	NY Col. Doc. VIII:794
"3 o'clock p.m. . . ."	Staff Rept.
"The right was . . ."	Simcoe 147
"Capt. Davis with . . ."	2 NJA 4:482
"to pursue the . . ."	Thacher 201
"several fresh graves . . ."	ibid
"fired 48 rounds . . ."	PNJHS (NS) VI:93
"constant firing"	Staff Rept.
"a full trot"	WP Sti/GW 6.23.80
"took fifteen prisoners"	Thacher 201
"were relieved by . . ."	Jung. 7:13
"The Regiment von . . ."	Staff Rept.
"between 12 and . . ."	Jung. 7:13
"moon-light"	2 NJA 4:464
"a heavy thunder . . ."	Popp 13
"Marched to Ryerson's . . ."	Staff Rept.
"embarked in available . . ."	Jung. 7:13
"by marching his . . ."	Clinton 194
"Horn Yappo seven . . ."	WP Hun/GW 6.25.80
"I could not . . ."	Clinton 193
"about 8 o'clock . . ."	WP Sta/GW 6.26.80

APPENDIX I

Following the so-called "Cambridge Army" of 1775, there were three Continental armies raised consecutively by Congress to fight the Revolutionary War. They were called the First Establishment, Second Establishment and Third Establishment.

Although many of the officer personnel carried over from one Establishment to the next, the enlisted personnel were quite different in each. Large numbers of enlisted men declined to sign-up for another enlistment period without first going home for awhile. For many of the enlisted men, one "hitch" was quite enough.

The First Establishment called for one-year enlistments that ended on various dates in December 1776, but the expiration dates were extended for six weeks in the Princeton emergency by the payment of a bonus to those who volunteered to stay-on for that period. This extension of service brought several thousand men of the First Establishment to Morristown after the Battle of Princeton on January 3, 1777. Then, as the men of the First Establishment began to leave Morristown in late January and early February, the new three-year enlistees for the Second Establishment began to arrive at Morristown.

Enlistments of the Second Establishment began to expire on December 31, 1779, running-on for four or five months, and Morristown became the setting for the dissolution of the Second Establishment army as it had been for the First Establishment army. Likewise, Morristown saw the arrival of the new enlistees of the Third Establishment during the winter and spring of 1779-1780. Thus, the bulk of the army in all three Establishments, amounting to many thousands of men, saw some service at Morristown.

Following is the composition and strength, by brigade, of Morristown forces on three critical dates during the First, Second and Third Establishments.

CONTINENTAL AND STATE TROOPS
MORRISTOWN
1.6.1777 (1)

FIRST ESTABLISHMENT

Mercer's brigade [mixed]	325
Stephen's brigade [Virginia]	400
Hitchcock's brigade [Mass. & R. I.]	353
St. Clair's brigade [mixed N. E.]	1400
Fermoy's brigade [Pa. & Md.]	610
Mifflin's brigade [Pa.]	1500 (2)
Mc Dougall's brigade [Mass.]	750 (3)

STATE TROOPS

Cadwallader's brigade [Pa.]	1147
Ewing's brigade [Pa.]	600
	6335

(1) This was the composition of the army on the first day at Morristown. For a breakdown of these brigades by regiment see (Pr. 34, 35). (For troop dispositions after the first few days at Morristown, see Appendix VI.)
(2) Some Pa. militia detachments with Mifflin.
(3) Mc Dougall's brigade was already at Morristown and included three Mass. continental regiments and two N. J. militia regiments.

WEEKLY STATE OF CONTINENTAL ARMY
MORRISTOWN
12.18.1779 (1)

SECOND ESTABLISHMENT

Smallwood's brigade [1st Md.]	955
Gist's brigade [2nd Md.]	984
Irvine's brigade [1st Pa.]	816
2nd Pennsylvania brigade	693
Hand's brigade	678
Maxwell's brigade [N. J.]	870
Clinton's brigade [N. Y.]	762
Parson's brigade [1st Ct.]	968
Huntington's brigade [2nd Ct.]	817
Stark's brigade	890
	8433

(1) (Rolls 246:137: 12.18.79 ret.) This appears to be the first return after the army's arrival at Morristown to spend the winter of 1779-80. For a breakdown of these brigades by regiment as they assembled at Morristown in the spring of 1777, see (WW 8:99, 100, opp. 170); (Rolls 246:137: 5.21.77 ret.) Shown are rank and file fit for duty.

WEEKLY STATE OF CONTINENTAL ARMY
MORRISTOWN
6.3.1780 (1)

THIRD ESTABLISHMENT

1st Pennsylvania brigade	635 (2)
2nd Pennsylvania brigade	514 (2)
Hand's brigade	543 (2)
Maxwell's brigade	741 (3)
1st Connecticut brigade	549
2nd Connecticut brigade	315
Stark's brigade	463
	3760

(1) (WP 6.3.80 ret.) This return was made three days before the army left Morristown for Springfield to repel the invasion of New Jersey. For a breakdown of these brigades by regiment see Appendix III. Shown are rank and file fit for duty. The Maryland Division under the command of Maj. Gen. John Kalb, consisting of the 1st and 2nd Maryland brigades, had departed Morristown for the south on 4.17.80. (WW 18:27) The 1st regiment of artillery left with the Maryland division. (WW 18:270) The New York brigade under the command of Brig. Gen. James Clinton had departed Morristown for the north on 5.30.80. (WW 18:448, 50)
(2) For the winter of 1780-81, the Pennsylvania troops returned to the 1779-80 Morristown encampment grounds where they rioted in early January 1781. (See *Mutiny in January,* Carl Van Doren, New York, 1943.)

Reproduced here is a tracing of a survey map titled "Draught of the Tract of Land on which the Deceased Mr. Henry Wick Lived Containing 1345 acres 132 Perches Strict Measure—Surveyd Jany 13th 1781 Wm Gray." The tracing was made by Mr. Henry Pilch of Madison, New Jersey, in January 1948 from the original map in the De Lancy Kountze Papers in the New Jersey Historical Society Manuscripts Collection. The original cannot now be found. The map is of special interest because it shows the placement of huts on the Wick property, which were occupied by the Pennsylvanians before they rioted on 1.1.1781 and then went home. Lt. Enos Reeves of the Pennsylvania line said that the huts were very much "out of repairs" (Pa. Mag. 20:470) but his brigade was able to make livable some of Hand's 1779-80 brigade huts. They also used the "logs of the old huts of the Maryland Brigade" (ibid) to extend the line of Hand's huts along present Tempe Wick Road "toward Kemble's" (ibid). It should be noted that this map shows additional huts along the present Jockey Hollow Road where the New York brigade was hutted during the winter of 1779-80. (See Rochefontaine map Chapter I for 1779-80 hutting arrangement.)

William Gray, the maker of this map, was Capt. William Gray of the 4th Pennsylvania regiment. Although his regiment and the bulk of the Pennsylvania troops had departed camp after rioting on January 1, Gray seems still to have been in camp on the 13th when this survey map was made. He did, however, retire from the army a few days later on 1.17.1781. This surely was not a military map ordered by Gray's superiors but probably was done as a favor for the Wick family. Lt. Reeves had noted on December 28, four days before the riots, as follows: "Mr. Wicks who has been sick for several days past, died and was buried yesterday." (Pa. Mag. 20:472) For Capt. William Gray's military record and his military map production see (AmM 21).
(3) While the eleven Pennsylvania continental regiments rioted early in January 1781, at Morristown, the two remaining New Jersey continental regiments also rioted late in January, at "Pompton," (WP Howe/GW 1.27.81) New Jersey. But the New Jersey revolt was soon quieted, and on February 7, 1781, Gen. Washington ordered the New Jersey troops to be moved "to Morris Town and dispose of them in the Huts lately occupied by the Pennsylvanians." (WW 21:196) To strengthen the Morristown garrison, Washington ordered Gen. Heath, commander in the New York Highlands, to send "the light companies of the troops under your command . . . to Morris Town." (WW 21:228) On July 7, five months to the day after the Jersey troops were ordered to Morristown, they were ordered "to march from Morris Town towards Dobbs Ferry," (WP GW/Day 7.7.81) New York, to join the main army. After participating in the victorious Yorktown campaign, the two New Jersey regiments were sent by boat to "The Head of Elk," (WP Lin/GW 11.22.81 encl.) Maryland. Then on November 22, 1781, they began a march to New Jersey, arriving home early in December. Their orders were to "take post in the Vicinity of Morris Town." (ibid) The location of this "post" was more precisely identified in a February 20, 1782 advertisement in the local Chatham newspaper, as follows: "To be sold at Public Vendue . . . A FARM, lying three miles from Morristown on the road to Chatham, where the Jersey troops are butted [hutted] it contains 157½ acres. Daniel Pierson." (N.J. Journal 2.20.82) During the spring, on the way north to his Newburgh, New York headquarters, Gen. Washington visited Morristown from "March 26, 1782—March 28, 1782." (WW 24:89-94) Then, after six months in the huts on the road to Chatham, the two New Jersey regiments were ordered to march "the 29 Inst. [August] towards the Hudson," (WW 25:61) and thence to Newburgh, again to be with the main army. Col. Elias Dayton, commander of the New Jersey regiments, was to leave behind "20 of the Invalids or Weakest Men from both regts. with a proportion of Non Commisd Officers . . . for the preservation of the Huts." (ibid) The New Jersey troops remained at Newburgh throughout the winter of 1782-83. Some of them were there as late as May 25, 1783, when "The Jersey regiment gives the Guards." (WW 26:454) The treaty of peace was concluded three months later on September 3, 1783.

Our attention was first directed to the advertisement of Daniel Pierson in the New Jersey Journal by Mr. Henry Pilch, of Madison, New Jersey, who had this to say about the location of the property: "The matter of Daniel Pierson's advertisement of sale raises some questions. According to available records Daniel Pierson owned no property in the area described in the advertisement on the date thereof.

"The Property situated southwest of Madison Avenue (route 24), lying on both sides of Tredwell Avenue in the Borough of Madison and township of Chatham, described by early local historians as the 'Loantaka camp site' was owned, prior to May 1, 1782,

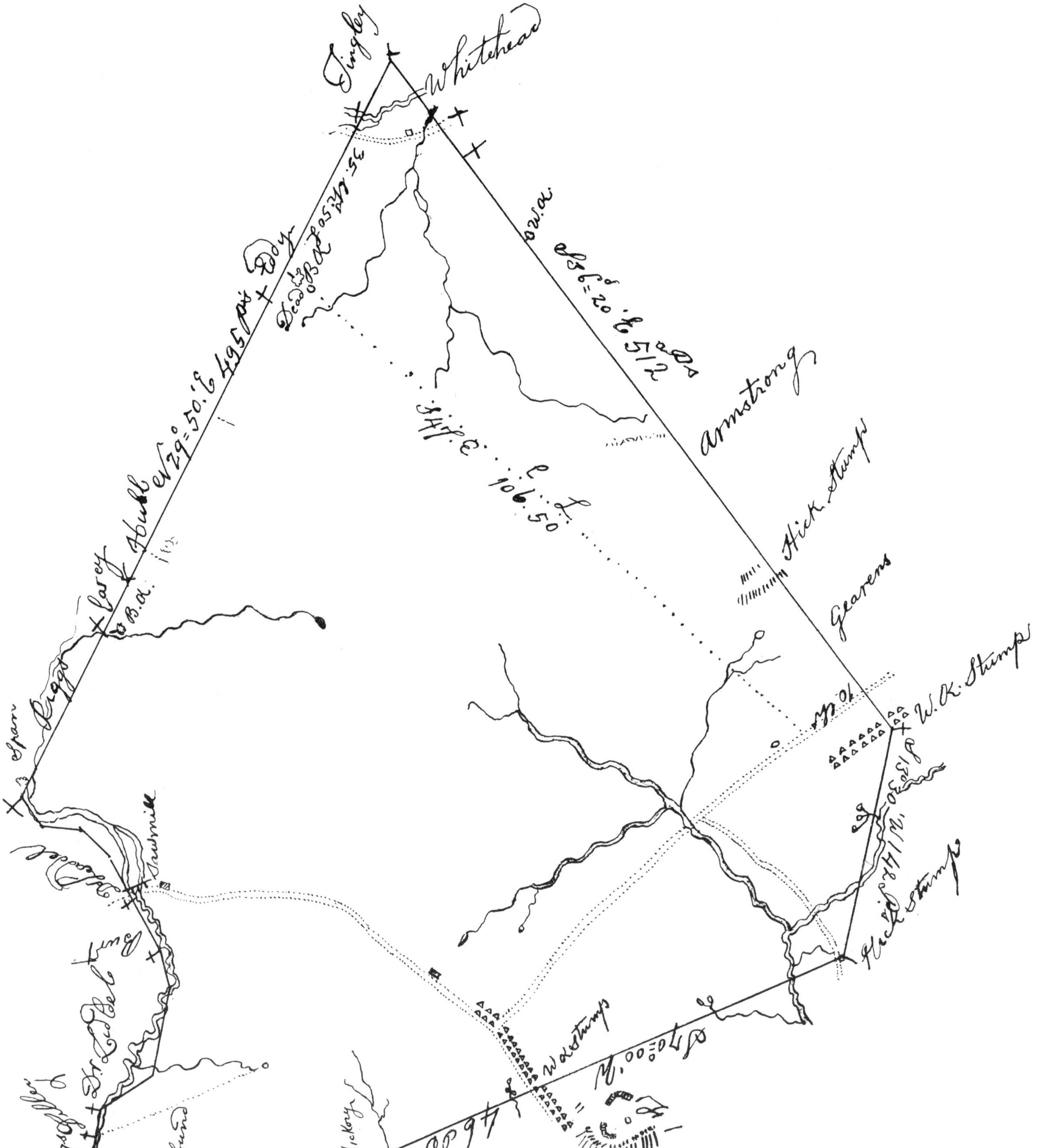

WILLIAM GRAY MAP OF HENRY WICK PROPERTY January 13, 1781—tracing by Mr. Henry Pilch January 1948. The original map also indicated courses and distances along the Passaic River on left edge of map, as follows: "Courses and Distances from the Chestnutt to the Spans Ok up the Pisiack N 67° 00 W 36 ps, N 17° 00 W 36, N 17° 00 E 45, N 57° E 35, N 20° E 50, N 9° W 30, N 27° W 68, N 47° W 24, N 80° W 26, N 47° W 17 to Spans Ok."

by Benjamin Pierson, the father of Daniel. On that date Benjamin Pierson apparently sold 157½ acres to John Easton and an adjoining 33 acres to Nathan Wilkerson. The Deeds are not of record, but Benjamin Pierson took back mortgages covering said properties on May 1, 1782. In a deed dated May 18, 1795, from John Scott (the then owner of part of the Easton 157½ acres) to Vincent Boisaubin, the property is described as 'being the land which John Easton formerly purchased of Benjamin Pierson deceased. . . .'

"Benjamin Pierson did not die until August 2, 1783. By the terms of his will, dated April 10, 1783, probated August 12, 1783, Benjamin Pierson bequeathed to his son Daniel, 'the bonds of John Easton & Nathan Wilkerson'—but no lands are mentioned.

"A careful examination of land and church records in Morristown reveal the existence of only one Daniel Pierson in the Morristown area prior to, during and after the Revolutionary War period. He was Daniel, the son of Benjamin, above mentioned, and was born in 1750, died December 15, 1831 in Dayton, Ohio. In the early 1800's this Daniel Pierson disposed of several tracts of land situated northeast of Madison Avenue (route 24) in the Convent area, nearly opposite the reputed Tredwell Avenue campsite, and extending northeasterly across what is now the College of St. Elizabeth property, to and beyond Park Avenue. There is no indication how, when or from whom he acquired title to this property."

APPENDIX II

AMERICAN CONTINENTAL DETACHMENT NEW JERSEY ADVANCE POSTS 12.26.1779 (1)

Brig. Gen. William Irvine in command

6th Md. regt. Lt. Col. Benjamin Ford		(2)
1st N.J. regt. Col. Matthias Ogden		(2)
3rd Pa. regt. Maj. Thomas Byles		(2)
5th Pa. regt. Maj. Christopher Stuart		(2) (3)
10th Pa. regt. Col. Richard Humpton		(2)
2nd R. I. regt. Lt. Col. Jeremiah Olney		(2)
	750	

(1) WW 17:380
(2) WW 17:321
(3) Maj. Stuart on furlough, Maj. James Reid of 2nd Canadian regt. took his command. (WW 17:327 and note); (Headquarters O.B. 12.26.79)

AMERICAN CONTINENTAL DETACHMENTS RAID ON STATEN ISLAND 1.15.1780 (1)

Maj. Gen. William Alexander (Lord Stirling) in command

Brig. Gen. William Irvine's detachment	750	(2)
Col. Moses Hazen's detachment	990	(3)
Col. Josias Hall's detachment	400	(4)
Col. Walter Stewart's detachment	500	(4)
	2550	

(1) (WW 17:380); (Irvine Papers II:16)
(2) For breakdown of detachment see above.
(3) For breakdown of detachment see below.
(4) Breakdown of this detachment not known.

AMERICAN CONTINENTAL DETACHMENT NEW JERSEY ADVANCE POSTS 1.25.1780 (1)

Col. Moses Hazen in command

1st Md. brigade	112
2nd Md. brigade	123
Hand's brigade	92
Maxwell's brigade	73
1st Ct. brigade	141
2nd Ct. brigade	101
1st Pa. brigade	93
2nd Pa. brigade	92
Clinton's brigade	65
Stark's brigade	98
	990

(1) (Hawkins, O. B. 1.24.80) This selected detachment was to be organized into "3 battalions 330 men each—8 platoons in each battalion—5 of 21 file and 3 of 20—5 captains, 8 subs., 16 sergts., 16 corps., 6 drum and fife to each battalion." (ibid) Colonels with the detachment were "Col. Ogden, Lt. Cols. Ford, Hait and Menges." (ibid) These were Col. Matthias Ogden of the 1st N. J. regt., Lt. Col. Benjamin Ford of the 6th Md. regt., Lt. Col. Joseph Hait of the 2nd Ct. regt., and Lt. Col. Francis Mentges of the 5th Pa. regt. Note: For a complete list of prisoners, continental, militia and civilian, taken in the actions at Elizabethtown and Newark in which this detachment was involved, see reports (Mackenzie 1.25.80, 1.26.80.) There also was a small detachment of Independent Dragoons with Hazen. These were under the command of Capt. Henry Bedkin. (WP Hazen/GW 1.29.80)

APPENDIX III

AMERICAN CONTINENTAL FORCE IN NEW JERSEY ACTION 6.6.80—6.23.80 (1)

FIRST LINE MAJ. GEN. NATHANAEL GREENE

PENNSYLVANIA DIVISION, MAJ. GEN. ARTHUR ST. CLAIR

1st Pa. brigade, Brig. Gen. William Irvine
Brig. Gen. Anthony Wayne as of 6.14.80
1st Pa. regt. Col. James Chambers
2nd Pa. regt. Col. Walter Stewart
7th Pa. regt. Maj. James Parr
10th Pa. regt. Col. Richard Humpton

2nd Pa. brigade, Col. Francis Johnston
Brig. Gen. William Irvine as of 6.14.80
3rd Pa. regt. Col. Thomas Craig
5th Pa. regt. Col. Francis Johnston
6th Pa. regt. Lt. Col. Josiah Harmar (2)
9th Pa. regt. Col. Richard Butler

CONNECTICUT DIVISION, MAJ. GEN. MARQUIS DE LAFAYETTE

1st Ct. brigade, Brig. Gen. Samuel Parsons (3)
3rd Ct. regt. Col. Samuel Wyllys
4th Ct. regt. Col. John Durkee
6th Ct. regt. Col. Return Meigs
8th Ct. regt. Lt. Col. Isaac Sherman

2nd Ct. brigade, Brig. Gen. Jedediah Huntington
1st Ct. regt. Col. Josiah Starr
2nd Ct. regt. Col. Zebulon Butler
5th Ct. regt. Col. Philip Bradley
7th Ct. regt. Col. Heman Swift

SECOND LINE
MAJ. GEN. FRIEDRICH STEUBEN
MAJ. GEN. LORD STIRLING AS OF 6.9.80

Hand's brigade, Brig. Gen. Edward Hand
1st Canadian regt. Col. James Livingston
2nd Canadian regt. Col. Moses Hazen
4th Pa. regt. Lt. Col. William Butler (4)
11th Pa. regt. Lt. Col. Adam Hubley

Stark's brigade, Brig. Gen. John Stark
2nd R. I. regt. Col. Israel Angell
Webb's Additional regt. Lt. Col. Ebenezer Huntington (5)
Jackson's Additional regt. Col. Henry Jackson
Sherburne's Additional regt. Maj. William Bradford (6)

ADVANCE CONTINENTAL FORCE
MAJ. GEN. LORD STIRLING, COMMANDER
MAJ. GEN. FRIEDRICH STEUBEN AS OF 6.9.80

New Jersey brigade, Brig. Gen. William Maxwell (7)
1st N. J. regt. Col. Matthias Ogden
2nd N. J. regt. Col. Israel Shreve
3rd N. J. regt. Col. Elias Dayton
Spencer's Additional regt. Lt. Col. William Smith (8)

MISCELLANEOUS CONTINENTAL DETACHMENTS

Hand's Detachment (9)
Maj. Caleb Gibbs Company (10)
Maj. Henry Lee's Corps (11)
Lt. Col. Thomas Forrest's Artillery (12)

(1) For brigade totals see Appendix I, 6.3.80 ret.
(2) Col. Robert Magaw captured at Ft. Washington 11.16.76, exchanged 10.25.80.
(3) Col. Meigs commanding this brigade 5.26.80 (WW 18:424).
(4) Col. Lambert Cadwalader captured at Ft. Washington 11.16.76, placed on parole.
(5) Col. Samuel Webb captured on Long Island 12.10.77, placed on parole.
(6) As of 5.1.80, the men of this regt. assigned to other regts. of Stark's brigade. (WW 18:319)
(7) Gen. Maxwell's letter to Gen. Washington of 5.15.80 refers to the five regiments of his brigade being at Connecticut Farms. (WP Max/GW 5.15.80) Presumably this was the 4th N. J. regt. whose records are very incomplete, and the regt. is usually regarded as broken-up in mid-1778. A return of prisoners taken at Elizabethtown in January 1780, however, includes a man designated as of the 4th N. J. regt. (Mackenzie 1.25.80, 1.26.80)
(8) Col. Oliver Spencer not with his regiment. (WP Smi/Ste 6.17.80)
(9) "120 Greene's [St. Clair's], 80 La Fayette's [Ct.], 100 Steuben's [Hand's and Stark's]." (WW 18:489)
(10) Maj. Caleb Gibbs commanded Washington's Guard prior to detached duty at the front with his unit. His force was "150 men." (WP 140:66 verso)
(11) "about 50" involved. (Jung. 7:14) Lee's dismounted troops were not with him at this time.
(12) (2 NJA 4:482).

APPENDIX IV

NEW JERSEY MILITIA FORCE
IN NEW JERSEY ACTION
6.6.80—6.23.80

MAJ. GEN. PHILEMON DICKINSON, COMMANDER

1st Burlington Col. [William] Shreve	56	(1)
1st Essex Col. [Moses] Jaques	303	(2)
2nd Essex Col. [Philip] van Cortland	300	(3)
1st Hunterdon Col. [Joseph] Philips	263	(4)
2nd Hunterdon Col. [Joseph] Beavers	168	(5)
3rd Hunterdon Capt. [George] Ely	53	(6)
4th Hunterdon Col. [John] Taylor	200	(7)
1st Middlesex Col. [John] Webster	143	(8)
2nd Middlesex Col. [John] Neilson	170	(9)
3rd Middlesex Lt. Col. [William] Scudder	224	(10)
Eastern Morris Col. [Sylvanus] Seeley	250	(11)
Western Morris Col. [John] Starke	250	(12)
1st Somerset Col. [Frederick] Frelinghuysen	350	(13)
2nd Somerset Col. [Henry] Vandyke	350	(14)
Hunterdon Cavalry Capt. [Israel] Carle	12	(15)
Somerset Cavalry Capt. [Peter] Stryker		(16)
Essex Cavalry Capt. [Samuel] Meeker		(17)
1st Hunterdon Artillery Capt. Yard		(18)
	3111	

(1) (Force 6.19.80 ret.) Col. Thomas "Reynolds" of the 2nd Burlington is "expected" to arrive according to (WP 137:31).
(2) (Force 6.19.80 ret.); (WP 137:31); (WP 140:66); (Felcone 1423).
(3) (Force 6.19.80 ret.); (WP 137:31); (WP 140:66); (Felcone 1423).
(4) (Force 6.19.80 ret.); (WP 137:31); (Felcone 1423).
(5) (Force 6.19.80 ret.) Col. Beavers not with his regt.; Lt. Col. [William] Chamberlain is mentioned in (WP 137:31); (Felcone 1423).
(6) (Force 6.19.80 ret.) In this return, Ely listed as senior officer present.
(7) (WP 137:31); (WP 140:66); (2 NJA 4:581).
(8) (WP 137:31); (WP 140:66); (Felcone 1423). Lt. Col. [Samuel] Crow is listed as senior officer present in (Force 6.19.80 ret.).
(9) (WP 140:66) Col. Neilson made brigadier general in 1777. Maj. [John] Emburgh is mentioned in (WP 137:31).
(10) (Force 6.19.80 ret.); (WP 137:31).
(11) (WP 137:31); (WP 140:66).
(12) (WP 137:31); (WP 140:66).
(13) (WP 140:66); (Felcone 1423). Lt. Col. [Derrick] Middah is mentioned in (WP 137:31).
(14) (WP 140:66). Maj. [Abraham] Nevius is mentioned in (WP 137:31).
(15) (Force 6.19.80 ret.).
(16) (ibid)
(17) (ibid)
(18) (ibid)

APPENDIX V

BRITISH—HESSIAN FORCE
IN NEW JERSEY ACTION
6.3.80—6.23.80

LT. GEN. WILHELM VON KNYPHAUSEN, COMMANDER

FIRST DIVISION, BRIG. GEN. THOMAS STIRLING
COL. FRIEDRICH VON WURMB AS OF 6.7.80

37th regt.	350
38th regt.	397
Leib regt. [du Corps]	428
Landgraf [Landgrave]	459
	1634

SECOND DIVISION, MAJ. GEN. EDWARD MATTHEW		
17th regt. (one company)	79	
22nd regt.	341	(2)
57th regt.	352	
Buneau regt.	554	
1st Skinner's batt. [N. J. Volunteers]	209	(3)
4th Skinner's batt. [N.J. Volunteers]	154	(3)
2 six-pounders		
"Some cavalry"		
	1689	
THIRD DIVISION, MAJ. GEN. WILLIAM TRYON		
Dismounted Jaeger Corps	482	(4)
1st & 2nd batt. Guards	732	
Pioneers	40	(5)
	1254	
FOURTH DIVISION, MAJ. GEN. CARL VON HACKENBERG		
43rd regt.	353	
1st Anspach-Bayreuth regt.	516	
Bose regt.	421	
2 three-pounders		
	1290	
FIFTH DIVISION, MAJ. GEN. FRIEDRICH VON LOSSBERG		
Donop regt.	414	(6)
"Cavalry"	271	(6)
[17th Dragoons and Mounted Queen's Rangers]		
Von Diemar's Hussars	88	(6)
Royal Artillery	115	(7)
German Artillery	132	(7)
Baggage		
	1020	
Total June 7, 1780	6887	(8)
ADDITIONAL TROOPS TO NEW JERSEY		
2nd Anspach-Bayreuth regt.	488	(9)
Dismounted Queen's Rangers	451	(10)
	936	
Grand Total June 23, 1780	7823	

(1) (Jung. 7:13); (CP Mackenzie ret. 6.18.80). All troops in invasion force listed in these two references, except as noted below.
(2) (Jung. 7:14).
(3) For Muster Rolls of these battalions see (NJSA).
(4) Hessian as well as Anspach Jaegers.
(5) A Loyalist unit sometimes referred to as "Guides and Pioneers."
(6) (Baur. 353); (Staff Rept.) The latter lists "Staten Island Dragoons." One return lists "Stuart's Dragoons" (Jung. Order of Battle 6.30.80)
(7) These totals include all artillery. One return shows 2 six-pounders, 6 three-pounders, and 2 howitzers with the 5th Division. (Jung. 7:13)
(8) "6,000" says Maj. Gen. Robertson to Germain. (NY Col. Doc. VIII:793)
(9) Sent to New Jersey June 17 from N. Y. (CP Mackenzie ret. 6.18.80)
(10) Sent to New Jersey June 22 being a part of the Charleston force. (Clinton 193). They consisted of "33 officers and 418 men" (CO 5:99:2044)

APPENDIX VI

WINTER OF 1776-1777 IN NEW JERSEY

The army that fought the Battle of Princeton shown in Appendix I, totaling 6,335 men, was an army about to disband. Just prior to the Battle of Princeton, Congress had agreed to pay to the continental soldiers of the army "a Bounty of Ten Dollars pr Man besides their pay running on" (WW 6:455) if they would stay in service for six weeks beyond their one year enlistment periods, which were to expire on various dates from December 1 through December 31, 1776. Thus, the continental soldiers who fought at Princeton on January 3, 1777 and who marched into Morristown on January 6, were only those who had accepted the bounty offer. These extended enlistments would begin to expire on January 15, and all of them would expire by February 15.

However, all in the Princeton army who marched to Morristown were not continental soldiers. Nearly half of them, or "2,847 men," (Pr. 34, 35) were Pennsylvania state troops. Being state troops, these men had not been presented with the federal bounty offer. During the Princeton emergency, many of the Pennsylvanians had stayed on past their 60 day terms of service and they were ready to go home as soon as they arrived at Morristown. As Gen. Washington wrote to Congress on his first day at Morristown, "The Severity of the Season has made our Troops, especially the Militia [i.e., state troops], extremely impatient, and has reduced our number considerably. Every day more or less leave us," (WW 6:477) indicating that some of the Pennsylvanians had left even before the army reached Morristown.

Although the army was impatient, as Washington noted, the men were also very tired when they arrived at Morristown. They had not had a good night's sleep since they left Trenton, a week past. As the army entered the town "at about sunset" (Rodney Diary) and the men were allowed to break ranks, everyone scrambled for a place to get some sleep. They had no tents with them and their baggage had been left behind on the Bordentown Road near Trenton as the army had marched to Princeton and then to Morristown.

Lt. Col. James Read wrote to his wife on the 8th that he had found a place to get some sleep in a house in Morristown, but "the house is exceedingly crouded." (de Coppett Rea/Rea 1.8.77) Lt. Charles Willson Peale said that he found a house in Morristown that would take him in but there was no available bed, so he "slept on the planks rather coldly." (Pa. Mag. 38:285) Probably many of the enlisted men were forced to settle for churches, schoolhouses, barns and other out-buildings. Every available sleeping quarter for miles around was taken up. As Lt. Peale noted, one would have to walk a "few miles" to find a house without soldiers. (Pa. Mag. 38:285)

Capt. Thomas Rodney said that a whole regiment consisting of his Kent County Delaware militia company and four companies of Pennsylvania light infantry, totaling "196 men," (Pr. 34); (Rodney Diary) occupied one house. Rodney wrote in his diary on January 6, "Our whole Light Infantry are quartered in a very large house belonging to Col. Ford having 4 Rooms on a floor and Two stories high." (Rodney Diary)

The first day or two at Morristown were days of rest. But as soon as the men had some sleep and had recovered somewhat from the ordeals of the Princeton battle, they were ordered back to war. The enemy in great numbers were still at Brunswick and Amboy, now New Brunswick and Perth Amboy, and they must be held to that area, if possible. Thus, men who were fit for duty and whose times were not yet up, were sent to the front lines.

As Capt. Stephen Olney, a continental officer, put it, "To complete the extra month's service I was in a detachment of about 300, under the command of Colonel Lippitt and Lieutenant Colonel Henshaw as a patrol or scouting party. We left our encampment near Morristown, and proceeded to within 20 or 30 rods of the road leading from Brunswick to Bonumtown." (Olney Diary) Even the Pennsylvania state troops were compelled to go to the front until their time was up. Lt. Col. James Read of the Chester County regt. wrote to his wife on January 8 that "I have been on guard duty all night but just come off and am now call'd to duty again." (Princeton Mss. Rea/Rea 1.8.77) The new duty was to go down to "Raritan Run," (LC Sullivan Papers 1.10.77) to stand against the enemy.

Maj. Gen. John Sullivan was sent to the front to command the forward troops of the Princeton army who were trying to contain the enemy on the northern sector. Sullivan made his headquarters at "Chatham." (WW 7:55) To contain the enemy on the southern sector Gen. Washington ordered Maj. Gen. Israel Putnam to gather what troops he could muster, in and around Philadelphia, and to advance to Princeton where he should make his headquarters. From Princeton he should send out false information to the enemy that his force was "twice as great as it is." (WW 6:471, 472)

But what would happen when the Princeton army went home? Washington would have to rely on the New Jersey militia and militia from neighboring states until he could raise a new continental army. Washington was well aware of this. Thus, while he was at Pluckemin on January 5, enroute to Morristown, he wrote to Maj. Gen. William Heath, American commander in the New York Highlands, as follows: "General Lincoln must cross the North River and come on with the remainder of the Militia to Morristown." (WW 6:473) This was Brigadier General Benjamin Lincoln and the militia was a force of Massachusetts militia assembled in the Highlands.

However, the Massachusetts militia who were soon on their way, plus some New Jersey state troops already in the front lines, would not be enough to contain the enemy. Thus, Gen. Washington urged Congress to appeal to the governors of the neighboring states for help, as follows: "As the militia must be our dependence, till we can get the New Army raised and properly arranged, I must entreat you to continue your endeavours with the States of Pennsylvania, Maryland and Virginia." (WW 7:30) The governors did respond, and some of the larger contingents that came to New Jersey were as follows:

MASSACHUSETTS

The Massachusetts militia was the first to arrive. On 1.18.77 Washington noted, "A few days ago Genl. Warner arrived, with about seven hundred Massachusetts Militia engaged to the 15th of March." (WW 7:29) This was a brigade under the command of Brig. Gen. Nathaniel Warner. The Massachusetts force was increased to about 1,000 men when on 1.14.77, Gen. Lincoln arrived from the New York Highlands with "a Regiment of Massachusetts Militia, consisting of about 250." (WW 7:146)

PENNSYLVANIA

Although loosely called militia by Gen. Washington, the troops that came from Pennsylvania at this time were not, in the strict sense militia or conscripted soldiers. The Pennsylvania Militia Act was not passed until 3.17.77. Instead, they were enlisted volunteers known as "Associators," who were engaged for a period of not over 60 days. Some Pennsylvania Associators may have arrived in New Jersey in January. On 1.16.77, the Pennsylvania Council of Safety wrote to Gen. Washington that "The Westmoreland Battalion consisting of 620 is on its way." (WP PCS/GW 1.16.77) Further, it was noted on 2.1.77, that a considerable number had "gone to camp, especially from County Cumberland." (WP Arm/GW 2.1.77) Also in the lines by 2.7.77, were the Associators from "Bedford County." (WP Dav/Put 2.7.77) There appears to have been no Pennsylvania brigadier with these troops, at this time.

MARYLAND

The Maryland militia also turned out in brigade strength. The first Maryland arrivals were under the command of Brig. Gen. Thomas Johnson, Jr. The Maryland militia under Johnson appear to have arrived sometime in early February and their terms would be up, according to Gen. Washington, "the 5th of Next Month," (WW 7:203) which would be March. To replace Johnson's men, "the Baltimore militia" (WW 7:249) under Brig. "Genl. Buckanan," (WW 7:249) (Brig. Gen. Andrew Buchanan) was said to be enroute.

However, as late as 3.5.77, Washington complained that "I cannot conceive upon what principle the Baltimore Militia were stopped, they ought to have been here in time to have relieved Genl. Johnston's Brigade, the last of whom go home today." (WW 7:249) It had been rumored as early as 2.5.77 that the militia units of "Hartford and Cecil Counties in Maryland" (WW 7:104) also had been ordered out, but as of 3.15.77, it appears that only the Cecil County militia, numbering 177 men, were present and accounted for.

Additional small units arrived from other states, but those from Massachusetts, Pennsylvania, and Maryland were the large contingents of state troops in brigade strength that came to New Jersey to fill the gap between the First Establishment and the Second Establishment of the American continental army. By March 15, however, most of these units from neighboring states had gone home, and were replaced by other units.

Following is a return of troops showing the strength of the American Army in New Jersey and their disposition, as of 3.15.77. Note that only "46 rank and file" out of 3,519 men were stationed at Morristown. The balance of the army, fit for duty, was in the front lines opposite the "8,361 rank and file" (CO 5:94:Part 1:212) of the enemy still at Brunswick and Amboy, and the bulk of the army would remain at the front for the rest of the winter and spring.

RETURN OF CONTINENTAL TROOPS UNDER THE COMMAND OF HIS EXCELLENCY GENERAL WASHINGTON AT THE DIFFERENT POSTS IN THE STATE OF NEW JERSEY
15th MARCH 1777 (1)

Post	*Regiment*	*Rank & file fit for duty*
Morristown	Part of Pennsylvania regt.	46 (2)
Bound Brook	8th Pennsylvania	342 (3)
Prince Town	Capt. Yates from Maryland	49 (4)
	1 comp. of Colo. Martin's Jersey	35 (5)
	Colo. Shreve's	200 (6)
Chatham	Colo. Ward's to serve to 15 May	235 (7)
	Pennsn. Rifle	25 (8)
Raritan	Wyoming War.	99 (9)
Westfield	3rd Pennsylvania	28 (10)
	1st Jersey	94 (11)
	4th Jersey	157 (12)
	12th Pennsylvania	162 (13)
Spank Town [Carteret]	1st Pennsylvania	171 (14)
	German Batt.	125 (15)
Whippany	1,2,3,4,5,6,9 Virginia 74 well/571 invalids	645 (16)
Different Posts	Colo. Proctor's artillery	130 (17)
		2543

RETURN OF MILITIA AT DIFFERENT
POSTS IN JERSEY
15th MARCH 1777 (1)

Post	*Corps*	*Time to wch they are engd.*	*Rank & file*
Quibble Town [New Market]	Ramsey's Mard.	1 April	177 (18)
	Morgan's Virgn.	do.	47 (19)
	Geo. Scott's do.	do.	63 (20)
	Jos. Scott's do.	do.	32 (21)
Raritan	Jersey militia	do.	423 (22)
Westfield	do.	do.	234 (23)
			976

There are besides the above three or four hundred Jersey and other militia whose time expires about the 20th March. (24)

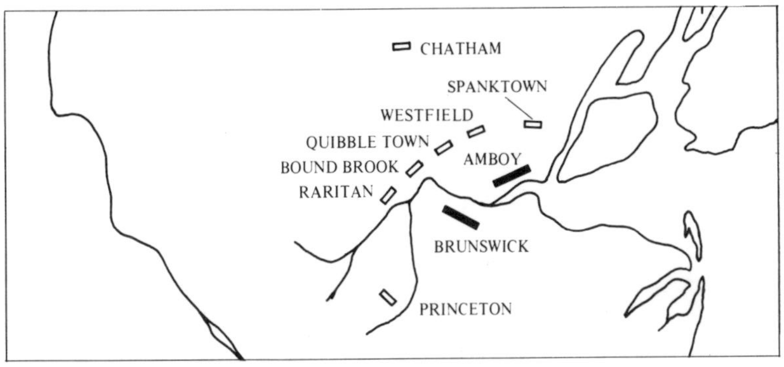

(1) (PCC Micro copy 247:167).
(2) The identity of this small force is not known, other than the fact that they were Pennsylvania continentals. They may have been the replacement for the "Light Infantry" (Rodney Diary) of the Princeton Army that had served as Washington's Guard before the Princeton Army was disbanded.
(3) On 2.26.77, Gen. Stirling wrote from Baskingridge, N. J. that "Col. Willson dyed the night before last. Maj. Butler is senior officer of regt." (WP Sti/GW 2.26.77) These men were Lt. Col. George Wilson and Maj. Richard Butler of the 8th regt. Col. Aneas Mackey of this regt. had died on 2.14.77. They had suffered great hardship in their January march across the mountains from Ft. Pitt to New Jersey.
(4) This appears to be Capt. Thomas Yates with his company of the 4th Md. regt.
(5) This was a company of Col. Ephraim Martin's 4th N. J. regt.
(6) This was Col. Israel Shreve's 2nd N. J. regt.
(7) This was Col. Andrew Ward's regt. of Ct. State Troops.
(8) These men appear to have been the last of the Princeton regt. They were under the command of "Lieut. [John] Robb . . . with 20 or 30 privates." (WP PCS/GW 2.8.77) As of 2.8.77, the Pa. Council of Safety was urging them to come home to form the nucleus of a new regt.
(9) "Wyoming Rangers" (WP Dic/GW 2.9.77); (WW 7:484) are mentioned as being in the N. J. front lines as early as 2.9.77. These were two "Independent Companies" commanded by Capt. Robert Durkee and Capt. Samuel Ransom. These two companies were also known as the "Wyoming Valley Rangers."
(10) As late as April 22, this regt. was not up to strength and it was ordered that "Detachments of 3rd, 4th, and 10th Pennsylvania Regiments are to form one Detachment and be under the command of Major Harmar till their respective regiments arrive." (WW 7:452) This was Maj. Joseph Harmar of the 3rd Pa. regt.
(11) This was the regt. of Col. Matthias Ogden, also known as the 1st N. J. regt. As early as 12.27.76, Maj. William De Hart was in "Morris Town" (WW 6:465); (WP DeH/GW 12.27.76) recruiting for this regt. As of 2.24.77, this regt. was forming at "Troy," (WW 7:200, 201), Morris County, New Jersey.
(12) This was the regt. of Col. Ephraim Martin, also known as the 4th N. J. regt. Martin had been shot through the chest at the Battle of Long Island, and after 1.1.77, the regt. appears to have been commanded by Lt. Col. David Rhea. Martin, however, does appear at Woodbridge, N. J. on 3.31.77 as the president of a court martial.
(13) This was the regt. of Col. William Cooke, also known as the 12th Pa.
(14) As of 3.3.77, Lt. Col. James Chambers of Hand's 1st Pa. regt. was "at Easton," (WW 7:241) Pa., and he was ordered to come to Jersey with as many men as he could bring. Col. Edward Hand was not with his troops as late as 3.28.77 on which date Gen. Washington noted that "By the Absence of Colo. Hand, the dismission of Lieut. Colo. Chambers, and the Resignation of Major Ross, (who I see is again promoted) the 1st regt. is likewise destitute of Field officers." (WW 7:326, 327) As of 3.12.77, Chambers was made colonel of the 10th Pa. regt. but was transferred back to be colonel of the 1st on 4.12.77, Col. Hand having been made a brigadier on 4.1.77. Although James Ross appears to have resigned, he certainly was back with the 1st Pa. as its "lieutenant colonel" (Br. 12) at the Battle of Brandywine, on 9.11.77.
(15) Lt. Col. George Stricker seems to have been the senior officer of the German batt., as Gen. Washington was seeking the advice of "Col. Stricker" (WW 7:20) as early as 1.16.77. However, Col. Henry D'Arendt was made commander of this regt. on 3.19.77, four days after the date of this return.
(16) As early as 1.13.77, Brig. Gen. Adam Stephen was ordered to take command of "five Virginia regiments," (WW 7:6) that had just entered into Jersey. More regts. were to follow. The Virginia regts. saw some action in January but soon many men of the Virginia regts. became ill, possibly of smallpox, whereupon the whole of the Va. force was sent to Whippany to recover. It would not be until after "April 19" (WW 7:438 note) that these troops would recover enough to take the field again.
(17) This was Col. Thomas Procter of the Pa. State Artillery. As late as 4.25.77, Washington noted, "I have not an Artillery Man here, but those belonging to the State of Pennsylvania." (WW 7:467) The day before this return was made, Gen. Washington wrote to Brig. Gen. Henry Knox who was in New England recruiting and arranging for armament, "your presence is necessary here, I hope you will make as much haste as possible to Join." (WW 7:289)
(18) Apparently this was the Cecil County militia, as Gen. Washington noted on 3.26.77, that "the Cecil County Militia . . . claim discharge the first of next Month." (WW 7:319)
(19, 20, 21) As of 2.25.77, Gen. Stirling asked that the "three Companies of Virginia Volunteers" (WW 7:201) be formed into a regiment for purposes of duty.
(22, 23) These were New Jersey "State Troops" or volunteer units as distinguished from New Jersey militia, which were conscript units. "State Troops" were recruited pursuant to a November 27, 1776 act of the New Jersey Legislature, for service until April 1, 1777. Many of the officers and men raised for this short term service came from existing militia regiments. The act called for the raising of four battalions under the command of Brigadier General Matthias Williamson. Williamson raised and commanded them until 2.6.77 having asked Gov. Livingston to accept his resignation "because of ill health." (WP Wil/GW 12.8.76) The composition of the four battalions of "State Troops" were as follows: Colonel David Chambers was appointed to command a battalion enlisted from Somerset, Sussex and Hunterdon Counties. Chambers, while on duty at Princeton, appears to have gotten into some trouble regarding "converting stores to personal use" (WP Cha/GW 2.9.77) and his lieutenant colonel, Jacob West, was next in command. Colonel David Potter was appointed to command a battalion en-

listed from Gloucester, Salem and Cumberland Counties. Potter, however, was made a brigadier on 2.22.77, and his batt. appears to have been commanded after that date by Lt. Col. Whittlow Cripps. Maj. Gen. Putnam noted from Princeton on 2.10.77, that "Lt. Collo. Cripps arrived here yesterday." (WP Put/Liv 2.10.77) Colonel Jacob Ford was appointed to command a battalion enlisted from Bergen, Essex and Morris Counties. As noted elsewhere, Col. Ford died on 1.10.77, and he was succeeded in command by his lieutenant colonel, Oliver Spencer. Spencer, however, as of 1.15.77, was given permission to raise one of the 16 Additional Continental Regiments, and he probably spent much of his time after that date in recruiting. Colonel Charles Read was appointed to command a battalion enlisted from Middlesex, Monmouth and Burlington Counties. Early in January, when the enemy advanced into New Jersey as far as Trenton, Col. Read sought the protection of the enemy. As noted by Gov. Livingston, "Colonel Charles Read of the Burlington Battalions, is in such a Situation with Respect to his having submitted to the Enemy, that it is not probable he will act any longer in that Office." (Assembly Votes 3.15.77) Next in command of Read's battalion was Lt. Col. Thomas Seabrook but he "is said to have refused taking the Oaths to the State." (ibid) Maj. John Taylor was the next ranking officer in the battalion.

(24) As far as New Jersey troops are concerned, this comment refers to the regular New Jersey militia consisting of from one to four regiments conscripted or drafted in each of the then 13 New Jersey counties. These regiments were called up for duty, one half or one third of them at a time, so as not to disrupt local farm and trade operations. As one part of each regiment would finish its tour of duty of two weeks or more, the remaining part would come out to relieve it. On 3.15.77, the New Jersey Militia Act was revised to give better control of the organization and operation of the militia. For the state of the militia as of 3.15.77, see (Assembly Votes 3.15.77). At this time, Gov. Livingston promoted two colonels to the rank of brigadier, Colonel William Winds on 3.4.77 and Colonel David Forman on 3.15.77. Nathaniel Heard had been a brigadier since 6.25.76. Gov. Livingston assigned three counties to each brigadier. To meet the militia tour of duty ending on March 20, 1777, noted in this return, Livingston "directed General Heard to collect 1/3 or if he thot proper half of the militia of Somerset, Hunterdon and Sussex, General Winds 1/3 of Bergen, Essex and Morris." (WP Liv/GW 4.4.77) General Forman, however, was finding it difficult to get the colonels in his counties to turn out with their men. Thus, Gov. Livingston "invested him with the power of calling out the militia of Monmouth, Middlesex and Burlington, without giving umbrage to the Colonels of those respective regiments. I have accordingly directed him to detach half of those of Monmouth and Burlington to join his brigade and doubt not that he will be of singular service." (ibid) There was no mention of Middlesex County militia being ordered to join Forman probably because they already had been supplying men to assist Gen. Putnam in the defense of the southern sector of the front. As to the Monmouth militia, they were heavily engaged during this period in the Sandy Hook area. (See The New York Times, 2.23.1896.) The Burlington militia were doing duty in the Little Egg Harbor area, and at the ferries on the Delaware. As to the militia of the unbrigaded counties, Gov. Livingston noted, "I have ordered Gloucester militia to assist the State of Pennsylvania in the works at Billingsport," (ibid) which was a new fort being built there. Livingston gave no specific assignment to Cape May County, "considering the remoteness of its situation." (ibid) As to the other two counties, Livingston remarked that "Salem and Cumberland have turned out with great spirit." (ibid) Senior New Jersey militia general, Philemon Dickinson, (a brigadier since 1775—made major general 6.6.77) was in overall command of New Jersey militia. He established his headquarters during this campaign at "Bell's Farm," (WP Dic/GW 2.13.77) located at "Raritan," (2 NJA 4:160); (Jones 25) referred to on a contemporary map as "Bells Head Qtrs." (Princeton Maps Jno. Clark 2.11.77)

As noted in the 3.15.77 return of the army, only 2543 Continental soldiers had reported for duty in three and a half months, and the situation was not soon to improve substantially. On March 25, Gen. Greene reported to Gen. Washington from Philadelphia, which was the principal Continental staging area of troops from the southern and midatlantic states, that "There have gone from this City [to New Jersey] about 700 men within a week past, a thousand more will be ready in eight to ten days." (WP Gre/GW 3.25.77) But these men would barely replace the New Jersey State Troops now in the Jersey front lines, and who were due to go home April 1.

In despair on April 9, Washington sent Gen. St. Clair to Philadelphia "to hasten the Troops on." (WW 7:372) Yet, while Washington lamented his enlistment problems, he observed a steady build-up of enemy forces in the Brunswick-Amboy area.

By May 11, Washington suspicioned that "The Enemy have certainly some Capital Object in view, either Philadelphia or Hudson's River." (WW 8:43) By May 27, he had eliminated the possibility of an enemy move up the Hudson when he noted that "Philadelphia is the destination talked of." (WW 8:131) Two days later Washington was more certain. He wrote Gen. Sullivan that "I am strongly apprehensive they will shortly push for Philadelphia." (WW 8:136)

Fortunately, by the last week in May, the flow of continental enlistees had increased considerably. (See ret. 5.20.77, WW 8:opp.170) Washington therefore decided to abandon his posts encircling the enemy at Brunswick and Amboy so as to place his main force more between the enemy and Philadelphia. To this end, Washington moved his entire army to Middle Brook, near Bound Brook. Further, on May 29, Washington moved his headquarters to "Middle Brook," (WW 8:137) thus ending his first, personal, winter's stay at Morristown.

For the placement of each unit of the army at Middlebrook see a map made by Brig. Gen. Henry Knox. It appears to have accompanied a letter from Knox to Col. Henry Jackson dated May 10, 1777. The letter stated in part, "I have repeatedly been upon the lines below and near Brunswick and very soon the whole army will encamp near to that place." The map is untitled and undated but the paper stock, as well as the folds of the map and letter, match. Both are in the Mellen Chamberlain Autograph Collection, Boston Public Library.

Gen. Washington returned to Morristown with a large part of his army for the period from July 4 through July 10, 1777, because of a renewed threat of an enemy movement up the Hudson. (See *Washington's Forgotten Encampment*, by Carl B. Scherzer, Morristown, 1977.)

INDEX OF NAMES*

---

* Appendix material is not indexed.